THE DYNAMICS OF
JUDAISM

THE DYNAMICS OF JUDAISM

A Study in Jewish Law

ROBERT GORDIS

INDIANA UNIVERSITY PRESS

Bloomington and Indianapolis

Library of Congress Cataloging-in-Publication Data

Gordis, Robert
    The dynamics of Judaism : a study of Jewish law / Robert Gordis.
      p.   cm.
    Bibliography: p.
    Includes index.
    ISBN 0-253-32602-8
    1. Jewish law—History.   2. Judaism—Essence, genius, nature.
I. Title.
BM520.5.G67 1990   88-45502
296.1′8—dc20   CIP
     1 2 3 4 5   94 93 92 91 90

CONTENTS

PREFACE

The character and contents of the present work will, I believe, be easily apparent to its readers. But perhaps a word of explanation is in order.

One of the characters in a P. D. James novel praises a sermon he has heard in these words: "That's all one asks of a sermon—no possible relevance to anything outside itself." A counterpart to this attitude is to be found in some academic circles, which rate the quality of a work of scholarship by its freedom from any involvement in the human condition or any concern with the living world. This Olympian detachment I cannot claim for myself.

In Boswell's *Life of Samuel Johnson*, a Dr. Edwards confesses, "When I was young I resolved to devote myself to philosophy, but I found cheerfulness always breaking in." In my youth, I decided to dedicate myself to the study of the Bible as well as the later stages of the Jewish heritage, but I found the problems and perplexities of the age always breaking in. I am thankful that I was able to devote myself to learning without turning my back on life. Though I often wished for more leisure for study, I have never envied the lofty isolation of the ivory tower.

Indeed, in the most creative periods of Judaism, its greatest exemplars did precisely that—they conserved and transmitted the values of the Torah with sensitivity to the life and thought of their times. They thus helped it to function as a guide to the good life in each generation. They held fast to two ideals: *Torah lishmah*, "learning for its own sake," and *Torat Hayyim*, "learning for the sake of life." By their creative activity, they demonstrated that these two principles do not contradict but complement each other.

The present work has been written in the spirit of this conviction. It seeks to explore the character of the Jewish ethos, the basic traits of the Jewish tradition, and the qualities that have endowed it with its enduring vitality. It is these attributes of Judaism that justify the contention that the eternal is always contemporary. I therefore venture to hope that the scholarship reflected in these pages will not be impugned by its concern for the grave problems confronting Jews and all human beings in the last decade of the twentieth century.

I wish it were possible to thank all the teachers, colleagues, students and friends from whom I have learned during a lifetime of study, teaching, and communal activity. Many of them are cited in the Notes. The greatest tribute to scholars or thinkers is having their ideas and insights enter the mainstream of culture and become part of the life of ordinary men and women, even though they may never have heard the authors' names.

Nearly all the contents of this volume were written especially for it. However, I should like to thank the publishers and editors of *Midstream*, *Judaism*, and *Moment* for the use, in substantially modified form, of material that originally appeared in their pages. My thanks are also extended to my associate, Ruth B. Waxman, for her assistance, and to my secretary, Beatrice Snyder, who labored loyally over the earlier forms of the manuscript.

And it is with pride and joy that I acknowledge the crucial assistance given me by my grandson Elie in the midst of his own busy career.

My dear wife, Fannie, and I recently celebrated our sixtieth wedding anniversary. That I was able, at this stage of life, to write this book is due in largest measure to her love and understanding of her husband and of his work. This sympathy was easier for her to generate because of her high intellectual gifts, her love of truth and the right, and her deep commitment to Judaism at its noblest. In the deepest sense, this is her book.

N.B.: While reviewing the edited manuscript for *the Dynamics of Judaism* Robert Gordis fell ill. The publisher is grateful to David Gordis for taking over for his father, confirming his revisions, and handling all the details that normally fall to the author during the publication process.

GLOSSARY AND GUIDE TO
RABBINIC SOURCES

ABOT (or PIKKE ABOT). "The Sayings of the Fathers." One of the tractates of the *Mishnah*. Collection of religious and ethical aphorisms attributed to various Sages.

AGGADAH (or HAGGADAH). Lit. "narrative." Material in the *Talmud* and the *Midrashim* of a nonlegal character. Encompasses traditions, legends, folklore, popular wisdom, ethical admonitions, and historical data.

APOCRYPHA. Greek, "hidden." Large and varied body of Jewish literature originating between 400 B.C.E. and 200 C.E. Reflects the viewpoints of various dissident sects who diverged from the dominant Pharisees.

CODES. Medieval manuals of Jewish law, encompassing rituals, ethics, civil and criminal jurisprudence, religious practices and observances, marriage, divorce, and inheritance. See also *Kashrut; Mishneh Torah; Shulhan Arukh*.

GEMARA. Aramaic, "study." The discussions and study of the *Mishnah* in the academies of Palestine and Babylonia. Later written and attached to relevant sections of the *Mishnah*, thus creating the Palestinian and Babylonian Talmuds, of which the latter is more extensive.

HALAKHAH. Lit. "the going," "the way." The entire corpus of Jewish law, from its biblical origins to the present. Also the accepted decision when there is a difference of opinion among scholars.

JUBILEES, BOOK OF. Part of the *Apocrypha*; retellings of the narratives in Genesis.

KASHRUT. The dietary laws contained in the *Halakhah*.

KETUBIM. Sacred writings; the third section of the Bible.

MIDRASH. Lit. "searching out the scriptures." Detailed study of the biblical text, primarily of the five books of the *Torah*. The *Midrash Aggadah* explores the narrative sections of the Bible; the *Midrash Halakhah* the legal passages. Originally oral, this material was collected into books called *Midrashim*.

MISHNAH. Lit. "repetition," "study." A compilation by Rabbi Judah the Patriarch (c. 200 C.E.) of legal discussions attributed to rabbinic Sages from the fourth century B.C.E. to the second century C.E. The first compendium of Jewish law. References to tractates in the *Mishnah* are preceded by the letter M; e.g., M. *Sanhedrin* 4:2 refers to *Mishnah Sanhedrin*, chapter 4, section 2.

MISHNEH TORAH. "The Double Torah," also called *Yad Hahazakah*, "The Mighty Hand," by Maimonides (Rabbi Moses ben Maimon, 1135–1204), divided into fourteen books. One of the three principal *Codes*.

RASHI. Acronym for Rabbi Shelomo Yizhaki (1040–1105), author of commentaries on the *Torah* and the *Talmud*.

RESPONSA. Lit. "answers." Questions that could not be resolved by recourse to the text of the *Talmud* or to the *Codes* were addressed to reputable scholars. Though the *Responsa* generally deal with the *Halakhah*, they also explore philosophic, theological, and historical issues.

SHULHAN ARUKH. "The Prepared Table," by Rabbi Joseph Karo (1488–1575). One of the three principal *Codes*; the authoritative guide to Hahlakhic practice for traditional Judaism.

SIFRA. *Midrash* on the Book of Leviticus.

SIFRE. *Midrash* on the books of Numbers and Deuteronomy.

TALMUD. Lit. "study." The massive collection of law and lore produced by rabbinic Judaism. The Babylonian Talmud consists of the *Mishnah* (400 B.C.E.–200 C.E.) and the *Gemara* of the Babylonia (200–500 C.E.). The Palestinian Talmud consists of the *Mishnah* (400 B.C.E.–200 C.E.) and the *Gemara* of Palestine (200–400 C.E.). All editions of the *Babylonian Talmud* follow the pagination of the first complete edition, printed by Daniel Bomberg in Venice in 1520–23. Its tractates are preceded by the letter B; e.g., B. *Menahot* 26b refers to the Babylonian Talmud, tractate *Menahot*, page 26, side 2. P. *Pesahim* 4:2 refers to the Palestinian Talmud, tractate *Pesahim*, chapter 4, section 2.

TORAH. Lit. "directive," "instruction," "teaching," "guidance," "law." The most fundamental and inclusive term in Judaism. Originally applied to brief instruction manuals for priests; then successively broadened to include the first five books of the Bible, the *Oral* and the *Written Torah*, the entire corpus of law and lore of the Rabbis (culminating in the *Mishnah*), the *Gemara*, all treatises and commentaries produced after the completion of the *Talmud*, and the entire *Aggadah*.

TOSEFTA. "Supplement." Collection of rabbinic material not included by Rabbi Judah in the *Mishnah*. Follows the order of the *Mishnah*. Compiled by Rabbi Hoshaya and Rabbi Hiyya (third century C.E.). Citations to tractates in the *Tosefta* are preceded by the letter T; e.g., T. *Yoma* 2:5 refers to *Tosefta Yoma* chapter 2, section 5.

WISDOM. The enlightenment taught by the Sages of the ancient Near East; embodied in the biblical books of Proverbs and Ecclesiastes and in *Ben Sira*, "The Wisdom of Solomon," in the *Apocrypha*.

THE DYNAMICS OF
JUDAISM

INTRODUCTION

OF JEWS AND JUDIASM

According to a well-known and probably apocryphal tale, the French philosopher Voltaire and Frederick the Great of Prussia were strolling about in the gardens of Sans Souci discussing the credibility of miracles. When the philosopher refused to rule out the phenomenon as impossible, the king challenged him to cite one authentic example. "Sire," Voltaire replied, "the Jews!"

Voltaire probably had in mind the longevity of the Jewish people, which has preserved its specific identity longer than any other group alive today on the face of the globe. Or he might have been thinking of Judaism, the oldest living religion in the world. Moreover, this identity has survived not in the depths of the African jungle or among the bushmen of Australia, far removed from other human contacts. The Jews' ancestral homeland, the land of Israel, lies at the heartland of the Eastern Hemisphere, at the intersection of Europe, Asia, and Africa. The land has been crisscrossed by the major trade routes of antiquity and has been conquered more than twenty times in the course of history.

Moreover, for nearly two thousand years, since the burning of the Second Temple by the Romans in the year 70 c.e., Jews have been in exile, exposed time and again to every possible peril, persecution, spoliation, expulsion, and massacre. These threats to Jewish survival have alternated with the "gentler" challenge of voluntary defection, which takes countless forms. At one end of the spectrum is unconscious alienation and indifference to community and tradition; at the other are formal conversions to another religion and the not infrequent pathological phenomenon of *juedischer Selbsthass*, hatred of self, expressed as a violent antipathy to one's origins and kin.

The full dimensions of the miracle of survival go further. Jews have not merely managed to cling to existence; they have manifested unparalleled vitality. Their creativity has continued unabated from the beginning of their collective history in the Bible, perhaps the greatest achievement of the human spirit, to the outpouring of genius and talent in modern times, highlighted by such seminal figures as Marx, Freud, and Einstein and by countless others slightly less gifted. The constant process of attrition from Jewish ranks, which has gained in intensity in modern times, has not appreciably reduced the emergence of men and women of talent and genius who have contributed to every area of human endeavor.

One is strongly tempted to apply the term *unique* to the Jewish people. The tradition views this quality as existing throughout its history, starting with the call to Abraham, and deriving from God's election of Israel, which was ratified by the covenant at Sinai. It attributes to King David the characterization "Who is like your people Israel, one nation on the earth?" (II Sam. 7:23).

This quality may also be explained in secular terms. When the ancient Hebrews first appeared on the stage of history, they were a tiny branch of the ancient Semitic peoples in the Middle East, their cult practices being similar and doubtless derived from the pool of traditions and practices that was their common patrimony. As variations developed, the Israelite religion continued to share many characteristics with its neighbors. Modern archaeologists, historians of religion, and biblical scholars have had a field day in pointing out countess similarities between the religion of the Hebrews and that of other Semites. All too often, however, these scholarly researches were marred by a methodological error—the resemblances were exaggerated and the differences overlooked. Perhaps an even more important consideration: had there been only similarities, the Hebrews and their religion would have disappeared with the destruction of their national polity, as has happened with all their ancient neighbors. While Yehezkel Kaufmann and other scholars have maintained that the distinctiveness of the religion of Israel was inherent since its inception, a more plausible view is that its special character was the fruit of a development over centuries, though it is no less genuine on that account. Because of its special experience and leadership, biblical religion developed several unique traits that marked it off from the pagan world.

First, the Hebrew faith represented the commitment of an entire people to its God, not merely that of a caste of priests or nobles to a sovereign. The whole people entered into a *brit*, a covenant to obey the will of God by observing His commandments. The Book of Deuteronomy mandates a practice without parallel elsewhere. Every seventh year, at the *Succot* festival, all the men, women, and children were commanded to assemble, and the entire Torah was read aloud to them. This practice of *hakhel*, "assembly," was probably a utopian enactment, but it underscored a fundamental principle already set forth at the giving of the Torah at Sinai, that God's covenant encompassed an entire people.

Second, the terms of the covenant are highly significant. Some modern biblical scholars claim to have found various "Decalogues" embedded in the biblical text that are largely ritual in character. The reality of these alleged "Ten Commandments" seems to me to be highly doubtful. In any event, what is clear beyond dispute is that the Decalogue *par excellence* is the famous one presented in Exodus 20 and Deuteronomy 5. It is the only one repeated in the biblical text. Even more significantly, it alone is described as establishing the covenantal relationship between God and Israel, and it is fundamentally ethical in character.

Third is the unique character of the religious leadership that arose in Israel. The Hebrew priests were not essentially different from their counterparts in other Semitic cultures. They were the guardians of the sanctuary, officiants at sacrifices and other ritual occasions, and the custodians of the sacred texts. Hebrew prophecy, in its early stages, as depicted in the historical books of Judges, Samuel, and Kings, had its analogues in the Semitic-culture world, as the discoveries in Mari on the Euphrates and elsewhere in the ancient Middle East have demonstrated. What is without parallel is the emergence in Israel of a line of Prophets, extending over centuries, whose single-minded and passionate concern was the demand for righteousness in the life of the individual and the nation.

The Hebrew Prophets differed among themselves in their evaluation of ritual, running the gamut from a deep interest in the cult, as in Ezekiel, through a more moderate attitude, as in Hosea and Isaiah, to the strongly negative attitude that is reflected in the prophecies of Amos. For all of them, however, the touchstone was the same: If ritual stimulated the practice of righteousness, it was useful; if it did not, it was a snare and a delusion. Undoubtedly there were men and women in Assyria and Babylonia, in Edom and Ammon, and among the Phoenicians and the Egyptians who were sensitive to the evils of their society and hungered after righteousness. But it was only in Israel that this preoccupation, this obsession, if you will, with doing justice, loving mercy, and walking humbly with God became a persistent tradition transmitted through generations and remaining central to the national ethos.

After the Babylonian exile the biblical books became sacred scripture. A passage, a verse, or even a word in the narrative portions of the Bible could serve as the starting point for an elaborate development in the Aggadah (literally, "narrative"), the mass of legend, ethical admonitions, religious doctrine, popular wisdom, and folk belief preserved in the Midrash and the Talmud. Similarly, every section in the legal portions of the Torah, and to a lesser degree in the other biblical books, was vastly expanded into an elaborate corpus of Halakhah, "law." The Rabbis were well aware that substantial sections of the Oral Law had only a tenuous relationship to the biblical text. Thus the Mishnah declares:

> The annulment of oaths is a procedure flying in the air, and has no basis in the written Torah. The laws of the sabbath, the offerings prescribed for the festivals and for ritual transgressions are like mountains hanging by a hair, for which there is a slight basis in Scripture, but with many rabbinic laws. The civil law and the regulations regarding the sacrificial system and the laws of purity and impurity, as well as the laws concerning prohibited sexual relationships do have a biblical basis to depend upon, and they are the essence of the Torah [*gufei torah*] [M. *Hagigah* 1:8].

The Mishnah and the Talmud added to the injunctions and prohibitions in Jewish law, which continued to grow in extent and complexity in the work of the medieval authorities. In sheer bulk, the ritual and ceremonial law—which included the Sabbath, the festivals, *kashrut* (the regulations regarding food), family relations, and the sacrificial cult—were more extensive than the sections dealing with civil and criminal law. Thus a specious plausibility was given to the charge frequently launched against rabbinic Judaism, that it was "arid legalism" from which the vital spirit of the Prophets had fled.

After the loss of the central elements of the cult, primarily the Temple and the sacrificial system, greater attention was given to the ritual observance of the individual and the community in order to compensate for the vacuum. This is entirely understandable. The particularistic character of the ritual rather than the universalistic injunctions of morality was essential, if Judaism and the Jewish people were to survive the constant perils to which they were now exposed. The Prophets had enunciated the principles of righteousness; the Rabbis sought to embody them in life through the law.

In sum, the secret of the survival of the Jewish people lies in its religion, and the heart of that religion is the conviction that the moral law is central to its covenant with God.

I have sought to demonstrate on historical grounds, the uniqueness of the Jewish people and its traditions, which the religious consciousness sees as the election of Israel. The idea may also be defended in sociological terms, if we recognize it not as a "congenital trait" but as an "acquired characteristic." Today Jews are virtually the only group that possesses a religion, a culture, and a sense of kinship specifically its own, distinct from those of other peoples. What is perhaps even more significant, these three elements are organically related to one another, each reinforcing the others. This linking of religion, culture, and ethnicity was sensed by the tradition and formulated in the kabbalistic text the *Zohar*: "The Holy One, blessed be He, the Torah and Israel are one." The great modern Jewish thinker Mordecai M. Kaplan has emphasized this triadic bond and the significance of its organic character today. Each element has its own values and has contributed richly to the content and vitality of the tradition as a whole.

In the ancient world, however, this organic relationship was universal. The Sumerians and the Babylonians, the Egyptians and the Phoenicians, the Greeks and the Romans, each possessed their individual religion, culture, and sense of kinship, distinct from the civilization of all other societies. Today all the nations of antiquity have disappeared; only the Jews have survived, still preserving this special characteristic, which goes back to their origin.

For most modern men and women, religion, national allegiance, and, to a lesser degree, culture are separate entities, largely independent of one another. What is more, they often are shared with other groups. German is spoken by the Swiss and the Austrians as well as by the Germans. Baptists in Memphis share a common faith with their coreligionists in Moscow. In Britain and the United States we speak the same language, or so we are led to believe!

When an anthropologist colleague challenged the observation that the organic relationship of ethnicity, religion, and culture makes Jews unique in the modern world, I asked him to offer another example. After considerable thought, he was able to come up with an exception not likely to disprove the rule: the Parsees of India, whose religion, culture, and sense of kinship are uniquely their own.

In sociological terms the Jewish community constitutes a religio-cultural-ethnic group without parallel in the modern world. For those who wish to avoid jargon, two other descriptions are available. The first is *am*, "people," derived from the Hebrew root meaning "togetherness," a designation frequently applied to the Jews in the Bible. The term is sufficiently general to be free of political connotations; Jews the world over obviously share no single political allegiance or nationality.

The second term is *mishpahah*, "family," which may be related to a root meaning "attachment." It, too, goes back to the Bible. "You alone have I singled out of all the families of the earth," the Prophet Amos declares, "therefore, I will call you to account for all your iniquities" (Amos 3:2). Whatever term is preferred, the sense of Jewish kinship is indubitable and fundamental.

Many Jews today are not religious believers. Some are not caught up by the vision of a Jewish homeland in the state of Israel. Many modern Jews have been deprived, particularly during their formative years, of any meaningful contact with the great sources of Jewish tradition and culture. As a result, in adult life they tend to arrive at the position of Alfred Kazin, "After years of search I have concluded there is no intellectual meaning to my Jewishness." They are left only with inchoate emotional ties, primarily nostalgia and love of family. Frequently this attitude is accompanied by an undercurrent of envy for those who appear happy within the Jewish tradition and yet thoroughly at home in society at large.

The term "family" is appropriate on several counts. It carries the emotional freight involved in the feeling of belonging, which may be the sole aspect of Jewishness remaining for many modern Jews, intellectuals and nonintellectuals alike. By indirection, at least, *mishpaḥah* reminds us that family feeling may be marked by controversy as well as by consensus. The sense of Jewish belonging often persists in the face of profound disagreements. Even when alienated from much of their heritage, many Jews continue to feel that they possess a common history from the past, a common tradition in the present, and a common destiny in the future, with each element being strengthened by the others.

This sense of kinship manifests itself in a strong feeling of responsibility, even among Jews who differ totally in background and outlook. The first international organization dedicated to the preservation of the lives and rights of Jews everywhere, founded in Paris in 1860, was the Alliance Israélite Universelle. It adopted as its motto the traditional Hebrew phrase *Kol Israel haverim*, which may be somewhat freely rendered as "All Israel are brothers." The most dramatic manifestation is the passionate concern of Jews everywhere for the state of Israel whenever its security and progress seem threatened.

Mohammed called the Jews "the people of the Book." The vast range of Jewish literature over the centuries may be described with little exaggeration as an extended commentary on the Bible from every conceivable point of view. Today Jewish culture expresses itself in music, dance, drama, and the plastic arts, but literature is still predominant. Many languages have served as the medium of communication. Obviously, the first and foremost is Hebrew, the language of the Bible and of the reborn state of Israel. Scarcely less sacred is Aramaic, the language of much of the Talmud and the Midrash and of basic prayers like the *Kaddish* and the *Kol Nidre*, as well as of the *Zohar*, the centerpiece of Jewish mysticism. In addition, Jews have molded many other languages to their use, creating rich literatures in Judeo-Arabic, Judeo-Spanish (or Ladino), and Yiddish. Today Jewish creativity is expressed in virtually every modern language.

The Jewish religion possesses a body of beliefs and insights regarding God, man, and the universe; the power to convince men and women of its truth; and the capacity to endow them with the strength to confront the problems inherent in the human condition. It contains a body of ethical teaching that reckons realistically with the limitations of human nature without losing faith in its potential. Perhaps the most obvious aspect of the Jewish religion is its rich and elaborate ritual governing daily life, the Sabbath, and the festivals; at home, in the synagogue, and in the street.

Both the ethical and the ritual teachings of Judaism were embodied in the imposing corpus of the Halakhah, a term generally though inadequately translated as "law." For the greater portion of Jewish history, the Halakhah was paramount in every aspect of human existence. The Roman-Jewish historian Josephus proudly remarked that while the laws of the Empire were enforced by the legions of Rome, the laws of Moses were being observed everywhere with no external power to compel obedience. Even today, in a period of weakened religious loyalty and in the face of the imperious demands of modern life and personal desire, Jewish law has considerable impact on the lives of Jews.

The destruction or even the decay of any of the three components of Jewishness would be a body blow to the Jewish heritage, but it is clear that one of the three is paramount. However unpalatable it may be to confess it in a secular age, it is clear that the Jewish religion, beyond all its other functions, is the guarantor of the Jewish future. Our century has witnessed the most colossal onslaught on the biological survival of the Jewish people, in the unspeakable horror of the Nazi Holocaust. Nor is the power of anti-Semitism spent today. Nevertheless, the major threat now is the nonviolent, ongoing process of assimilation in all its forms and degrees.

The history of the past two hundred years has demonstrated that the most dedicated concern for Jewish culture, be it literature, art, or music, cannot stem the tide of defection from the Jewish community. The gifted artist Leonid Pasternak was a close friend of the most important Zionist leaders and Hebrew writers of his day. His son, Boris, the famous Russian poet and novelist, found his spiritual home in the Russian Orthodox Church. The most passionate attachment to the Jewish name and defense of Jewish rights are no more efficacious in preserving Jewish identity. The British politician Benjamin Disraeli aggressively proclaimed his Jewish descent, but that did not prevent his being a communicant of the Church of England.

It is only the Jewish religion that stands guard over the perpetuation of the Jewish people. Its cultural and national aspects remain vital and fruitful only when nourished by its religion. Cut off from it, the Jews linger, languish, and die. The Jewish religion itself, however, is a complex and variegated phenomenon. It embraces doctrines of belief, ritual practices, and ethical guidance both personal and collective, all embodied in a system of law that gave these teachings concrete form and made them operative in human lives. Jewish law, in all its aspects—ethical, ritual, civil, and criminal; individual and family—has maintained Jewish existence through time. Whenever the observance of Jewish law becomes attenuated in a Jewish community, the other manifestations of the Jewish spirit are weakened and ultimately face extinction.

The future of Judaism, not as a fossilized relic of the past but as a vital force, is by no means assured. Uniqueness—or, to use a less value-laden term, singularity—is no guarantee of preservation; on the contrary, it may heighten the degree of vulnerability.

Many factors have conspired to undermine loyalty to the Jewish religion, its fabric of faith, and its structure of observance. Two major phenomena that ushered in the modern world, the Emancipation and the Enlightenment, wreaked havoc with traditional Jewish life. At the end of the eighteenth century, the Emancipation admitted Jews to individual citizenship in central and western Europe, and later throughout the world; in return it demanded and received the dissolution of the autonomous Jewish community, with its power to compel obedience from its members.

Simultaneously, the Enlightenment attacked the validity of religion in general. Judaism, for centuries immured within ghetto walls and largely unaware of the new currents of thought and patterns of action in the world at large, was far less prepared than Christianity to face the challenge. For many Jews, traditional Judaism had forfeited its authority over their lives and thoughts. The extraordinary technological progress of the past two centuries, coupled with the demands of a new economy, made it difficult, if not impossible, to maintain the regimen of Jewish law and practice. For centuries, the Jewish way of life had been prized as a bulwark; now it was decried as a barrier to the brave new world outside.

The defenders of tradition, with few exceptions, were either unwilling or unable to understand the nature of the modernist challenge. They threw down the gauntlet to the modern age: "either all or nothing." Modern Jews by the hundreds of thousands enthusiastically chose the latter alternative. Millions of Jews defected from the tradition or from the community or from both. The rabbis were unable to turn back the clock to a bygone age, and the rebels were left with bad consciences for not being "good Jews."

What was and is clearly needed is the exercise of wise judgment. We must recognize what of the past belongs to the past alone, what is viable and indeed indispensable in the present, and what contains the seeds of growth and development in the future.

A major aim of this book is to assist in this enterprise of revitalizing the Jewish tradition for the modern world. It seeks to achieve that goal by analyzing the theoretical foundations of Jewish tradition and law and by spelling out the factors, both internal and external, that made it possible for the Torah to remain relevant and life-giving through the centuries. Understanding the dynamism of Jewish law is indispensable for making it come alive for men and women of today and tomorrow.

Biologists tell us that in a living organism there is a constant process in which existing cells break down and are replaced by new ones. After seven years every cell in a human body is new, none surviving from an earlier stage. In what sense then can we speak of the same person after an eight-year interval? The answer is obvious. If a man went to sleep one night and awoke on the morrow with every cell in his body changed, there would be a sharp break in his identity. But since the process is gradual, over an extended period, the minute changes preserve the continuity of the organism. Also, throughout the process certain basic traits, physical or psychological, persist, in spite of modifications, so that even after an interval of many years, the person can be recognized. Growth is the result of the ongoing dialectic between continuity and change.

Both these factors must be reckoned with if we wish to understand the life and growth of Judaism and help assure its meaningful survival. In this volume I have sought to reckon fairly with points of view other than my own. However, this book is not intended as a purely academic exercise in antiquarianism. It seeks to avoid the state of mind of the nineteenth-century authority on medieval Jewish literature Moritz Steinschneider. When the modern Hebrew poet Judah Leib Gordon visited him, Steinschneider is reported to have asked him, "Young man, in what century did you live?"

The greatest scholars and teachers in Judaism responded actively to the needs and interests of the people and grappled with the problems of the tradition without abandoning the scholarly search for truth. For them, the two ideals of *Torah lishmah*, "learning for its own sake," without any ulterior or practical motive, and *Torat hayyim*, "learning in the service of life," were not contradictory. Israel's greatest Sages—Ezra, Johanan ben Zakkai, Hillel, Akiba, Judah the Patriarch, Saadia Gaon, Rabbenu Gershom, Maimonides—all served both ideals. Admittedly, it is more comfortable to immerse oneself in the silent past than to wrestle with the complexities of the strident present, but the service of life must be our goal.

The first stage of the scholar's quest must be to discover *wie es eigentlich gewesen*, "as it actually was," to use the phrase coined by Leopold von Ranke (1795–1862), or, more accurately, *wie es eigentlich geworden*, "as it actually became." The next must be a realistic yet sympathetic appraisal of the state of society, its qualities and its defects, its achievements and its problems. The third stage is the articulation of a vision of *tiqqun haᶜolam*, the improvement of the world and the enhancement of human existence. The final and crucial step is to move toward translating the ideal into reality. As we strive toward this ultimate stage we must remain aware that it can never be fully attained, but that the effort is both feasible and necessary.

What is true of the world at large applies to Judaism as well. The goal of a meaningful Jewish tradition in the modern world can best be advanced, I believe, by utilizing, together with all other sources of learning and insight, the methods and results of historical-critical scholarship. The present book is not written in a partisan spirit, but recognizes the contributions that all the movements in contemporary Judaism are making to the treasure house of Jewish life and thought. Moreover, I believe that the outlook expressed here cuts across denominational lines and is accepted by thoughful men and women in all sectors of the Jewish community.

This volume seeks to discover the dynamics of Judaism and the factors hat have led to its growth and development, as well as to its enduring vitality through time. The first part, "Principles," describes the fundamental traits of the Jewish tradition that molded Jewish law from its inception to the present day. The chapters in this part serve as a theoretical foundation and provide a sense of direction for the concrete and vital issues discussed in the second part, "Practices." Here I demonstrate the two strengths of the Halakhah—its stability and its flexibility in confronting the problems of Jewish life in modern Western society. Prominent in these discussions are questions concerning the rights and status of women.

The enduring spirit of the Jewish tradition has given it continuity through time, while various factors, both internal and external, have stimulated its development, the interplay among them assuring its survival. If loyalty to Judaism today can be reinforced by an understanding of its innermost nature, its future is safe. To that goal this volume is dedicated.

Principles

I

THE BASIC TRAITS OF THE JEWISH TRADITION

Ever since Matthew Arnold, it has been generally recognized that the two great sources of Western civilization are Hellenism and Hebraism, the culture of ancient Greece and ancient Israel. The art, science, and philosophy of the Greeks were the point of departure for the extraordinary development of these disciplines in medieval and modern civilization. The Hebrews, on the other hand, were the source of the religion and ethics of the Western world. The noblest embodiment of the Greek genius was the philosopher; the most exalted symbol of the Hebrew ethos was the Prophet.[1] The loss or absence of either would be an incalculable impoverishment of the human spirit, and civilization is the richer for both. Like all generalizations Matthew Arnold's pronouncement may suffer from oversimplification, but it is by no means devoid of truth. None of the other nations of antiquity, not even Sumer, Babylonia, or Egypt, had nearly as powerful an impact on the character and content of the Western world as did ancient Israel and Hellas.

The Power of the Hebraic Tradition

Nevertheless, the subsequent history of the Greek and the Hebrew impact on civilization has been radically different. To be sure, the Hellenic achievement remains important as part of the background of Western culture, but Greek philosophy, science, and even art have all been transcended by medieval and modern achievements in these areas. The religion and ethics of ancient Israel, on the other hand, are not merely of historical interest; they remain very much alive in the modern age. Whatever religious faith lives on in the Western world, within the major denominations as well as among the smaller and often more dynamic sects, generally claims the Bible as its living source and authority. It should be noted, too, that the Western world includes Islam, which is indebted to biblical and postbiblical Judaism scarcely less than is Christianity.[2]

There is, of course, a very respectable intellectual tradition of philosophic ethics beginning with Socrates, Plato, and Aristotle and extending to John Rawls, Robert Nisbet, and their colleagues in our own day. But the analyses of ethical philosophers, however brilliant and profound, have largely remained the province of academics. The great social and ethical controversies in our day are not generally carried on in terms of the categories of secular philosophic ethics; they are affected by perspectives, rightly or wrongly deduced from biblical teaching.

The mounting concern regarding war and peace, nuclear weapons and total annihilation, as well as the issue of nationalism and its relationship to the international community, finds its basis in the biblical text and its varied interpretations. The far-flung struggle over women's rights and obligations, the future of the family, the relations of the sexes, and the mutual attitudes of parents and children are all strongly colored by the narratives, laws, and admonitions in the Scripture. Abortion, contraception, divorce, extramarital relations, homosexuality— phenomena that have come to the forefront of modern consciousness— are argued in terms of biblical teaching, real or alleged. The debate on social justice and racial equality, like earlier conflicts over black slavery, take their point of departure from the Bible. To be sure, both defenders and opponents of the status quo are able to quote Scripture for their own purposes. By and large, however, as historians have noted, the impetus toward achieving a greater measure of justice, freedom, and peace for all human beings has drawn its inspiration, during the Middle Ages as well as in our own day, from the Hebrew Bible.

In sum, the great moral issues being debated in our day are rarely related to the abstract concepts found in philosophy, ancient, medieval, or modern. Instead, it is generally taken as axiomatic that people know right from wrong without the need for ratiocination. As the Prophet Micah put it, "He has told you, O man, what is good and what the Lord your God requires of you, to do justice, to love mercy and to walk humbly with your God" (Mic. 6:7). It is the Hebrew Prophets not the Greek philosophers who have been the source of inspiration for virtually every movement seeking to advance justice, freedom, and peace in human affairs. Hence, understanding the nature of the Hebrew tradition and penetrating to its dynamics and its techniques for dealing with the problems posed by the far too eventful history of the Jewish people is a highly significant enterprise for anyone interested in humankind or in the segment that is the people of Israel.

By the same token, the undertaking is both extensive and complex. It requires broad knowledge in many areas, a sense of balance, and the intellectual integrity to do justice to the luxuriant variety of phenomena within Judaism. Two centuries of gifted and dedicated research in all phases of Jewish life and thought have demonstrated that the spectrum of Judaism is far wider than was originally understood. Only after the scholar has worked thoroughly and objectively is it possible—and necessary—to establish the major and minor elements of the tradition. With the results of scholarship to hand, the thinker has both the right and the duty to evaluate the various elements in the tradition and to determine which are worth preserving and cultivating and which are best minimized or set aside.

There is no more preposterous statement than the claim that one maintains "the entire tradition," particularly in the case of Judaism, where controversy and conflict have been its very lifeblood, as the Bible and the Talmud abundantly attest. Anyone who loves a tradition is perforce selecting some elements and discarding others, making some central and others peripheral. Since human existence is finite, living is a never-ending process of selectivity.

The brief statement of mysticism and asceticism at the close of this chapter indicates the pitfalls involved in facile generalizations about the nature of Judaism and underscores the need for thorough sympathy for its varied manifestations. It is clear that mysticism and asceticism are legitimate expressions of Jewish religiosity, a claim long denied in some quarters. At the same time, neither tendency can claim to be a dominant influence in the Jewish tradition, except perhaps for limited periods. While their impact has waxed and waned with varying conditions, they are not central to the Jewish view of life, present-day fashions notwithstanding.

The Affirmation of Life

It may plausibly be argued that the first principle in Judaism is recognition of the One God—"In the beginning God. . . . " But the first chapter of Genesis, which articulates this belief, ends with an all-embracing view of the world and its creator that remains a fundamental characteristic of the Jewish tradition. It is its *affirmation of life as a good here and now*, including all its physical and spiritual aspects, and in spite of all its frustrations and agonies.

Thus the opening chapter of Genesis climaxes the account of creation with the statement "God saw all He had made, and behold it was very good" (Gen. 1:31). The Rabbis read the last word *meʾod*, "very," as *mot*, "death," to indicate that even death is part of life and is powerless to negate its essential goodness (Midrash Genesis Rabbah 7:5). In view of the tragic Jewish experience through the centuries, both individual and collective, culminating in the Holocaust, the tradition would have had ample warrant for regarding this world as a vale of tears and human existence as a living hell. Who would have blamed those who are overwhelmed by evil triumphant in the world? But the dominant attitude embodied in Jewish ethics has been life-affirming, although thinkers have been acutely conscious of its limitations.

Thus the Mishnah taught that this world is a corridor leading to the hall of the world to come and declared that "One hour of the bliss in the world to come is better than all the life of this world." But that statement is prefaced by another, "One hour of repentance and good deeds in this world is greater than all the life of the world to come" (M. *Abot* 4:1). Although the world to come is the area of perfect reward and boundless bliss, it cannot equal this world, imperfect as it is, which is the field of human activity and striving.

According to biblical law, the *nazir* (literally, "consecrated person"), who had taken a vow to abstain from wine and strong drink, had to bring a sin offering after he had fulfilled the obligations of this vow of abstinence (Num. 6:14). Why the sin offering? The Rabbis of the Talmud explained this provision by setting down a striking generalization regarding the entire ascetic impulse: "If he who has deprived himself only of wine is called a 'sinner,' how much more so is he who denies himself of any of the joys of life?" (B. *Nedarim* 10a).

The third-century Babylonian Sage Samuel counseled his students, "Take hold and eat, take hold and drink, for this world from which we depart is like a wedding feast" (B. *Erubin* 54a). His great contemporary, Rab, following in the footsteps of the biblical Sage Ecclesiastes, though in a far different mood, declared it a supreme religious duty to enjoy the pleasures available in the world: "Every human being is destined to render an account before God for all the blessings of the world that his eyes beheld and he did not enjoy" (P. *Kiddushin*, end).[3]

A modern Hasidic tale reveals that at least one source of hesitation with regard to the ascetic life derives from ethical concerns. A rich Hasid once visited a rabbi and asked to be blessed. "Before I do so, tell me what your manner of life is," the rabbi said. "Rabbi, I am very frugal in my food, I wear the cheapest garments, I fast Mondays and Thursdays every week." "I cannot offer you a blessing, my son," the rabbi replied, "unless you promise forthwith to change your way of life completely. You must begin to eat meat and drink wine. You must dress in accordance with your station, and enjoy the blessings of this world." After the rich Hasid promised to obey and had received his blessing, the rabbi's disciples asked, "Rabbi, why did you insist that he forsake his abstemious way of life?" "The answer is simple," said the rabbi. "If he eats nothing but bread and water, he will regard it entirely proper for the poor to starve altogether. If he eats meat and drinks wine, he will recognize that the poor should at least have bread to eat."

The Appraisal of Human Nature

The affirmation of life, in spite of all its limitations, goes hand in hand with a realistic assessment of human nature. In the cosmic hierarchy of divine creation, human beings occupy a middle position between the animals and the angels. With the beasts, humans share the animal instincts and appetites. They are bidden not to suppress them but to control and channel them for higher goals through the medium of the *mitzvot*, which "were given in order to refine human nature." (Midrash Genesis Rabbah 44). Humans share with the angels the duty of worship and obedience to God. But one crucial difference makes them greater than the angels: Unlike the heavenly beings, humans are endowed with free will—the capacity to choose between good and evil, between loyalty and rebellion. The angelic nature deprives the angels of this freedom of choice, which is the glory of man and the purpose of creation. Time and again the Talmud repeats: "The Torah was not given to angels, but to human beings" (B. *Yoma* 30a and 54a).

It was an axiom of biblical thought that "there is no man that lives and does not sin" (I Kings 8:46; Eccles. 7:20; II Chron. 6:36). Building on this biblical foundation, normative Judaism developed the view that human nature is malleable, in the concept of "the two *yetzers*," an evil impulse as well as a good impulse, with which every human being is endowed.[4]

In the agonizing decades before the destruction of the Second Temple by the Romans, there arose in Palestine a few apocalyptic sects who believed that human beings had inherited an ineradicable taint of evil from Adam's sin in the Garden of Eden.[5] The doctrine of the Fall of Adam emerges full-blown in the Apocrypha, in IV Ezra, the author of which witnessed the destruction of the Temple in 70 C.E.:

> Oh thou Adam, what hast done?
> For though it was thou that sinned,
> The Fall was not thine alone
> But ours also who are thy descendants.[6]

But II Baruch, written in the same age of chaos and corruption, opposes this view energetically and gives clear expression to what was and has remained the basic Jewish viewpoint:

> Adam is therefore not the cause, save for his own sin,
> But each of us has been the Adam of his own soul.[7]

Even the Gospels, which have marked affinities with the groups that produced the pseudepigraphical literature, nowhere express the idea that the human race has been corrupted irremediably by Adam's sin. The doctrine appears only in the Epistles of Paul, who makes it the cornerstone of his theology. Since then, the Fall of Man has remained fundamental to Christian theology.[8] In the following centuries, it underwent considerable development and modification, and the process of reinterpretation is still very much alive. But a basic difference emerges between Judaism and Christianity: In classical Christianity, man sins because he is a sinner; in classical Judaism, man is a sinner when he sins.

To be sure, the darker side of life found its expression in the tradition as well. One of the few overtly philosophical discussions in the Talmud reads, "The school of Shammai taught, 'It is better for man not to have been created, than to have been created.' The school of Hillel taught: 'It is better for man to have been created than not to have been created.' The Sages decided according to the school of Shammai, but added: 'Now that man has been created, let him scrutinize his actions'" (B. *Erubin* 13b).

In the vast number of controversies between Shammai and Hillel and their schools, it is Hillel who prevails; rabbinic law is emphatically Hillelite rather than Shammaiate in spirit and content. Moreover, the detailed prescriptions of rabbinic law for the conduct of life, including all of its minutiae, testify to the high valuation of life here and now. That the goal of the Halakhah is enhancing human welfare and minimizing suffering is clear from the Talmudic comment: "'You shall keep My laws and My ordinances, by which man shall live' [Lev. 18:5]. This means, 'Ye shall live by them and not die through them' [B. *Sanhedrin* 74a]." The mainstream in rabbinic Judaism persisted in finding life a good; *leḥayyim*, "to life," being the universal toast to the present day.

The most noteworthy area for self-fulfilment, often suppressed or denigrated in other traditions, is to be found in the realm of sexual experience.[9] The creation narrative in Genesis 2:18 declares categorically: "It is not good for man to dwell alone." The Hebrew word *ɔadam*, used in the passage and in the first chapter, means "human being" and is not limited to males. Because of a clear awareness of the perils that lurk in sexual desire, it was called *yetzer haraᶜ*, "the evil impulse." But the Talmud observes, "Without the sexual impulse, no man would build a house, marry a woman or engage in useful occupation" (Midrash Genesis Rabbah 9:7). A wise and witty legend declares that when Satan, the personification of the *yetzer haraᶜ* was once taken captive, there was not a chicken's egg to be found anywhere.

In *Iggeret Hakodesh*, attributed to the medieval legalist and commentator Nahmanides, the classic Jewish attitude toward the sexual component is clearly and vigorously expressed:

We who are the descendants of those who received the sacred Torah believe that God, blessed be He, created everything as His wisdom dictated, and He created nothing containing obscenity or ugliness [*genai ʾo kiyyur*]. For if we were to say that intercourse [*ha-ḥibbur*] is obscene, it would follow that the sexual organs are obscene.

How could God, blessed be He, create something containing a blemish or obscenity or a defect? For we would then find that His deeds are not perfect, though Moses, the greatest of the Prophets, proclaims and says, "The Rock, whose work is perfect" [Deut. 32:4]. However, the truth is, as it is said, that God is pure-eyed, so that He sees no evil. Before Him there is neither degradation nor obscenity. He created man and woman, fashioning all their organs and setting them in their proper function, with nothing obscene in them.[10]

The Jewish tradition never embraced the myth that "good women don't want sex." Based on Exodus 21:10, rabbinic law ordains that a man must not withhold from his wife her three basic rights of food, clothing, and sexual intercourse (B. *Ketubbot* 47b).

Marriage, not celibacy, constitutes the highest state of holiness in Judaism. The term for the contract of betrothal, *kiddushin* (originally meaning "set apart, denied to others"), has been taken for centuries to mean "state of holiness." It is not merely permissible but mandatory for a man and his wife to derive pleasure from the sexual act, which has been ordained by God and by that token is holy. Thus Jewish tradition established the practice of the husband's reading The Song of Songs on the sabbath eve. Though the book was interpreted allegorically to refer to the love of God and Israel, its literal meaning as the joyous expression of the love of man and woman was not lost upon the Jew.

The Talmudic injunction that scholars and their wives have conjugal relations on the sabbath eve is explained by Rashi, the great medieval commentator, on the grounds that conjugal relations are a source of pleasure and that the sabbath is intended for pleasure, rest, and enjoyment.[11] Nahmanides justifies the rule on mystical grounds, "A holy act should be performed on a holy day."[12]

In this important aspect of life, the attitude of normative Judaism is at the furthest possible remove from that of classical Christianity. The early Christians, like other Jewish apocalyptic sects living in an atmosphere of crisis, developed a sense of "imminent eschatology," a conviction that a cosmic catastrophe climaxed by God's intervention in the world was about to occur. As a result, the Gospels and the Epistles of the New Testament express an ethics of self-abnegation, not only in the areas of sex and the family but also with regard to the social and political order.[13] The effects of this approach are written large in the life of Western civilization to the present day.

When Francis Bacon declared that the blessing of the Old Testament is prosperity and that of the New is adversity, his intention was to exalt the new dispensation at the expense of the old. Judaism, however, would feel not at all uncomfortable with Bacon's pejorative description. Living in a world created by a righteous God must by definition be a blessing. Hence, enjoying the gifts of nature provided by Him is perforce a duty as well as a privilege.

This affirmation of life finds a striking and unique embodiment in the structure of Jewish ritual. An elaborate system of benedictions has been created by the tradition for every experience in life. Special blessings are ordained for spiritual occasions, such as the study of the Torah; meeting with a great scholar, whether Jewish or gentile; beholding a person of great beauty; seeing a natural wonder; or witnessing thunder or lightning. But the most frequently used blessings are offered for normal physical pleasures, such as partaking of bread, water, fruit, or wine or donning new clothes. Most fundamental of all is the *sheheḥeyanu*, "thanksgiving for being alive." A tradition that looked down on the enjoyment of the physical world could never have created this structure of blessings. Their importance in Judaism is eloquent testimony that the enjoyment of life is recognized as a divine imperative.

The Quest for Self-Fulfilment

The affirmation of life as a blessing is a great leap of faith in Judaism. From it flow two cardinal principles: the quest for self-fulfilment as the cornerstone of personal ethics, and the drive for justice as the foundation of ethics in society.

The commands of Judaism, unlike those of the New Testament, are designed to serve as canons of behavior for a perdurable society. The ethical code is rooted in the faith that the world is governed by a righteous God, so that right doing leads to well-being and wrongdoing to disaster. In pre-exilic Israel, where the bulk of the Bible had its origin, the center of religious concern was the group rather than the individual. The Torah promises prosperity to the nation if it obeys God's will and punishment if it violates His law. The Prophets were even more consistent in their concern with national destiny.

During the Babylonian Exile and the period of the Return, the individual became increasingly important. His actions and hopes, his beliefs and doubts, moved to center stage in Jewish religious thought, when the fortunes of the nation declined as a succession of foreign rulers—Persian, Egyptian, Syrian, and Roman—held sway over Palestine. Now the Wisdom teachers transferred the basic attitudes of biblical faith and ethics from the group to the individual and continued to maintain the ethic of self-fulfilment and the primacy of justice.[14]

The most succinct formulation of the biblical world view is to be found in the Book of Proverbs: "Righteousness exalts a nation, but sin is a reproach to any people" (14:34). The indispensable role of the law and the Prophets in molding the national ethos is set forth in the same book: "Lacking the vision [of the Prophets], a people grows wild, but happy is he who keeps the Law" (29:18). The ethic of self-fulfilment was expressed by Hillel in the first century B.C.E. in his matchless utterance: "If I am not for myself, who will be for me? But if I am only for myself, of what good am I? And if not now, when?" (M. *Abot* 1:14).

His words should guard us against the error of identifying self-fulfilment with self-interest or selfishness. What is crucial is the concept of selfhood, which is not exhausted by the boundaries of one's physical organism, the body from tip to toe, with its needs and appetites. Basic to the ethics of self-fulfilment is the emphasis on the total personality, which has a thousand invisible strands linking it to others in the family, the community, the nation, and the human race.

The preference in Judaism for the ethics of self-fulfilment over the ethics of self-abnegation, which some other religious traditions held out, is clearly indicated in an interesting passage in the Talmud. It sets out the hypothetical case of two men in a desert. One possesses a flask of water that is adequate to sustain only one life. An otherwise little-known Sage, Ben Patura, suggests that they share the water so that neither may look upon his companion dying before his eyes. But the famous Sage Rabbi Akiba cites the biblical verse "Thy brother shall live with thee [italics mine]" (Lev. 25:36), from which he deduces that "Thy life takes precedence over the life of thy neighbor" (B. *Baba Mezia* 62a). Akiba declares that in such a tragic circumstance the owner of the flask would be morally justified in drinking the water himself, thus preserving at least one human life instead of having both men die out of a sentimental impulse. It goes without saying that he would be free to give his bottle to his companion, out of love for him or out of the conviction that there was a greater gain in preserving the life of his companion than his own. Akiba rejects the idea that both lives ought to be lost, when one can be saved.

On the other hand, the Talmud insists that if A threatens to kill B unless B kills C, B is forbidden to murder C in order to save his own life. B must be prepared to die at the hand of A, since in either event one innocent life would be lost, and B would thus keep himself free from the crime of murder: "Who is prepared to say that your blood is redder than that of your proposed victim?" (B. *Pesahim* 25b).

Justice and Love

The affirmation of life as against the ethic of self-abnegation is the source of the ethic of self-fulfilment for the individual. It is also the philosophic basis for the concern in Judaism with the ideal of justice in society. It is because each human being has a right and a duty to enjoy the blessings of the world that justice is a universal obligation. Injustice in all its forms means the encroachment by one person or group on the legitimate and inalienable right of another to partake of the joys available in this world, in which all human beings have a share.

If denying oneself the blessings of the world were the ideal, the tyrant and the exploiter could scarcely be faulted for aiding their victims to fulfil their religious duty and thus attain to eternal life in the world to come! Indeed, in some circles in pre–Civil War America similar arguments were actually invoked. In 1829, Charles Coatesworth Pinckney, a nephew of the Founding Father of the same name, urged an audience in South Carolina to be more zealous in evangelizing their black slaves on the ground that the imparting of Christianity would tend to make them more docile, obedient, and tractable:

> Nothing is better calculated to render man satisfied with his destiny in this world than a conviction that its hardships and trials are as transitory as its honors and enjoyments; and that good conduct, founded on Christian principles, will ensure superior rewards in that which is future and eternal.

Quite different was the attitude of a Hasidic master who declared, "Why do you worry about my soul and your own body? Worry about my body and your own soul!"

Injustice is a violation of the moral order. It has its analogue in the physical world in the principle of "impenetrability," which states that two objects cannot occupy the same place—when the attempt is made, a collision occurs. The Prophet's insistence that "justice is God's law for the universe" could be described as "the law of moral impenetrability"; when injustice is perpetrated by one individual, group, or nation upon another, disaster must result.[15] The Hebrew Prophets rang untold changes on this basic theme, as enunciated in the Torah— "Righteousness, righteousness, you must pursue" (Deut. 16:20).

To be sure, no analogy is ever complete, and here there is a discrepancy of tragic proportions between the physical world and the moral universe. While scientific law apparently operates universally in the physical realm, Heisenberg's principle of indeterminancy notwithstanding, there are glaring "exceptions" to the law of "moral impenetrability." They constitute the problem of evil, the greatest stumbling block to religious faith. Answers and approaches without number have been proposed on every possible level of sensitivity and logic to explain the existence of evil in God's world. Ultimately the most profound response is that of God's speeches in the Book of Job—the world is beautiful, but evil remains a mystery, a residue of chaos in the cosmos. The Prophets themselves wrestled with the problem, but they would nevertheless insist that righteousness is an indispensable law of life.

The basic characteristics of the Jewish tradition that we have noted—the affirmation of life, the duty and the right to share in the blessings of the world, and the realistic perception of both the limitations and the potential of human nature—all unite to establish the ideal of justice as the cornerstone of Jewish ethics.

To evaluate fairly the impact on life of the ethics of self-fulfilment, it is worth recalling that Akiba himself died a martyr's death during the Hadrianic persecutions. What is perhaps even more to the point, rabbinic law declares that he who sees his neighbor drowning in a river or being dragged off by a wild animal or being attacked by bandits is obliged to save him. In this connection, the biblical command in Leviticus 19:16, which I regard as one of the most far-reaching principles of biblical ethics, is adduced, "You shall not stand idly by the blood of your fellow-man" (B. *Sanhedrin* 73a). In the eighteen centuries since Akiba, untold Jews were taught to live by the ethics of self-fulfilment. Yet they died for other human beings, for their faith, for their people, or for the advancement of some other ideal.

In sum, the ethics of self-fulfilment regards the preservation of one's life, which is the gift of God, as the highest good, so long as it is not achieved by the destruction of other life, which is equally the creation of God and has an equal right to survival.

We are now in a position to relate the practice of martyrdom to these two conceptions of ethics. At first blush, martyrdom would seem to be consistent only with the ethics of self-abnegation, of which it would be the highest manifestation. But while the martyr may indeed be actuated by this ideal, in reality the justification for the act is to be sought in the ethics of self-fulfilment. For martyrdom flows out of the individual's conviction that self-sacrifice will ultimately redound to the enhancement of life for the commonalty. The martyr, as its Greek etymology indicates, is a witness. By his heroic action he seeks to testify to the truth by which he lives and to help advance the cause to which he is dedicated, or to express his love for a being outside himself, be it on earth or in heaven. In a word, he loses his life so that what is for him the essence of life may live.

One of the oldest clichés declares that justice is the ethic of the Old Testament and love is the ethic of the New, or that Judaism is the religion of justice and Christianity is the religion of love. The symmetry and the contrast break down at the very outset.

First, Judaism is not the religion of the Old Testament. The Hebrew
Bible is only the first stage in the history of Judaism, which has continued to develop for more than two thousand years after the biblical period; indeed modern Judaism in all its forms resembles rabbinic Judaism far more than it does biblical religion.

Second, the formulation of the love ethic at its highest, the Golden
Rule, is to be found in the Hebrew Bible (Lev. 19:18); it is a quotation
not an original statement in the New Testament. Even its negative formulation, "What is hateful to you, do not do to your neighbor," was set
forth by Hillel decades before the rise of Christianity.

Third, and most important, the virtues of self-abnegation and love
were preached in the Sermon on the Mount and elsewhere to a community of believers, who expected the imminent destruction of the present
order and the miraculous establishment of a supernatural Kingdom of
God within a few days or weeks at the outside. Such extreme modes
of behavior as turning the other cheek to violence, or offering no resistance to tyranny, or selling all one's possessions and giving everything
to the poor could be enjoined upon the faithful only for a brief span of
time. Such patterns of conduct could scarcely serve as a permanent regimen for everyday life over an extended period. When the early Christian church recognized that the Kingdom of God was not imminent, it
developed an elaborate system of laws and institutions.

Moreover, the contention that "love" ought to be the guiding principle
in all human relations is frequently preached but rarely subjected to
analysis. No matter what definition of "love" is adopted, the term must
embody two factors: there must be an emotional content in the relationship between the subject and the object of the love; and this, in turn,
requires that there be some direct, palpable contact between them.

That nations and nation-states could relate to one another and conduct their foreign affairs in the spirit of love seems incredible even
as an ideal. Even the practice of enlightened self-interest and fair play
is generally beyond the capacity of national leaders. Accordingly,
Reinhold Niebuhr, who possessed a clear-eyed view of the realities of
human nature and yet sought to preserve the Christian doctrine of love,
proposed a bifurcation—nations should treat one another in the spirit
of justice, while individuals should react to each other in love.[16]

I believe, however, that love has a major limitation even as a principle governing the relations among individuals. We may be able to rise
to the level of love in our attitude toward other human beings within
our purview with whose suffering we may empathize and whose needs
we can feel. But "love" can rarely be used meaningfully with regard to
individuals with whom we have no contact or sense of identity, where
there is no true emotional content in the relationship. It is noteworthy
that the Golden Rule calls upon us to "love our *neighbor*," while Hillel's

negative formulation uses the term "friend." Both the biblical term *re'a* and Hillel's Aramaic *ḥabhra* are Semitic locutions meaning "the next person," whose presence impacts upon us and for whom we may be expected to feel compassion.

Perhaps some great-souled men and women can experience the same emotion of love for people on the other side of the globe whom they have never seen and with whom they have no contact. For the overwhelming majority of us, however, using "love" in such a context borders dangerously on cant. The most that can—and must—be realistically demanded of us is that we respond to all other human beings in the spirit of justice, no matter how far away or how different they may be. Nor do we require any other standard. Justice is enough. It applies equally to all persons by virtue of their common humanity, their innate dignity as children of God, and their inalienable right to the blessings of life, liberty, and the pursuit of happiness. It should hardly be necessary to emphasize that justice includes the exercise of sympathy and concern for anyone whose elemental rights are limited or lacking.

A striking instance of the blending of these attributes may be found in the biblical injunctions regarding the treatment of the needy. Thus the Book of Exodus commands:

> If you take your neighbor's garment in pledge, you must return it to him before the sun sets; it is his only clothing, the sole covering for his skin. In what else shall he sleep? Therefore, if he cried out to Me, I will pay heed, for I am compassionate [22:25, 26].

The Book of Deuteronomy repeats the injunction with a significant addition that reveals a delicate concern for the poor man's personal dignity. The pledged garment was returned to the borrower at nightfall, but when the lender returned in the morning to pick it up again, he was commanded,

> You shall not enter his house to take his pledge; you shall stand outside, while the man to whom you made the loan brings the pledge out to you ... [24:11].[17]

This injunction is probably the first adumbration of privacy as an inherent human right, an issue being warmly debated today in the American legal system.

Ethics in Wisdom Literature

The dimensions of biblical ethics are not exhausted by the Torah and the Prophets. Biblical Wisdom supplies some basic elements generally overlooked. Biblical Wisdom is embodied primarily but not exclusively in the Book of Proverbs and in the Apocryphal book of Ben Sira, the repositories of practical *ḥokhmah*. The Wisdom teachers built their ethical instruction for the individual on the biblical faith that the world is governed by a righteous God, so that a man's conduct determines his destiny. The ethics of biblical Wisdom rests on the conviction that "morality is the best policy."

What has not received due recognition is the special contribution of biblical Wisdom literature to ethical thought, indicated by its very name and its synonyms: *ḥokhmah*, "wisdom"; *binah*, "understanding"; and *deʿah*, "knowledge." Another term, *ʿormah*, which elsewhere in the Bible means "craft, cunning," is used in Proverbs in the favorable sense of "prudence, good sense" (1:4; 8:5, 12; 22:3; 27:12). Wisdom emphatically rejects the doctrine of *sancta simplicitas*, the notion that stupidity is the badge of holiness and ignorance the mark of piety. On the contrary, biblical Wisdom emphasizes a realistic understanding of human nature, the uncertainties of life, and the pitfalls of the unexpected, and it stresses the need for prudence in confronting them.

The Wisdom teachers extol the virtues of sobriety, truth telling, a sense of responsibility, and hard work. They warn against the vices of gluttony and drunkenness and such traits as impetuousness, conceit, greed, or bad temper. Above all, they describe the dangers to personal success and well-being posed by sexual entanglements with streetwalkers and, what was far worse, adulterous married women. In fact, what is generally called "the Protestant work ethic" is actually the teaching of the biblical Sages. It entered the world view of the Anglo-Saxon peoples because of the Protestant "addiction" to the Bible, which was particularly marked among the Puritans, who have been described as "Old Testament Christians."

As is the case with many aspects of biblical thought, the work ethic presented in biblical Wisdom is deepened and extended in rabbinic literature. In an eloquent passage, the modern historian Gedalya Alon summarizes the salient features of the work ethic of normative Judaism:

> Several principles are involved, the first of which is the social one: that is to say, every person is to some degree responsible for maintaining the social order. Next comes the individual factor: idleness is thought of as destructive to character; the person who does no work is like a ship adrift, a prey to every passing wind; while at the same time work is a sovereign remedy against the trials and crises from which no one is exempt. Thirdly, work is perceived as a value in itself, a potential source of deep satisfaction, a distinctive mark of the human being—God's gift to man. Finally, work is seen as an indispensable prerequisite for reaching the higher levels of spiritual exaltation. It was a doctrine of the Rabbis that revelation and prophecy were available only to those who first engaged in manual labor, witness for example Moses or Elisha.[18]

Their faith in God notwithstanding, the biblical Wisdom teachers knew that the correspondence between virtue and reward was less than exact, automatic, or universal. They were also keenly aware of the less-attractive aspects of human nature. Accordingly, they tempered their teaching by injecting a healthy dose of realistic understanding into their idealistic aspiration.

The Wisdom teachers constantly urge the practice of charity toward the poor, but they are conscious of the perils involved in going surety for one's neighbor, a practice in which one often loses both one's money and one's friend (Prov. 6:1–2; 11:15; 20:26; 22:26; 27:13).

The Sage in Proverbs is aware, too, of the utility of a bribe in making one's way and removing obstacles to one's advancement: "A man's gift eases his way and gives him access to the great" (18:16). Similarly, "A gift in secret subdues anger; a present in private, fierce rage" (21:12).

Another instance of the predilection for the concrete over the abstract may be cited. There is, to be sure, no explicit injunction in the Torah to "Love your enemy," as is enjoined in the Sermon on the Mount. But neither is there a command, "Hate your enemy," the claim in Matthew 5:43 notwithstanding. Instead, the Holiness Code urges: "You shall not hate your kinsman in your heart. Reprove your neighbor, lest you incur guilt because of him. You shall not take vengeance or bear a grudge against your kinsfolk. Love your neighbor as yourself: I am the Lord" (Lev. 19:17–18). Even more specifically, the Torah commands, "When you encounter your enemy's ox or ass wandering you must take it back to him. When you see the ass of your enemy prostrate under its burden and would refrain from helping him, you must nevertheless help him with it" (Exod. 23:4–5).

The Book of Proverbs, sensitive to human weaknesses, seeks to motivate such action toward one's enemies by pointing out that not only will it win God's favor but that it constitutes a subtle form of "revenge" upon one's foe: "If your enemy is hungry, give him bread to eat. If he is thirsty, give him water to drink. You will be heaping live coals on his head, and the Lord will reward you" (Prov. 25:21–22).

Justice and the Law

Justice is the cornerstone of Jewish ethics, but it is not identical with law, because justice includes aspects of human relationships that are beyond the power of the law. These are the categories for which the Talmud has a series of significant names: "acts punishable by Heaven but not punishable by human courts," "forbidden but unpunishable," and "matters handed over to the heart." Thus the law makes it punishable to injure one's fellow; justice requires that we help him. Beating one's father is a legal crime enforceable with sanctions; no system of law can compel a man to love or revere his parent. There thus emerges the paradox that law, which arises in order to make justice operative in society, falls perpetually behind it. In a rational and just society, the goal will always be to close the gap and bring legal practice as close to equity as possible. This observation may appear elementary, but the truth is that it has frequently been lost sight of in modern society.

The Halakhic category of offenses "punishable by Heaven but unpunishable by human courts" reminds us that there are immoral acts beyond the power of the police and the courts to deal with; when the effort is made through legal and government agencies, more harm than good generally results. The cause of temperance was scarcely promoted by the Eighteenth Amendment; instead, Prohibition created an array of law enforcement problems and a proliferation of crime that are still with us. Americans are notoriously impatient with problems, and so the cry goes up, "There ought to be a law against it." The intractable fact remains, however, that there are antisocial and immoral patterns of behavior that cannot be suppressed by the agencies of the law; they can be overcome, if at all, only by the slow process of ethical education.

A striking case in point is the matter of pornography. For years persistent and unavailing efforts have been made to deal with it through legal means. A long succession of definitions and redefinitions of obscenity have been advanced in legislation and judicial decisions. Justice Woolsey's famous ruling in the case of James Joyce's *Ulysses*, that a work is to be judged by its social value as a whole, was a landmark decision of enduring value, but it is obviously not a sufficient guide. The more-recent and more-restrictive judicial declaration that if the moral standards of the community are violated the work is obscene is of little value or help. Which community is to serve as the norm—San Francisco or Greenwich Village, or all of New York City, or the Bible Belt, or all of the East, or the entire country? And how are these standards to be determined? By the sermons preached, by the statements of politicians or by the actual practices of the given society? The net result of antiobscenity legislation and judicial decisions has been censorship and punishment of the true artist or writer, while the purveyors of filth go free and wax rich.

At the beginning of this century, George Bernard Shaw wrote,

> Let nobody dream for a moment that what is wrong with censorship is the shortcoming of the gentleman who happens at any moment to be acting as censor. Replace him tomorrow by an Academy of Letters and Poetry . . . and the new filter will still exclude original, epoch-making work, while passing conventional, old-fashioned and vulgar work.[19]

The lack of resolution of the obscenity issue points up an insight of Jewish law—that particularly in the area of human relations, external, positive law is incapable of meeting the problem. What is required is a source of inner direction for moral conduct. The frustrations and failures encountered by law enforcement officials in the campaign against drugs underscores the same truth.

Since Judaism finds its origin and authority in the will of a moral being, who at the Exodus presented Himself to His people as the champion of justice and freedom, its legal system must constantly pass muster before the moral conscience. To be sure, the human conscience is often as obtuse among Jews as among others, and its capacity for self-deception is endless. But the goal is always present to close the gap between law and ethics and make the law the practical expression of ethical aspiration.

Pluralism in the Tradition

It may be argued that the task essayed in this chapter, the fair and adequate delineation of the contours of the Jewish tradition, is an elusive undertaking. Indeed some would insist that it is an impossibility.

The problems involved in doing justice to a tradition drive from both the character of the observer and the nature of the phenomenon being observed. Every student approaches his task through his own personality, with all his limitations of knowledge and insight. Moreover, every era has its own blind spots and special fields of vision. These inevitably affect the work and attitude of the scholar, who is the child of his age as well as the product of his own specific development. His conclusions will inevitably be colored by his predilections and prejudices.

At least equally important is the fact that a tradition is never monochromatic—it will contain contradictions and inconsistencies. Some of these differences emanate from the same period, when they represent the deposit of opposing groups or aberrant sects. They may derive from isolated communities or influential individuals. Others go back to different eras and reflect the changes stimulated by the flux of events.

What has been presented above as the basic traits of the Jewish religion must of necessity represent a selection from the limitless spectrum of Jewish differences in outlook and timbre. Thus we have emphasized the basically rational approach to the problems of life as characteristic of the Jewish tradition. We have also pointed out that the principle of the enjoyment of the world's blessings is a major imperative taught by Judaism.

The attentive reader will have noticed that in this sketch of the Jewish tradition two major phenomena in religion have apparently not been taken into account. One is asceticism, which is not especially popular today, in an age dedicated to instant gratification. The other is mysticism, a trend that is now greatly in vogue, at least as a conversation piece. In a period hostile to the intellect and scornful of reason, mysticism on every conceivable level is "in."

In the past, what role have asceticism and mysticism played in the Jewish tradition? What function, if any, can they perform in the present and future? These questions have been answered differently during the relatively short history of the scientific study of Judaism. On the one hand, modern historical-critical scholarship serves to indicate the complex problems facing the scholar and the thinker in their work. On the other, it offers an opportunity to evaluate the place of mysticism and asceticism in Judaism without exaggerating or minimizing their roles.

Today there is a growing recognition of the variety in Jewish belief and practice, together with a deeper appreciation of the contributions that the different schools have made to the content of Jewish life and thought. As a result, some thinkers and scholars now espouse the view that the concept of "normative Judaism" is a misnomer; whatever has been accepted by some Jews at one time or another is "Jewish" and is therefore equally valid as part of Judaism. Hence, they argue, value judgments on "authenticity" must not be applied to the history or the content of Judaism.

Undoubtedly, a good deal of merit inheres in this view. There is a substantial moral gain in adopting a position of tolerance and open-mindedness toward the various currents in the stream of Jewish thought. This attitude is far superior, ethically as well as intellectually, to the narrow and arrogant claim made in some quarters to possess the whole truth and nothing but the truth. Justice Learned Hand once defined liberty as "the spirit that is never quite sure it is right." It may be added that this attitude is essential not only to the cause of liberty but also to the quest for truth.

Particularly in recent years we have become increasingly conscious of the many pitfalls that lurk in the search for truth. Sensational episodes in the contemporary history of science have demonstrated that completely objective research scarcely exists even in the physical sciences. In the humanistic disciplines, where the background and outlook of the scholar are central to the enterprise, the proclivities and prejudices of the investigator will often distort the evidence and affect the conclusions.

In addition, the problems involved in determining the basic features of a tradition may inhere not only in the varying attitudes of the observer but in the divergence to be found within the data itself. Hence the self-evident truths of one age may be questioned in another and totally rejected in a third one.

The critical-historical research into Jewish history, literature, beliefs, and institutions is less than two centuries old. There were individual precursors of the scientific method in medieval Spain, Provence, and Italy in the Middle Ages, but as a sustained and conscious enterprise, it began in the nineteenth century. Because most of its early great practitioners hailed from the German-speaking areas of Europe or were educated there, the discipline was called *Die Wissenschaft des Judentums*, which is inadequately translated as "the science of Judaism."

Its early exemplars in the nineteenth century reflected the rationalistic and evolutionary emphasis of the Emancipation era, which followed upon the French Revolution. Thus, Heinrich Graetz, the first great Jewish historian, like his colleagues, tended to emphasize the contributions of Jewish philosophy and the achievements of Hebrew philology and biblical exegesis, both of which, by a striking coincidence, had their inception in the genius of the gaon Saadia (882–942). Rabbinic scholars such as Abraham Geiger, Zacharias Frankel, and Isaac Hirsch Weiss undertook to trace the history of Jewish law from the Bible through the Talmudic and medieval periods. The vast structure of medieval Hebrew poetry and other literary texts in which Jewish literature was preserved—though previously neglected—were cultivated by Leopold Zunz, Israel Davidson, Chaim Brody, and other scholars.

There were exceptions, to be sure, but in general the features in the history of Judaism that seemed to accord best with the *Zeitgeist*, "the spirit of the age," were given the lion's share of scholarly interest and energy, while other elements were downgraded or neglected. Jewish mysticism and its great classics were dismissed as a farrago of superstition. Thus Graetz treated Shabbetei Zevi, "the false Messiah," as a charlatan and his followers as dupes. Only grudging attention was paid to Hasidism, and its literature was not even studied. Asceticism was regarded as indigenous to Christianity but foreign to Judaism. Yiddish was dismissed as a jargon, a debased form of German. In general, the vast masses of East European Jewry in the Czarist empire were regarded with an admixture of scorn for their intellectual backwardness and pity for their poverty and rightlessness.

Asceticism and Mysticism

An about-face has occurred with regard to both asceticism and mysticism. It has long been regarded as a truism that Judaism, unlike early Christianity, is a nonascetic religion. To disprove this widely held notion, a distinguished American biblical scholar, James A. Montgomery, undertook to assemble all the evidence for ascetic practices in ancient Israel.[20]

The most important phenonenon in this connection was the Nazirate, an institution that existed in the biblical period and for a few centuries after the return from the Babylonian Exile. A *nazir* (literally, "set apart, consecrated"), was a person, male or female, who took certain restrictions upon himself or herself for a fixed period of time in order to adhere to a higher standard of purity than was enjoined upon the generality of men and women. Nazirites had to let their hair grow long, abstain from liquor, and avoid defilement by contact with a dead body (Num. 6). Apparently they were also called upon to refrain from sexual relations, though the most famous Nazirite of all, Samson, hardly testifies to such abstinence.

During the period of the Hebrew monarchy, there was also a sect or clan called Rechabites. In obedience to the commands they ascribed to their founder, Yonadab ben Rechab, they were required to live in tents instead of stone houses and to abstain from wine and liquor. They were not to plant crops and were evidently to support themselves by raising cattle (Jer. 25).

Our information with regard to both groups is tantalizingly meager. Clearly, both the individual Nazirites and the communally oriented Rechabites represented a symbolic protest against the sophisticated urban culture of the late Hebrew monarchy, with all its blandishments and corruptions. Hence they insisted on returning to the ambiance of the early nomadic stage in Israel's experience.

The Hebrew Prophets also glorified the nomadic period in Israel's Golden Age, but they were not interested in a mechanical reversion to a dead past. They sought to perpetuate the ideals of equality, mutual responsibility, and social justice, which they believed had prevailed in the nomadic era, and to integrate them into the new and more-advanced rural and urban society of the monarchy. The Nazirites and the Rechabites, on the other hand, lacked this capacity for the creative use of tradition. Their goal of preserving the outward marks of the earlier age was an essentially reactionary enterprise that was doomed to failure.

After the Babylonian Exile, the Rechabites are lost to view, but the institution of the Nazirites continued for several centuries after the building of the Second Temple. In addition, various groups called "Essenes" in Greek and Latin sources came into existence. The name "Essenes" is a Greek transcription of the Aramaic equivalent of the Hebrew *Hasidim*, "saints, holy men." The Essenes observed rigorous rules of ritual purity and generally, but not always, abstained from marriage. Only one group among them, the Dead Sea sectarians or Qumranites, left an extensive literature, which has only come to light in the mid-twentieth century.

The Essenes lived in communal settlements, generally in sparsely populated desert areas. Their wealth was held in common, and they were governed by a council of priests and laymen apparently chosen by the members. They supported themselves by husbandry and the care of sheep. They hated the pomp and pageantry of the Temple in Jerusalem, the leadership of which they regarded as usurpers and perverters of God's will. Their personal abstemiousness and their absorption in pious exercises and the study of sacred books gave them a cachet of holiness. Though generally pacific in temperament, some of them participated in the war against Rome, which ended in the burning of the Temple and the destruction of the Jewish polity in 70 c.e. Thereafter monastic communities no longer existed in Jewish life.

Asceticism as an individual proclivity continued among Jews in the Middle Ages and down to modern times. Traditional Jewish communities had *perushim* (literally, "set apart"), who are not to be confused with the ancient Pharisees. These holy men took vows of personal deprivation in order to "reenact the Exile" and thus hasten the Redemption. Their practices included flagellation, bathing in icy streams during the winter, abstemiousness in food as well as frequent fasting, and long periods of wandering as exiles away from home. Their modest needs were generally supplied by the inhabitants of the villages and the towns to which they came in their wanderings.

It is, therefore, obvious that asceticism was not unknown in biblical and postbiblical Judaism; its legitimacy cannot be denied as an expression of Jewish piety. There will always be temperaments that find in the voluntary withdrawal from such pleasures as food, love, and friendship the formula for the attainment of holiness.

Such goals have always resonated in some spirits, and Judaism is no exception. The ascetic's motto might well be the injunction recorded in the Talmud, "Sanctify yourself by [abstaining even from] what is permitted to you" (B. *Yebamot* 20a). Nonetheless, it is clear that ascetic practices were not the norm; they penetrated only to limited circles and always remained the regimen of a small minority of the people. So far, no ascetic groups like the monastic orders in Christendom are to be found in Judaism. It is only individuals who choose to mortify the flesh by ascetic practices.

Even more revolutionary has been the relatively recent change of attitude with regard to the role of mysticism. The genius and energy of the twentieth-century scholar Gershom Scholem has transformed our understanding of Jewish history by highlighting the importance of the mystical impulse in Judaism, a scholarly discipline that he virtually created from scratch. He gave a positive evaluation to the messianic movements that arose many times during the eighteen hundred years of Jewish exile, seeing in them the indestructible yearning of the people for redemption from exile. With incredible erudition and brilliance, Scholem argued that Jewish vitality lay precisely in the mystical and messianic movements, rather than in the rationalism of the philosophers, the scientific achievements of the scholars, or the legal acumen of the Rabbis.

So thoroughly were the tables turned that in the *Encyclopedia Judaica* published in 1972 in Israel, Scholem's masterful article, "Kabbalah," occupies 164 columns, a volume in itself;[21] while Pharisaism, the seedbed of normative Judaism, receives only three columns; and "Philosophy, Jewish" is treated in six. The Talmud occupies 28 columns, and even the Bible, the foundation of modern Israeli culture, is alloted only 100.

The phenomena of mysticism had always been present in Judaism, but an appreciation of their importance emerged only at the conjunction of a powerful creative scholar and an era prepared to give them respect and attention. Our age is marked by the flight from reason and by the yearning for refuge in mystical experience, Occidental and Oriental, genuine and counterfeit. Hence, astrology and computers, the signs of the zodiac and the tracking of satellites, are all featured on the same newspaper page. The presence of both Scholem the man and an age of triumphant fundamentalism combined to reveal the historical dimension of mysticism in Jewish religion and history—and exaggerate it.

It is to be expected that when the inevitable reaction makes itself felt in both scholarship and life, a better balance will emerge between the denigration of mysticism in earlier historical critical research and the exaggerated claim made for it by Scholem and his followers. Undoubtedly mysticism is an important factor in Jewish history, but it is not the vital source of all creativity nor is it more important than any other major manifestation of the Jewish spirit.[22] In sum, while mysticism and asceticism are authentic expressions of the Jewish ethos, they are not dominant traits in the tradition.

At present, a powerful surge to fundamentalism is making itself felt throughout the world. In Christianity and Judaism as well as in Islam it is marked by several closely related attributes. The most basic is intolerance of any divergence, a refusal to hear any view that differs from the accepted "truth." The bigotry is supported by triumphalism, the passionate conviction that the victory of "our side" is assured and that all who disagree are consigned to outer darkness. Finally, the suppression of dissent is morally justified by the claim to "authenticity," which is not inhibited in the least by the existence of identical claims by rival factions and creeds.

Nonetheless, the virtues of tolerance and the appreciation of differences remain. They do not require a retreat either from history or from reason. Scholars have the obligation to carry out the most rigorous and unbiased research they can, utilizing all available sources. It is their task to describe as fairly as possible the principles and practices of all the groups and movements in the history of Judaism. At all times, they must strive to draw the conclusions that best satisfy the canons of scientific method, following their lead without fear or favor. However, when the scholarly research is completed, the thinker is called upon to judge the value and the importance of the competing movements and tendencies and their contributions to the content of Judaism.

Conscious of the risks involved in running counter to the tide, I continue to believe that the relative importance and value of asceticism and mysticism for religion and for life are exaggerated today. What Max Kadushin has called "normal mysticism,"[23] the piety fostered by traditional Halakhic Judaism in the past, has, and deserves to have, a central place in Jewish life. On the other hand, the extreme forms in which mysticism often manifests itself today are in my view an aberration that will be abandoned when men and women once again recognize the power of reason and constructive action. These are the instruments needed for facing the problems of life, both individual and collective, and for doing battle against oppression, cruelty, and ignorance.

Several other important attributes may be sought and found in Judaism, but what is fundamental is a passion for justice, a bias for the right, an identification with the persecuted. This trait, a miracle to some and a scandal to others, was stamped on the psyche of the Jewish people at the Exodus from Egypt. We now turn to the powerful impact of this unique event on the history of Israel and mankind.

II

BONDAGE AND LIBERATION
THE EGYPTIAN EXPERIENCE

Throughout its history, the Jewish tradition reveals the pervasiveness of the ethical impulse within it. This concern with justice as the cardinal principle that must govern human affairs is not rooted in Jewish genes, nor is it a whim or a passing fashion. It is the consequence of the exposure of the biblical Hebrews to three factors that, particularly in combination, had an indelible effect on the outlook on life of biblical and post-biblical Judaism: the experience of the Hebrew tribes under Egyptian bondage, ending with the Exodus; their period of wandering in the wilderness, which culminated with their entrance into the Promised Land; and the activity in their midst of the Hebrew Prophets, who never permitted the people to forget their lowly origin or to falsify it. The first factor is the subject of this chapter; the other two are treated in chapter 3.

Israel's Egyptian experience stands like a mighty colossus at the inception of its national life, dominating the spiritual landscape of Israel and casting a powerful light on the faith and imagination of mankind for all time.[1] Both the period of bondage and the Exodus served as a paradigm for revolutionary leaders through the centuries, who interpreted the biblical narrative in the light of conditions in their own times and circumstances and found in it an earnest of the ultimate triumph of their particular causes. They included such religiously motivated figures as the fifteenth-century Italian reformer Savonarola, the Swiss Protestant theologian John Calvin, the English Puritan leader Oliver Cromwell, and the contemporary Latin-American exponents of "liberation theology." Even secular and antireligious figures, such as Karl Marx, Lincoln Steffens, and Ernst Bloch, have fallen under the spell of the biblical Exodus.

We shall limit ourselves here to two illustrations of its impact on Americans. Black Africans, kidnapped from their homes by Arab traders and sold into slavery in America, kept alive for some two hundred years the faith that one day they would be free. They were sustained by the sermons they heard, the prayers they pronounced, and the spirituals they sang, all of which helped them to identify themselves with the ancient Israelites:

> When Israel was in Egypt land,
> Oppressed so hard they could not stand,
> Let my people go.

White Americans also drew inspiration and hope from the biblical Exodus. In the controversies between the American colonists and the British government in Westminster, the colonists saw themselves as the Israelites, Washington as Moses, George III as Pharaoh, the British as the Egyptian oppressors, and the Atlantic Ocean as the Red Sea. In a word, the Book of Exodus was the guidebook to their future, bringing the prophetic assurance of victory in their battle for liberty.

When the Continental Congress voted to adopt an appropriate seal for the newborn republic, a committee consisting of Benjamin Franklin, John Adams, and Thomas Jefferson proposed a scene depicting the drowning of the Egyptians in the Red Sea and the inscription "Rebellion to tyrants is obedience to God."

Whenever men were enslaved or exploited, but dared to hope and fight for freedom, the Exodus was a beacon on their path, bearing the promise of victory over their enemies.[2]

Important as the role of the Exodus is in the consciousness of mankind as a whole, it is at the very heart of the Jewish tradition. The Exodus divides into two major concepts: *shicbud mizrayim*, the bondage in Egypt, and *yezibat mizrayim*, the Exodus from Egypt. Since each became a cornerstone in Jewish religious and ethical thought, they deserve to be analyzed separately.

The Memory of Bondage

The experience—and later the memory—of slavery in Egypt laid the foundation for the Jews' identification with the oppressed rather than with the oppressors. The subsequent history of the Jewish people, heroic and tragic both, reinforced this trait, until it became virtually second nature in the Jew. The source of this feeling was poignantly expressed in the Torah: "You know how it feels to be a stranger, for you were strangers in the land of Egypt" (Exod. 23:9). This theme is repeated time without number in the Bible.

This constant reminder of the slave background of the Jewish people ran counter to normal human behavior. Usually people tend to glorify their origins and to invent for themselves a resplendent past; the lowly beginnings from which all human groups began are conveniently forgotten, and myths are created with gods and heroes as progenitors. To turn to American history once more, members of today's high society in the state of Georgia are not likely to relish a reminder that they are descendants of convicts transported to the colony as a philanthropic venture by General James Oglethorpe.

Infinitely more pernicious has been the Nazi myth of an Aryan race—brave, blond, and beautiful—from which, Hitler declared, the Germans were descended, though he himself hardly qualified for the image. The living descendants of the imaginary "blond beast" concocted by Nazi mythology then proceeded to live up to that designation and gave the world its most horrible demonstration of beastliness, both moral and physical.

The Bible never permitted the Jewish people this luxury of forgetting and pretending. Their lowly beginnings were constantly recalled. The Decalogue declares, "Remember that you were once slaves in the land of Egypt, and that the Eternal your God brought you out by sheer strength and main force" (Deut. 5:15). This injunction did not remain a mere state of mind. It was directly applied to the elements in society who were weak and unprotected—the foreigner, the widow, the orphan, and the slave—and was extended to the lower orders of creation.

In the ancient world, even more than today, the alien had no rights. The Torah emphatically breaks with this universal pattern by the ringing declaration:

> There shall be one statute both for you and for the stranger who resides with you, a statute forever throughout your generations. As you are, so shall the stranger be before the Lord. One law and one ordinance shall be both for you and for the stranger that resides with you [Num. 15:15–16].

This sentiment is repeated again and again (Exod. 12:19; Num. 15:29).

More than legal justice is called for. "Therefore *love* [italics mine] the stranger; for you were strangers in the land of Egypt" (Deut. 10:19). Oppressing or cheating the alien or taking advantage of him in the courts because of his inferior legal position was a temptation not easily resisted. Hence it is forbidden again and again by the Torah (Exod. 22:20; 23:9; Deut. 23:17; 27:19) and is vigorously denounced by the Prophets (Jer. 7:6; 22:2; Ezek. 22:7; 29; Zech. 7:10; Mal. 3:5).

In the preceding chapter, we noted some limitations on the applicability of the Golden Rule, "You shall love your neighbor as yourself" (Lev. 19:18). Nevertheless, it is generally regarded as embodying the highest level of human conduct. It may be argued, however, that exalted as the principle is, it is based on the similarity between a man and his neighbor: "your neighbor—as yourself." A still higher rung on the ladder of love is reached in loving those who are different. This higher principle is laid down in the same Holiness Code in Leviticus:

> When a stranger resides with you in your land, you shall not do him wrong. The stranger who resides with you shall be to you as the native among you, and you shall love him as yourself; for you were strangers in the land of Egypt; I am the Lord your God [19:33–34].

When the Bible speaks of God as the Redeemer of Israel, it is using a legal term in its technical sense. By liberating the Israelites from their Egyptian masters, God became their master and they his *abadim*, a term generally translated as "servants" but literally meaning "slaves," morally bound to obey His will.

The Book of Deuteronomy repeats this great injunction no fewer than five times: "You shall remember that you were slaves in the land of Egypt" (5:15; 15:15; 16:12; 24:18; 22). Thus the Torah fashioned a powerful sense of identification of the Jew with the slave, the lowest stratum in society. The Exodus is the antithesis of human slavery.

To be sure, the Torah did not abolish human bondage. Slavery was the universal economic order in the ancient world. At a time when technology was generally primitive and productivity correspondingly low, the only viable economic system had to be based on slave labor. It is less than 150 years since slavery was abolished in the United States, in Czarist Russia, and in the British overseas possessions. Slavery remained characteristic of human society virtually until the end of the nineteenth century. There are reports that even today slavery continues to prevail on the Arabian peninsula and in parts of Africa.

A poor, technologically underdeveloped people like the Hebrews in Palestine three thousand years ago could not abolish the institution of slavery as such. The low productivity of the ancient world made an economy based on free labor impossible. What the Torah did was to transform the institution of slavery radically, all but eliminating it. It set a limit of six years of service for Hebrew slaves. Thus by a masterstroke, lifelong bondage was converted into a period of bond service. Even during these six years, the slave was safeguarded by the law. He had rights to his family relationships and could not be physically beaten, maltreated, starved, or underfed. Jewish law protected the slave with so many provisions that the Talmud declares, "He who acquires a Hebrew slave acquires a master for himself."[3] Non-Hebrew slaves did not enjoy the same limitation on the period of service (aliens in any society are far less privileged than citizens), but the basic physical protections of the law were extended to them as well.

Biblical Wisdom literature, which emanated from the upper classes in society, was less concerned with social justice and personal freedom

than were the Torah and the Prophets. Nevertheless it is in the Book
of Job, which transcends the limitations of class, culture, and ethnicity,
that the all-embracing doctrine of human equality is most clearly enunciated.

In the great "Code of Integrity" at the close of his debate with the
Friends, the suffering Job sets forth the ethical standards by which he
has lived. Citing fourteen infractions of morality of which he has not
been guilty, Job declares that during his days of prosperity and power
he had never been guilty of injustice toward his slaves. He was always
aware of God's seeing eye and of the common origin of all His children:

> "Have I despised the cause of my man-servant or of my maid-servant
>   When they contended with me?
>   For I always remembered,
>   What shall I do when God rises up,
>   and when he examines me,
>   how shall I answer Him?
>   Did not He make him in the womb as He made me
>   and fashion us alike in the womb?
>
>   [Job 31:13–15]

In every way possible, biblical and postbiblical Judaism sought to
protect the slave while in bondage and, more fundamentally, to convert
slavery into a limited period of bond service. Nevertheless, in spite of
all these provisions and safeguards, slavery was slavery, and the entire
thrust in the biblical tradition was antislavery. This basic attitude is
clearly evident in a remarkable law that had important consequences
in American history. On two occasions before the American Civil War,
Congress adopted a Fugitive Slave Law, according to which a black
slave who escaped from the South had to be returned to his original
master. There were many law-abiding citizens throughout the country
who refused to obey this law. Through the Underground Railroad they
helped speed these slaves into freedom, either in the North or in Canada. These practitioners of civil disobedience were not scofflaws or enemies of the American system. They held that the law of God took precedence even over Congress:

> You shall not give up to his master a slave who has escaped from his mas-
> ter to you; he shall dwell with you, in your midst, in the place which he
> shall choose within one of your towns, where it pleases him best; you
> shall not oppress him [Deut. 23:16–17].

Implicit in the biblical law of the fugitive slave is the conviction that
slavery is sinful. The illegitimacy of one man's being enslaved to another was explicitly stated by one of the greatest of the Sages, Rabbi
Johanan ben Zakkai. According to the Book of Exodus, a slave who re-

fuses to go free after his term of service and prefers to remain in bondage has his ear bored through (21:5–6). The Rabbis explain that this branding of the slave is a punishment: "His ear heard God proclaim, 'Unto Me shall the children of Israel be servants, for they are My servants' [Lev. 25:55] and not servants to servants. Yet this man took a human master for himself; he deserves to have his ear pierced through" (B. *Kiddushin* 22b). For Judaism, freedom from slavery is not merely a God-given right; it is a divinely ordained command.

The sympathy for the weak nurtured by the memory of Egyptian bondage extended to the lower orders of creation as well. Many remarkable provisions for the merciful treatment of animals were laid down in the Torah. Deuteronomy forbids the farmer to plow with an ox and a donkey yoked together, because that practice obviously imposes great hardship on the weaker animal (22:10). Nor was the farmer permitted to muzzle an ox during the threshing period to prevent its eating any other grain (Deut. 25:4).

A sensitivity to the feelings of living creatures and a simultaneous desire to inculcate compassion in human beings finds exquisite expression in another enactment in Deuteronomy:

> If you chance to come upon a bird's nest, in any tree, or on the ground, with young ones or eggs, and the mother sitting upon the young or upon the eggs, you shall not take the mother with the young. You shall let the mother go, but the young you may take to yourself, that it may go well with you, and that you may live long [22:6, 7].

Many factors undoubtedly enter into the complex structure of the laws of *kashrut* (food permitted to be eaten); these include the traditional laws of kosher slaughtering. The latter in particular are designed to keep alive the sense of reverence for life by minimizing the pain of the animal and by forbidding the eating of blood, which is the seat of life.

The juxtaposition of two verses in the Fourth Commandment, the first one ordaining rest for all living creatures on the sabbath day, and the second linking it immediately to the remembrance of the suffering in Egypt (Deut. 5:14, 15), demonstrates the pervasive impact of the bondage experience on the Jewish psyche for all time.

Building on these biblical foundations, rabbinic law and tradition elaborated an entire concept bearing the poignant name *zaʿar baʿalei ḥayyim*, "the pain of living creatures." Albert Einstein is reported to have credited the German-Jewish statesman Walter Rathenau with the saying "When a Jew says that he enjoys hunting, he lies." Whether or not this trait is true of modern Jews, the tradition strongly condemns hunting for sport as "not being the way of the seed of Abraham, Isaac, and Jacob." This sense of sympathy for suffering was not permitted to remain merely emotional or theoretic. Normative Judaism has always sought to translate attitudes into actions and feelings into conduct, to infuse ritual with ethics and inculcate ethics through ritual.

The period of bondage in Egypt served also as the rationale for the single most important observance in Judaism and the only ritual commandment to be found in the Decalogue. While the version in Exodus ordains the sabbath on theological grounds, to serve as a memorial of God's creation of the world and His resting on the seventh day, the Decalogue in Deuteronomy offers a socioethical rationale. The sabbath is explicitly linked to the period of Egyptian bondage:

> Observe the sabbath day, to keep it holy, as the Lord thy God commanded you. Six days you may labor, and do all your work; but on the seventh day is a sabbath for the Lord your God, on it you shall do no manner of work, you, nor your son, nor your daughter, nor your man-servant, nor your maid-servant, nor your ox, nor your ass, nor any of your cattle, nor your stranger that is within your gates; so that your man-servant and your maid-servant may rest as well as you. And you shall remember that you were slaves in the land of Egypt, and the Lord your God brought you out from there by a mighty hand and by an outstretched arm; therefore the Lord your God commanded you to keep the sabbath day [Deut. 5:12–15].

In Exodus 23:12, the theme of sabbath rest for all living creatures is repeated, but a strikingly new emphasis is added, "so that the slave and the stranger may be refreshed."

As has been pointed out above, Hebraism and Hellenism have been the most powerful influences from antiquity on the modern world, and deservedly so; the loss of either would mean an impoverishment of the human spirit. Both Moses and Aristotle understood the importance of leisure for raising people above the level of the beasts. Both knew that unless humans have freedom from unceasing toil, they cannot develop their spiritual attributes and rise to their full potential.

What were the consequences? Aristotle argued that since human beings need leisure to develop their highest capacities, slavery is justified, for the existence of some as slaves makes it possible for others to be free. The Torah realized equally the importance of liberty for the unfolding of human personality, but it drew radically different conclusions. It established the institution of the sabbath rest, one day in seven, which was applied not only to free persons, but to slaves and to all living creatures. *Shi‹bud mizrayim*, "the bondage in Egypt," was the matrix in which the Jewish spirit was fashioned and the Jewish tradition received its basic stamp, which could never be obliterated.

The Exodus in Judaism

As significant as *shi‹bud mizrayim*, the bondage in Egypt, is the second aspect of the Exodus, *yezi‹at mizrayim*, the liberation of the Israelites and their setting out for the Promised Land under the leadership of Moses.

The Exodus is the single most significant event in Jewish history. Forever after Jews saw in the Exodus living testimony of God's boundless love for his people and His faithfulness in fulfilling the promises He had made to the patriarchs Abraham, Isaac, and Jacob. These themes are stressed throughout the Torah, are reiterated by the Prophets, and are the subject of many of the psalms that praise God's saving power. Classical postbiblical literature—the Midrash, the Talmud, and the prayer book—rings many changes on the theme of God's special relationship to Israel, founded on mutual love and faithfulness and demonstrated for all time by the Exodus. Countless rituals observed on weekdays, sabbaths, and festivals recall the Exodus; they culminate in the spring Passover holiday and the *Seder*.

However, this all-pervasive influence of the Exodus on the Jewish consciousness has within it the seeds of a major moral and intellectual defect, the egregious error of believing that God is concerned exclusively with the Jewish people, a misconception that leads directly to the sin of chauvinism. The first of the great literary Prophets, Amos of Tekoa, was keenly aware of this malady, which affected many of his contemporaries as it does many of ours. He cited the Exodus, which was univerally regarded as proof positive of God's special concern for Israel. But then he added the all-important conclusion to be drawn from this event—Israel's special position imposed upon him a higher standard of conduct and a greater measure of responsibility than is required of members of nations that were not granted this unique privilege. In his words:

> Hear this word, O people of Israel, that the Lord has spoken concerning you, concerning the whole family that I brought up from Egypt: You alone have I singled out of all the families of the earth. Therefore will I call you to account for all your iniquities [Amos 3:1–2].

It is true that God had brought Israel out of Egypt, but, Amos contended, as the governor of history, He directs the migrations of all other nations as well. Indeed Israel is on a par before Him with the Ethiopians: "Indeed you are like the Ethiopians to Me, O house of Israel, declares the Lord. True, I brought Israel up from the land of Egypt but also the Philistines from Caphtor and the Arameans from Kir" (Amos 9:7). The message of the Exodus is clear—a uniqueness, yes; special privilege, no. Israel's one claim to distinction lies in its adherence to a higher standard of moral accountability.

Coming at the beginning of Jewish history, the Exodus imbued the Jew with a sense of hope, a conviction that the Jewish people is indestructible, a faith that even the Holocaust could not destroy. But this was not all; the physical liberation of the Exodus culminated six weeks later in the spiritual freedom conferred upon the Jewish people by the Torah. By the covenant at Sinai, Israel dedicated itself for all time to the war against idolatry, cruelty, and injustice. As the bearer of an immortal Torah, Israel itself is endowed with immortality. In the words of the traditional blessing, "He has given us a Torah of truth and planted in us the seed of eternal life."

The Exodus as a Paradigm of World History

The significance of the Exodus extends beyond the confines of the Jewish people; it offers insight into the meaning and direction of human history. The Exodus, bearing its message of the triumph of right over the forces of evil, stimulated the emergence of what the American philosopher Morris Raphael Cohen has called the greatest Jewish contribution to civilization—the concept of a philosophy of history.

When one first observes the succession of events, large and small, in the experience of nations, they seem to be a concatenation of separate incidents, often accidental and generally unrelated to one another. In the ancient world, men wrote chronicles, recording major occurrences as they happened, whether for good or for ill, but finding no underlying meaning or pattern in human events. In our individual lives, more bad things than good seem to happen. In public affairs, the forces of evil always seem to be in the ascendant. In the words of James Russell Lowell, "Right forever on the scaffold; Wrong forever on the throne."

This dismal view of human existence is contradicted in purely human terms by the Exodus, the first known instance in history of the victory of freedom over slavery. God's presence in history cannot be demonstrated mathematically; it is an act of faith, but it rests on the testimony of Israel's history, preeminently as it is revealed in the Exodus.

Ancient history traces all the great empires rising and falling in succession—Babylonia, Assyria, Bablylonia-Media, Persia, Greece, and Rome. The Middle Ages continued the trajectory of one nation rising from the ruins of another and falling victim in turn to a new aggressor. The twentieth century has seen the destruction of the Russian, British, German, and French empires. Communist imperialism has replaced much of earlier colonialism, but, if the past is any clue to the future, it too will not prove eternal.

Is there any meaning to this awesome chronicle of human cruelty and misery? The Hebrew Prophets were the first to see history as a process directed by God in which evil is doomed to fail and good is destined to emerge triumphant. The world of human society is governed by a law of consequence—right actions lead to well-being; wrongdoing to disaster. This law in the moral sphere can no more be violated with impunity than the law of gravitation can be disregarded in the physical world.[4]

To be sure, at any particular time, the hand of God is not easy to discern, in either the public or the private domain. The Hebrew Prophets would insist that apparently haphazard events reveal the presence of God in history. As Kierkegaard pointed out, we must look to the past to see the hand of God in history. It may be added that to see events in the present as God's intervention in history is a gift reserved only to prophets. For lesser mortals to make the claim is both arrogant and dangerous, as the various manifestations of active messianism in contemporary Muslim, Christian, and Jewish fundamentalism make all too tragically clear.

Thus modern historians explain the fall of Rome in terms of political, economic, demographic, and ecological factors; and they may well be right. The Prophets of Israel would not have quarreled with these explanations. But they would have insisted that underlying all causes is the one dominant fact—each empire was created by violence, sustained by force, and preserved by oppression. In trying to escape the operation of the law of consequence or retribution in history, these empires doomed themselves to destruction.

As Judah Halevi pointed out in another connection, God presents Himself to His people in the Decalogue not as "the Creator of heaven and earth" but in the words "I am the Lord your God who brought you forth out of the land of Egypt, out of the house of bondage." God is not merely sympathetic to those languishing under tyranny; He is actively on their side and will bring them victory. Right will not be on the scaffold forever; the Exodus is a prophecy that mankind will move on to liberty and justice.

Therein lies the hope for democracy. It is not that democratic government is perfect. As Winston Churchill reminded us, "Democracy is the worst form of government possible, except that all others are worse." The saving grace of the democratic order is that it possesses an inner, built-in capacity for self-correction and self-regeneration without recourse to violence and force. The history of democracy, symbolized by the ballot box in North America, Western Europe, and Israel, has shown that a society can face its problems, overcome its defects, and improve its condition without resorting to military coup or bloody revolution. If the democratic spirit remains truly alive and does not develop a hardening of its spiritual arteries, democracy will survive and flourish.

God Works in History

Perhaps the most beloved ritual in Judaism is the Passover Seder, which commemorates the Exodus. The Seder ends with the popular children's song *Had Gadya*, "One Kid," a charming round designed to keep the youngsters awake and interested in the evening's proceedings. But some traditional commentators have interpreted *Had Gadya* as an allegory of human history. The one kid bought with two *zuzim* is the people of Israel acquired by God with the two Tablets of the Law. Each succeeding actor in the song—the cat, the dog, the stick, the water, the ox, the slaughterer, and the Angel of Death—refers to one of the great empires, each rising from the ruins of the other: Egypt, Babylonia, Persia, Greece, and Rome. Finally, God, the Holy One blessed be He, will arise, and destroy evil, the Angel of Death, thus ushering in the Kingdom of God.

That God works in history is the basic faith of the Prophets; how He works is very often a mystery. But some clues come to light now and again. The Exodus as an event testifies to the reality of the law of righteousness working itself out in history; the Exodus as a narrative in the Bible discloses the dynamics of liberation.

From earliest times, readers of the story of the Exodus have been troubled by one aspect of the biblical text. Several times in the account of the ten plagues that preceded the liberation of the Israelites, the Torah uses the phrase "God hardened the heart of Pharaoh." The moral difficulty is obvious—if God hardened the heart of Pharaoh, was it just for Him to punish Pharaoh for his hardness of heart? This is no mere schoolboy difficulty. It deals with the fundamental issue of man's freedom of will and consequently his responsibility for his actions. The problem can be met by responses on three levels: literal, psychological, and historical, each of which is a valuable contribution to our understanding.

First, the literal meaning of the text: Biblical thought recognizes that God is the cause of all causes, and, therefore, He is ultimately the source of all human actions. Hence there is no difference in meaning between the two formulations we find in the story of the ten plagues. When the Torah says, "God hardened the heart of Pharaoh," it is simply an alternate mode in biblical language of saying that "Pharaoh hardened his heart," a phrase that occurs several times in Exodus as well.

One instance of this usage occurs when the Prophet Elijah enters into a contest with the prophets of Baal on Mount Carmel. He offers a prayer for God's intercession, declaring, "You have turned the heart of the people backward [away from Yourself]" (I Kings 18:37). This is a biblical mode of saying, "The people have turned away from You." On the literal level, therefore, the theological and ethical problem involved in the "hardening of Pharaoh's heart" is solved when it is seen that both idioms are at one in making Pharaoh the source of the evil and therefore deserving of punishment.

In psychological terms, if the biblical account is given a "close reading," an interesting fact emerges. Throughout the saga in Exodus, the phrase that is used for the first six of the ten plagues is "Pharaoh hardened his heart." Each time that Moses warned him of the catastrophe that threatened, the king of Egypt hardened his heart, and the blow descended. Then he would come cringing to Moses, imploring him to remove the plague, and promising to let the Israelites go free. When the calamity was removed, Pharaoh would renege on his word and the charade would be repeated—not once or twice, but six times. Only with the seventh plague does the Torah introduce the phrase "God hardened the heart of Pharaoh."

Here the book of Exodus reveals its insight into human psychology. When we persevere in a given course of conduct and repeat it, it becomes second nature and ultimately dominates our behavior. Rabbinic literature expresses this truth in its apothegm "One good deed brings on another good deed, but one transgression leads to another transgression" (M. *Abot* 4:21). Or, even more vividly, "To the place I love, my feet take me" (B. *Sukkah* 53a). It was only after the king of Egypt had been repeatedly warned and remained obdurate that "God hardened Pharaoh's heart." Only with the last four plagues—hail, locusts, darkness, and the smiting of the firstborn—does God, so to speak, enter the picture. He hardens Pharaoh's heart only because Pharaoh has already done it himself. Thus the oppressor finally learns the lesson that he should have learned long before.

Finally, the biblical idiom used in the narrative of the ten plagues may be read as a clue to the processes of history. On the most profound level the narrative reveals the dynamics of revolution and change, the technique of struggle by which freedom and indeed all progress are achieved. Throughout history, whenever a people has sought to throw off the tyrants' yoke, the rulers have resisted any concessions and have fought to crush dissent and opposition. Had the oppressors been willing to modify their behavior, the bondage might never have been cast off.

When Moses began the struggle, he asked only, "Let us go into the wilderness and offer sacrifices to our God for three days" (Exod. 3:34). Had Pharaoh made this concession, most of the Israelites would probably have been content to return to Egypt and remain in bondage rather than brave the rigors and dangers associated with liberty in the wilderness. This is clear from the fact that when they were a free nation in the desert, they complained at every turn of their hardships and wailed for a return to Egypt.[5] All of Moses' courage and faith in God could not of itself have overcome this natural human weakness—the desire to take the course of least resistance, to stay and face the ills we know rather than brave new perils we know not. Slavery is more comfortable for many slaves than the hardships of liberty. In other words, the escape from Egyptian bondage required not only the courage and leadership of Moses but also the hard heart of Pharaoh. Both the liberator and the tyrant are essential actors in the drama of liberation.

Human history repeatedly reveals this pattern of events. In 1776, when the thirteen American colonies rose in revolt against King George of England, their rallying cry was "No taxation without representation." If the British government had had the good sense and moderation to say, "Very well, you may send five or ten members to represent you in the House of Commons in London," most of the colonists would have been satisfied, and there would have been no War of Independence.

In France, if the Bourbon monarchs Louis XV and Louis XVI had heeded the counsels of their more moderate ministers, who favored some reforms in response to the grievances of the people before it was too late, they could have retained most of their powers and privileges. Instead, they remained intransigent, and the result was the French Revolution and the guillotine.

In the twentieth century the same pattern was repeated in Czarist Russia. Years of oppression and corruption had finally brought matters to the boiling point. In 1905 the Czar had been compelled to establish a Duma, or parliament, but it was soon apparent that this body would have no real power. Nicholas II was able to sit on the lid only until 1917, when the Russian Revolution broke out. Even at that late date, the first leaders of the revolution, Alexander Kerensky and Prince Lvov, wanted only a constitutional monarchy, but the Czar was advised by his associates to stand firm. What followed was the overthrow of the monarchy, the execution of the royal family, and the establishment of the Communist regime. In this instance, to be sure, the remedy was not much better than the plague. Yet the dynamic of liberation remains the same. In this painful process, the obstinacy of the oppressor is no less essential than the courage of the revolutionary.

The same principle has revealed itself in the state of Israel in our own time. In 1948 the United Nations, following the recommendations of the Peel Commission, voted to partition Palestine into two states, one Arab and one Jewish. The Jewish territory was pitifully small, but the Jewish National Council, headed by so staunch a patriot as David Ben Gurion, felt that even a small Jewish state living in peace was better than blood-shed and the hostility of one's neighbors. The Jewish community in Palestine therefore accepted the partition plan.

Had the Arabs done likewise, the state of Israel would have emerged as a tiny state, a fraction of its present dimensions. But the Arab leaders were adamant in their refusal, and the rest is history. Once again the "historical law" seems to have operated. Two participants—and not one—are needed for the triumph of freedom. To be sure, the establishment of a viable state of Israel depended on the heroism of a small Jewish community, fighting all its neighbors against incredible odds. But it also required the implacable hostility and the stubbornness of the Arab leaders. The new Pharaoh was the Mufti, the Muslim religious leader, who announced that the Arabs would drive the Jews into the sea and take over all Jewish settlements and property.

Time and again, the expansion of the borders of the state of Israel, as in the Six Day War of 1967, was the direct consequence of the obstinacy of its Arab neighbors, who initiated one war after another in order to destroy Israel. Is it completely far-fetched to note that the only war Israel lost was the one it initiated, the conflict in Lebanon begun in 1982? Be this as it may, the brief history of modern Israel discloses the same principle at work: "God hardens the hearts" of the modern Pharaohs, and the cause of liberty moves forward.

Reading the saga of the Exodus in the Bible and reenacting the drama of liberation at the Seder ritual are not antiquarian exercises. The Exodus strengthens the faith that God works in history, giving men and women the courage and the incentive to do battle for justice, freedom, and peace. The beginning of Israel's history at the Exodus points to the consummation of men's hopes for the End-Time. Moses is the precursor of the Messiah. The Passover in Egypt points to the future Passover, when all mankind will fulfil its destiny and move forward from slavery to freedom, from darkness to light.

III

THE PRIMACY OF ETHICS

When we seek to penetrate the content of the Jewish tradition we are confronted by a mystery. The ancient Hebrews were not distinguished by their contributions to science, philosophy, or art—those achievements they left for their modern descendants. They displayed no marked talent for government or politics, industry or commerce. How are we to explain the depth and range of the contribution of Israel to religion, ethics, and human thought?

While the Greeks cultivated philosophic speculation and created the scientific method, it was the Book of Genesis that first saw the world not as a *pluri*verse governed by a multiplicity of gods, but as a *uni*verse, the product of one divine will. Most remarkable of all, it is this pattern of a cosmos that laid the foundation for the conception of universal laws in nature. Why was it not the highly advanced civilizations of Sumer and Babylonia, Assyria and Egypt, but the relatively uncivilized Hebrews who proclaimed the Decalogue, the succinct code setting forth the fundamentals of human behavior?

Where did Amos, a wandering shepherd and farmhand, derive the knowledge of international affairs affecting several foreign states besides his own country? Whence came his insight, which led him confidently to proclaim the operation of a universal law of consequence affecting the destiny of all men and nations, friend and foe? How could the Prophet Hosea see in his marital troubles and their resolution a paradigm of the love, fidelity, estrangement, and reconciliation marking the relationship of Israel and its God?

When Plato, perhaps the noblest of the Greeks, after Socrates, delineated the outlines of his ideal republic of the future, he saw mankind as forever divided into Greeks and barbarians, with the state being protected against the barbarians by a standing army. Four centuries before Plato, how could Isaiah, a citizen of the tiny state of Judah, the battleground of two world powers, Egypt and Assyria, enunciate the ideal of international peace, and what is more, declare that it was a divinely ordained goal toward which human history was inevitably moving? How could Ezekiel, like Jeremiah before him, dare to oppose the concept of group responsibility, which was universal in the ancient world, and insist that each individual was morally free and therefore accountable for his own actions? When the Babylonians burned the Temple, destroyed the kingdom of Judah, and exiled its leadership, the nation was apparently doomed, as had happened with countless other conquered peoples. How did Deutero-Isaiah derive the prophetic *huzpah* ("impudence") to insist that this decimated and exiled community had a central role to play in history by promulgating to all the world the faith in the one God and adherence to His law?

In a word, how could the literature of a tiny, weak people become the Bible of mankind? The religious believer has a clear-cut answer: Israel through its greatest sons, the Prophets and the Sages, was the bearer of the revelation of God; the Bible has the stamp of eternity, because it is the expression of an eternal God.

It would be difficult, if not impossible, to offer a better rationale for the abiding vitality and truth of the biblical message, which at many points goes beyond normal expectations. After all historical and sociological explanations are offered, there remains a core of mystery and wonder with regard to the insights of the biblical Prophets and Sages that defies explanation. To this miracle we shall return. Nonetheless, to the extent that causation plays its part in human life, it is possible to note three principal factors that endowed ancient Israel with its unique overriding concern for morality on every level of human existence.

We have already seen how the experience of Egyptian bondage and liberation exerted a powerful influence on all later generations. The other two elements that played significant roles were the nomadic period of wandering in the desert after the Exodus and the emergence of the unique group of men and women called the Prophets. They kept alive the memory of the two earlier historical epochs and derived from them fundamental religious and moral truths for their contemporaries, for all succeeding generations, and ultimately for the world.

The impact on the Hebrew psyche of both aspects of the Egyptian experience, slavery and liberation, cannot be exaggerated. The bitter memories of bondage taught the Jew to identify himself, in the Talmudic phrase, with the persecuted rather than with the persecutor. A sense of sympathy with the underdog became deeply ingrained in the Jewish spirit and has not been eradicated even in an age of blatant self-assertion and aggressiveness. The Exodus reminded Jews that their God had first revealed Himself by setting slaves free.

The Wilderness Tradition

According to the biblical tradition, the Israelites spent 40 years in the wilderness. Even after their entrance into the land of Canaan, a considerable portion of the people, two and a half tribes according to the Bible, remained in eastern Trans-Jordan under seminomadic conditions, as shepherds and cattle farmers.

In 1895, the German biblical scholar Karl Budde suggested that the wilderness period had exerted a powerful effect on the ideals of the Hebrews after they had settled in the Promised Land and passed from the nomadic to the agricultural and early urban stages.[1] By a striking coincidence, at almost the same time, in 1893, the American historian F. J. Turner, in an address entitled "The Significance of the Frontier in American History," called attention to the importance of the open frontier in molding the ideals of American democracy and in the development of its institutions.

There is a pattern characteristic of seminal ideas. When first proposed, they exert a tremendous influence. They are enthusiastically embraced and elaborated upon by scholars. Then comes the inevitable reaction, and the ideas are severely criticized and even dismissed as mistaken. Finally, a balance is struck between excessive claims and extreme denials. The significant contribution of the new idea is recognized and incorporated into the body of accepted knowledge. Precisely this destiny overtook Turner's contribution. After the period of initial enthusiasm, it was subjected to massive criticism, but few scholars today would completely deny the influence of the frontier on American life and thought.

Similarly, Budde's idea, expanded and exaggerated by other scholars, came under severe criticism in succeeding decades.[2] It is clear that there was no sharp line of demarcation between nomadism and settled agricultural life. In the Middle East, at least, seminomadism was prevalent, in which pastoral life was supplemented by the tilling of the soil.

More recently, Budde's emphasis on nomadic ideals has been attacked from another direction. Some scholars have denied the traditional account of the conquest of Canaan by the Israelites, as well as the alternative theory, the gradual infiltration by the Hebrew tribes from the desert and the eventual fusion of the two groups. Instead, these scholars have argued for a socioeconomic reading of Israelite history—the Hebrews were landless outsiders who carried out a revolt against the rulers of the Canaanite city-states in Palestine.[3]

Understandably, biblical scholars are concerned with establishing the facts of Hebrew history as objectively as possible. A more detailed analysis of the fascinating scholarly issues involved is presented in

Notes 1–4 of this chapter. However, historical research is not our present concern. Moreover, with all due regard for the value of the critiques and rival theories proposed, it is undeniable that ancient peoples went through a nomadic stage before moving on to agricultural society and finally to urbanization.

The nomadic or seminomadic stage was far from idyllic; it had its crudities and cruelties, but it also possessed several positive traits that the Prophets were able to use as material from the past in their efforts to build the future.

What matters for our theme is the perception of the wilderness period, rather than the highly elusive reality. What was decisive for Hebraic thought was not what actually happened but what became enshrined in the folk memory. The recollections of the past were undoubtedly idealized by later generations confronted by the massive problems of a more complicated age. The harsher aspects of the seminomadic stage were softened or obliterated, and its virtues were exaggerated by the power of nostalgia. Nor were the traits of the wilderness era, as pictured by the Prophets, merely a figment of their imagination; they had their basis in reality, albeit in cruder form.

Nomadism is fiercely egalitarian; there is no hierarchy of kings and rulers, no hereditary monarchy or nobility. Each member of the clan is on a par with his fellows; in a time of crisis, such as war, some leader will emerge because of greater sagacity or courage, but he remains at all times *primus inter pares* and nothing more. When the crisis has passed and the war is over, he reverts to his previous position in the ranks. Decisions are reached by the assemblage of all adult males of the tribe.

This primitive democracy has its analogues in early Semitic and Indo-European societies, and it is somewhat reminiscent of the New England town meeting, *mutatis mutandis*. This gathering made all decisions of peace and war, executed judgment in civil and criminal matters, adopted new laws and regulations, and was the ultimate source of authority. Elsewhere I have called attention to the evidence for this primitive democracy in ancient Israelite society.[4] Its Hebrew name *ʿedah* or *qahal*, erroneously translated as "congregation" in our Bible versions, should be rendered "commonalty" or "assembly."

Another characteristic of the nomadic stage is the communal ownership of property, or at least of income-producing wealth. The flocks, for example, were not the property of an individual but belonged to the tribe as a whole. The rights to pasture lands and to wells were vested in the clan or the tribe as a unit, and private property was virtually nonexistent.

The communal ownership of property and the acute sense of equality were accompanied by a strong feeling of mutual responsibility. The law of the clan, then as later, is "one for all and all for one." A negative consequence of this feeling was the blood feud, which migratory tribes might maintain for centuries and which began because of an offense committed against a single member. The practice was, of course, not restricted to the Semites, as *Romeo and Juliet* and the Hatfield-McCoy feuds in Kentucky remind us.

Tribal morality in ancient times was, to be sure, limited to the members of the tribe. Within the tribe there was a passion for fair and equal treatment of all its members that brooked no intereference from high or low. It was this idealized picture of nomadism that lived on in the Prophets.

The Prophetic Message

The bondage and the Exodus from Egypt, as well as the nomadic period, both real and idealized, would never have sufficed to produce the unique heritage of Israel. All ancient peoples passed from the nomadic and seminomadic to the agricultural and urban stages, but generally the ideals of the nomadic period disappeared, leaving scarcely a trace. Normally, too, a nation, like an individual, strives to forget rather than to emphasize a lowly past and would prefer to invent an exalted origin for itself.

The Jewish people, however, did not forget their past; they were not allowed to. Both their bondage in Egypt and the early nomadic and seminomadic stages remained a potent influence because of the emergence of another unique factor—the Prophets of Israel. As agricultural and urban life patterns developed, a fundamental change occurred; private property, with all its social consequences, came into existence. However, the egalitarian nonhierarchical character of the society survived through the period of the Judges. It was not until the rise of the monarchy as a response to the Philistine menace that class divisions along social, economic, and political lines came into being.

In spite of these new trends, the Prophets continued to recall the wilderness period as the ideal age in Israel's relationship to its maker. The harsher and cruder aspects of this primitive era were forgotten. The Prophets emphasized instead the equality, the mutual responsibility, the freedom from corruption, the absence of luxury, and the total loyalty to the God of Israel that they saw as characterizing this period in Israel's history. "I remember for you the kindness of your youth, the love of your bridal state, when you followed Me in the wilderness, in a land unsown," the Prophet Jeremiah proclaimed in the last decades before the destruction of the Judean kingdom (2:2). He was echoing the sentiments that had been adumbrated earlier by his spiritual progenitor, Hosea, as well as by Amos and Isaiah.

The role of the desert motif is attested even earlier in the life of the Prophet Elijah. Despairing of his cause, because of the relentless persecution he and the Prophets of the Lord were suffering at the hands of Queen Jezebel, he fled to Mount Horeb. It was here in the wilderness that Elijah heard the still, small voice that renewed his zeal for his mission.

The Hebrew Prophets were not nostalgic advocates of a bygone past. Israel had those too in the seminomadic orders of the Nazirites and the Rechabites. These groups, briefly discussed above, sought to register their protest against the material and spiritual ills of their age by retaining ritual and other practices of the earlier period.

The Prophets utilized the past creatively; that is to say, they retained those elements of the seminomadic stage that were vital, such as its sense of equality and justice. They rejected those elements that were of purely external character and hence of no real consequence, like the long hair and the abstinence from wine characteristic of the Nazirites, or the sheep herding and the dwelling in tents practiced by the Rechabites.

The Prophets accepted the inevitable social transformations of agricultural life, including the concept of private property that has characterized farmers throughout history. But they demanded the retention of those ethical ideals of nomadism that are valid in every system of society. It is significant that Hosea put it in an agricultural metaphor, "Sow for yourselves in righteousness, reap according to kindness, break up your fresh ground. For it is time to seek the Lord, till He come and rain righteousness down upon you" (Hos. 10:12).

Above all, the Prophets deepened such nomadic ideals as family morality beyond the physical relationship to include love and loyalty. They extended the ethics of the tribe to include the nation. For them, the tribes did not exist, only the people of Israel, worshipping the one God. The biblical historians who wrote in their spirit regarded the division of the Two Kingdoms as a major crime nationally and religiously.

Nor did the expanding loyalties of the Prophets halt at the frontier. Their patriotism went beyond the nation to include the entire human race. Thus the Prophets were the creators of Jewish nationalism on the one hand, and of the concept of world citizenship on the other. All too often, it has not been understood that these two aspects of their thought, far from being contradictory, complement and reinforce each other.

For the religious consciousness, the emergence of Hebrew prophecy is the mark of divine revelation. The secularist will seek to explain it in rationalistic terms, but the uniqueness of the phenomenon is beyond question. Prophecy was a universal phenomenon in ancient religion. Archeological discoveries and the reading of ancient documents from Egypt, Syria, and Mesopotamia, notably the tablets of Mari, have revealed various categories of Prophets who were consulted by kings, nobles, and commoners because of their access to the deity and their power to foretell events. These practitioners of divination had their analogues in ancient Israel as well, as is clear from incidents reported in the books of Samuel and Kings. The great Prophets, who would have indignantly denied any relationship with the soothsayers and professional prophets, nevertheless came out of their ranks and employed virtually the same techniques.

In two respects the great Prophets were a unique Israelite phenomenon. First, a chain of tradition extended over centuries from Moses to Malachi. Second, for all the differences among them, they shared the faith in a world created by a just God and governed by the law of moral consequence. For them, the touchstone of national policy was not the narrow national interest as conceived by the ruling powers, but the standard of righteousness that alone could stave off catastrophe. Indeed, for the Prophets, the pursuit of justice and peace was identical with the national interest.

Hence, in the eighth century B.C.E. Amos and Hosea did not hesitate to contradict the movers and shakers of their time—the royal court, the officials, and the great merchants—by declaring in the face of ostensible prosperity and national self-confidence that catastrophe was imminent for the northern kingdom of Israel. A century and a half later, Jeremiah and Ezekiel warned their fellow citizens in Judah that the same fate would overtake them.

When the Babylonians drove the national leadership into exile, burned the Temple, and killed the king, the nation seemed to be destroyed. At this point, the prophetic paradox emerged—the former heralds of doom became the purveyors of hope. Ezekiel and Deutero-Isaiah now flew in the face of reality and proclaimed that God had decreed a rebirth of Israel and the restoration of its people to its homeland, a prophecy fulfilled by the Declaration of Cyrus.

The Hebrew Prophets ineradicably placed the stamp of ethical concern on the Jewish tradition for all the centuries to follow. It is often forgotten that there were others besides the "literary Prophets"—Amos, Hosea, Isaiah, Jeremiah, Ezekiel, and their colleagues. Centuries earlier, Abraham, the founder of the Hebrew people is called a Prophet (Gen. 20:7); and Moses, the liberator and lawgiver of Israel, is described in the Torah as the greatest one of all (Num. 12:6–8). Even more significant is the prophetic challenge Abraham hurls at his God when he pleads for the sinful inhabitants of Sodom,

Far be it for You to do such a thing, to bring death upon the innocent as well as the guilty, so that innocent and guilty fare alike. Far be it for You! Shall not the judge of all the earth deal justly? [Gen. 18:25]

Centuries later, Moses demanded God's forbearance for his people, who he knew was guilty: "And if not, blot me out from the book You have written!" (Exod. 32:32).

By the same token, the Hebrew Prophets declared that justice and compassion are the true objectives of religion. Speaking in the name of his God, Amos commanded: "Hate evil, and love good, and establish justice in the gate" (5:15). He warned against the replacement of ethics by ritual, a temptation that remains a constant peril to the religious enterprise. He declared:

> I hate, I despise your feasts,
> I take no delight in your solemn assemblies.
> Even though you offer me your burnt sacrifices and cereal offerings,
> I will not accept them. . . .
> Remove the noise of your songs,
> The melody of your harps I refuse to hear.
> But let justice well up like the waters,
> and righteousness like a mighty stream.
>
> [Amos 5:21–22]

His spiritual disciple, Isaiah of Jerusalem, had attacked the alliance of plunder and piety with equal passion and eloquence and set forth the goals of true religion:

> Wash yourselves, make yourselves clean;
> Remove the evil of your doings from before my eyes;
> Cease to do evil, learn to do good;
> Seek justice, correct oppression;
> Defend the fatherless, plead for the widow.
>
> [Isa. 1:16–17]

What loyalty to the God of Israel entails is clear: "The Lord of hosts is exalted in justice, and the Holy God is made holy by righteousness" (Isa. 5:16).

When in 586 B.C.E. the Babylonians burned the Temple in Jerusalem, destroyed the Jewish state, and carried off the leadership to exile, the survival of the Jewish people was gravely threatened. There was a danger that with the loss of all these symbols and aspects of national existence, Jews both in Palestine and in the Diaspora would be absorbed into the surrounding population within a few generations. This had happened in the previous century, after the Assyrians had destroyed the northern kingdom of Israel in 721 B.C.E. A new appreciation now developed for the ritual aspects of Judaism, such as the sabbath, the dietary laws, and circumcision, which could be observed outside the borders of the Holy Land. They would not only deepen the religious consciousness but also strengthen the sense of national unity among the people and thus prove a bulwark against assimilation and eventual disappearance.

The three great sixth-century Prophets, Jeremiah, Ezekiel, and Deutero-Isaiah, all called for the observance of the sabbath, which, more than any other ritual, is permeated by religious and ethical values (Jer. 17:21; Ezek. 46:1–12; Isa. 56:2–6). Nevertheless, the national crisis did not weaken the vigor of the Prophets' insistence that morality is the heart and essence of the worship of God.

The great Prophet of the Exile, often called Second Isaiah, reminded his pious contemporaries of the true meaning of the Day of Atonement:

> Indeed this is the fast that I have chosen,
> to loose the bonds of wickedness and undo the
> thongs of the yoke,
> to let the oppressed go free, and to break
> every yoke.
> It is to share your bread with the hungry,
> and bring the homeless poor into your house,
> When you see the naked, to cover him,
> not to hide yourself from your own flesh.
> Then shall your light break forth like the dawn,
> and your healing spring up speedily;
> Your righteousness shall go before you.
> The glory of the Lord shall be your rearguard.
>
> [Isa. 58:5–7]

To underscore the primacy of ethics over ritual, the Prophets Amos and Jeremiah did not hesitate to deny altogether that the ritual law had been promulgated in the wilderness period when Moses was the leader of his people. Amos asked his hearers in the name of his God: "Did you bring Me sacrifices and offerings the forty years in the wilderness, O house of Israel?" (Amos 5:25). Jeremiah flatly declared: "For in the day that I brought them out of the land of Egypt, I did not speak to your fathers or command them concerning burnt offerings and sacrifices" (Jer. 7:22).

The Prophets' purpose was not to deny the antiquity of the sacrificial system, a practice universal in all ancient religion, but to stress the far greater importance of conduct. The next verse in Jeremiah makes this intention abundantly clear: "But this command I did give them, 'Obey My voice, and I will be your God, and you shall be my people, and walk in all the way that I command you, that it may be well with you'" (Jer.

7:23). Reverence for God and righteous conduct are for him the two tablets of the law.

From a totally different perspective, the biblical Wisdom writers make the same point. We have already referred to Job's great "Code of a Man of Honor" (Job 31). In declaring that he has been free from any infractions of God's will, Job lists no fewer than fourteen sins that he might have committed; all save one, the worship of heavenly bodies, are not ritual crimes, but subtle sins affecting his relationship to his fellows. These are offenses largely beyond the power of the law to punish, such as cheating in business and expropriating land belonging to others, because they operate within the letter of the law. He lists using unfair influence in the courts against slaves, callousness toward the resident poor, lack of pity for the stranger, and perversion of the just claims of the widow and the orphan. In the area of personal relationships, he includes lusting after women and the practice of adultery in secret. Most remarkable of all in indicating the sensitivity of biblical ethics, are three sins from which, Job protests, he has been free. He has never been complacent because of his wealth, nor has he rejoiced in the misfortunes of his enemies, nor has he concealed his shortcomings because of the fear of mob opinion. The "Hymn to Wisdom" in Job culminates with the line: "He has said to man, 'Reverence for the Lord—that is wisdom. The avoidance of evil, that is understanding'" (28:29).

Moses and the Decalogue

The highest role to which a human being could aspire was that of the Prophet who directly experienced the presence of God and became the spokesman who brought His message to His people. It is noteworthy that it is Moses who is called the greatest of Prophets, "trusted throughout My household, with whom I speak mouth to mouth, plainly and not in riddles" (Num. 12:7–8). In describing his death, the Torah declares: "There has not arisen a Prophet since in Israel like Moses, whom the Lord knew face to face" (Deut. 34:10). Later tradition reinforced this judgment, calling Moses "the father of the Prophets" and emphasizing his unique relationship as more intimate and direct than that of his successors.

The reason for this preeminence is highly significant—Moses' message was not limited to purely abstract ethical principles, however eloquent and soul-stirring; it was embodied in *mitzvot*, "concrete commands," specific canons of conduct. Some were legal norms intended to make ethical principles come alive in human affairs; others were ritual practices designed to dramatize fundamental religious and ethical truths and give them a grip on human lives. Thus, there is no command in the Torah, "Be free"; instead Passover reenacts the epic of liberation. No single biblical passage proclaims the equality of all human beings. Instead, the regulations governing the humane treatment of slaves and the provisions for setting them free and not returning them to bondage were more-prosaic but more-potent instruments for achieving justice and compassion. Moses did not preach morality; he created practices for embodying it in life.

Both in the biblical text and in the rabbinic tradition, Moses' encounter with God on Sinai is the central event in revelation. The Decalogue is the basic product of that encounter; this, the most famous of all codes, underscores the primacy of ethics as the heart of Jewish religion.

The First Commandment, "I am the Lord your God who brought you from out of the land of Egypt, the house of bondage," deals with the fundamentals of faith, the only one, incidentally, in the Decalogue concerned with belief. It uses the singular pronoun "I," without explicitly negating the existence of other gods, because for Israel there is only one God to be worshipped and obeyed. Though God is the creator of heaven and earth, He presents Himself to His people as the liberator from bondage and oppression, thus identifying Himself with justice and freedom.

Implicit in the commandment is another concept—God holds sway not only over Canaan, His "national territory," as was the prevalent pagan notion of divine rule, but even over Egypt, which was not His "original" domain. Thus the First Commandment enjoins loyalty to one God, who is identified with the cause of justice and, by implication at least, holds universal sway.

The next two commandments are ritual in character. The Second Commandment, "You shall have no other gods besides Me," addresses the exclusive worship of the God of Israel.[5] The Third, "You shall not take the name of the Lord your God in vain," is cryptic and apparently forbids involving God with any object, act, or word unworthy of Him.

The Fourth Commandment, "Remember the sabbath day to keep it holy," is both ritual and ethical in character and thus serves as a bridge to the six remaining ones. In enjoining rest on the sabbath, the commandment has served as the starting point for the elaborate details of sabbath observance as developed in postbiblical Judaism. The explanation given in Exodus, "For in six days the Lord made heaven and earth, the seas and all that is in them, and He rested on the sabbath day, therefore the Lord blessed the sabbath day and hallowed it," is religio-cosmic. The version of the Decalogue in Deuteronomy 5 motivates the observance in socio-ethical terms: "Remember that you were a slave in the land of Egypt, and the Lord your God freed you from there, with a mighty hand and an outstretched arm, therefore the Lord your God has commanded you to observe the sabbath day." Both versions emphasize the right and duty of slaves, strangers, and even animals to rest on the sabbath.

The last six commandments are exclusively ethical. The Fifth says, "Honor your father and your mother"; the Sixth, "You shall not murder"; the Seventh, "You shall not commit adultery"; the Eighth, "You shall not steal"; the Ninth, "You shall not bear false witness"; and the Tenth, "You shall not covet your neighbor's house . . . your neighbor's wife, his male or female slave, his ox or his ass or anything that is your neighbor's."

It is characteristic of the pragmatic nature of Judaism that nine of the Ten Commandments deal with overt actions and not with feelings or states of mind. Only the last, "You shall not covet," deals with an emotion, that of envy, undoubtedly because it is at the root of so much evil in the world.

The Evolution of the Torah

The Torah of Moses contained the earliest traditions of Israel: creation and the Garden of Eden; the Flood and the Tower of Babel; the lives of the Patriarchs Abraham, Isaac, and Jacob; Joseph and the sojourn in Egypt; the Exodus and the revelation at Sinai; Israel's wandering in the wilderness; and the death of Moses. Interspersed among these narratives are the laws promulgated for the Israelites. These two strands in the Torah were not merely preserved by later generations; they were studied minutely, interpreted, and amplified by all the various movements in postbiblical Judaism, including the Sadducees, the Essenes and Qumranites, the Judeo-Christians, and other sects now lost to history. However, it was preeminently proto-rabbinic and rabbinic Judaism that developed most fully the two aspects of the written Torah, the narratives and the laws. The former were the basis of the *Aggadah* (literally, "the telling," "the narrative"), a body of ethical admonition, religious thought, folklore, and legend; the latter grew into the *Halakhah*, an elaborate system of civil, criminal, family, and ritual law.

Originally this new material was transmitted orally from generation to generation. It was therefore called the Oral Torah, even later when it was put into writing. The transition from the Aggadah to the Halakhah may occur anywhere in the text simply by association with a name, a phrase, a catchword, or a formula. Just as the narratives of the Torah are juxtaposed with its legal sections, so the Aggadah and the Halakhah are constantly interwoven in rabbinic literature.

Moreover, the standards of ethical conduct enjoined by the Aggadah are regarded as no less normative than the provisions of the Halakhah. The principal difference is that the latter are enforceable by human agency, while the former are subject only to the judgment of God. It is possible to speak of the Aggadah as corresponding roughly to "ethics" and the Halakhah as basically equivalent to "law," but only if it is kept in mind that the two sets of correlatives are not identical, because the Halakhah is motivated by powerful ethical impulses. What is most important, there is a constant effort to embody the moral vision of the Aggadah in the institutions and regulations of the Halakhah. A standard advanced by a teacher of the Aggadah in one generation as the optimum may later become the accepted norm and ultimately be the minimum required by the Halakhah.

Strictly speaking, it was not the Written Torah that was meticulously observed by the masses of the Jewish people, but the Oral Law, the vast deposit of tradition that had grown up after the canonization of scripture which took place from the fifth to the second centuries B.C.E. Thereafter nothing could be added to or subtracted from the text of Holy Writ.

Over the next thousand years, from Ezra to the compilation of the Talmud, the body of oral tradition continued to grow as a result of the cumulative teachings of the Rabbis. It was consigned to writing in two principal stages, though the name Oral Law continued as its designation. In the third century C.E. the Mishnah was codified by Rabbi Judah the Patriarch. Some three hundred years later, the Gemara was compiled in two forms, Palestinian and Babylonian; the two works together constitute the Talmud. In addition, the Oral Law included the Tosefta, which is largely legal in nature, and the Midrash, a vast literature, primarily Aggadic in content. During the Talmudic period, the Rabbis had created a rich ethical literature consisting of individual apothegms and insights scattered in the Talmud and the Midrash; some of them were collected in the popular Mishnaic tractate *Abot*, "The Sayings of the Fathers."

The ethical quest was never abandoned. Throughout the Middle Ages, ethical treatises, which exerted considerable influence on the people, such as the closing chapter of Saadia's *Emunot Vede∘ot*, the *Eight Chapters* of Maimonides, and the *Duties of the Heart* by Bahya Ibn Paquda, continued to appear. The tradition was carried on in modern times by Moses Hayyim Luzzato, in his *Path of the Upright*, and in an extraordinary body of ethical teaching, originally oral in character, produced by Hasidism in its greatest period. The impulse lived on in the Musar literature of the ethical movement created by Rabbi Israel Salanter, in the *Hafetz Hayyim*, and in other works that continue to influence the ethical behavior of Jews.

But the position of primacy was always accorded not to ethical analysis or moral admonition but to the Halakhah, the body of biblical and postbiblical law that embodied these principles and established the

Torah as the highest authority in Judaism. While the broad, all-inclusive ideals enunciated by the Prophets needed little modification or extension with the passing of time, the concrete practices and institutions of the law were constantly affected by the changes in the shifting social, economic, political, and cultural conditions under which Jews lived. The historian Josephus, writing during the heyday of the Roman Empire, after the burning of the Second Temple and the destruction of the Jewish polity at the hands of the conquerors, nevertheless boasts that Moses, unlike the Emperor, has no legions at his command, yet the laws he promulgated in the Torah are being observed throughout the world.

In sum, the entire history of postbiblical law represents an unremitting effort to embody in life the idealistic aspirations of Moses, the Prophets, and their rabbinic successors. The Halakhah, however, like the Torah itself, is not limited to ethical conduct, *mitzvot bein ›adam laḥavero*, "commandments between man and man." In fact, much of Jewish law deals with ritual and ceremony, *mitzvot bein ›adam lamakom*, "commandments between man and God."

Today, a third category should be formulated, *mitzvot bein ›adam le ‹azmo*, "commandments between man and himself," the obligation of a human being to preserve his physical and mental well-being and above all to safeguard his personal integrity and purity—in a word, to refrain from sinning against himself. The recognition of such a category would effectively rebut the notion of "victimless crimes" and stigmatize practices like alcoholism, prostitution, drug abuse, and suicide as infractions of the moral law. Indeed the Jewish tradition considers the biblical injunction "Take utmost care and watch yourselves scrupulously" (Deut. 4:9, cf. v. 15) as the basis for the religious duty to take care of one's health and well-being.

In evaluating the role of ethics in Jewish law, it is important to recognize that the structure of the Talmud differs fundamentally from that of Western literature. While Western thought is based on the logic of relevance and coherence, the Talmud adheres to the logic of association, not unlike the "free-association" techniques developed in modern psychoanalysis. Thus a detailed analysis of a legal Halakhic issue may be followed by an element of the Aggadah, be it an ethical admonition, a bit of folklore, or an anecdote. Moreover, a discussion of a ritual procedure will frequently occur cheek by jowl with a theme from civil or criminal jurisprudence.

Ethics and Ritual In Judaism

As a result of the centrality of law in Judaism, the charge has been leveled for centuries, from the days of Paul to our own, that Jewish tradition is primarily legalistic; that is, preoccupied with the law rather than with ethics, with observance rather than with faith. Judaism has therefore been attacked as *external*, devoted to the letter rather than to the spirit; ritualistic, obsessed with minutiae of practice rather than with the presence of God; and legalistic, more concerned with adding to the sum of one's merits in the heavenly account book than with establishing a warm personal relationship with God and one's fellow beings.

Undoubtedly, these charges point to some genuine perils confronting the religious life, to which the biblical Prophets were sensitive. In the words of Isaiah:

> The Lord said, "Because this people draw near with their mouth
> and honor Me with their lips,
> While their hearts are far from Me,
> And their reverence for Me
> is a commandment of men learned by rote;
> Therefore, behold, I will again astonish this people
> with wonders and marvels;
> The wisdom of its wise men shall perish,
> and the prudence of its prudent men shall be destroyed."
> [29:13–14]

People have found it easier to reach for the shadow rather than to grasp the substance of religion; ritual observance all too easily degenerates into the be-all and end-all of piety. Bluntly put, observance of ritual is less expensive than obedience to moral imperatives, both psychologically and financially.

Traditional Judaism in every stage of its history has been acutely conscious of the peril of soulless conformity to ritual usurping the role of ethical sensitivity and moral concern. It emphasizes the overriding importance of right conduct, but it continues to regard both ritual and ethics, "the commandments between man and God" as well as those "between man and man," as embodiments of the divine will and hence binding upon the Jew.

But what of the relative importance of ritual and ethics in Judaism? Is it possible to discern any hierarchy of values in the tradition? Where a choice must be made between them, which is to be preferred? Here the evidence in both the Bible and the Talmud, though often overlooked, is extensive and unequivocal—ritual is important but ethics is paramount.

A comprehensive statement of the fundamentals of Judaism is recorded in the Talmud (B. *Makkot* 23b–24a) in the name of Rabbi Simlai:

> Six hundred thirteen commandments were given to Moses, 365 negative ones, equal to the number of days of the year, and 248 positive ones, corresponding to the number of organs in the human body.

Then David came and reduced them to eleven:

> "Lord, who shall sojourn in your tent?
> Who shall dwell on your holy mountain?
> He who walks uprightly and does the right,
>   and speaks the truth in his heart.
> He who does not slander with his tongue
>   nor does evil to his friend,
>   nor takes up a reproach against his neighbor;
> He, in whose eyes a reprobate is despised,
>   but who honors those who fear the Lord;
> who swears to his own hurt and does not change;
>   who does not put out his money at interest,
>   and takes no bribe against the innocent.
> He who does these things shall never be moved."
>
> [Psalm 15]

Then came Isaiah and reduced them to six: "He who walks righteously and speaks uprightly, who despises the gain of oppression, who shakes his hands free from holding a bribe, stops his ears from hearing of bloodshed and shuts his eyes from looking upon evil" [Isa. 33:15].

Then came Micah and reduced them to three: "He has told you, O man, what is good; and what does the Lord require of you, Only to do justice, and to love kindness, and to walk humbly with your God" [Mic. 6:8].

Then Isaiah came again and reduced them to two: "Keep judgment and do righteousness" [Isa. 56:1].

Finally Amos came and reduced them to one: "Seek Me and live" [Amos 5:4].

So did Habakkuk, who said: "The righteous shall live by his faithfulness" [Hab. 2:4].

The most familiar lapidary summation of the essence of Judaism is that of Hillel. When a proselyte came to him demanding to learn the entire Torah while he stood on one foot, Hillel's answer was brief, "What is hateful to you, do not do to your neighbor—that is the essence. Everything else is commentary. Go and study" (B. *Shabbat* 31a). Unfortunately, the final injunction in Hillel's utterance "study," is all too often overlooked! Incidentally, this uncompromising ethical summation of the Jewish tradition occurs in a Talmudic tractate concerned with the observance of sabbath prohibitions with all their minutiae.

Two centuries later, the famous Sages Akiba and Ben Azzai debated the question "Which is the most important verse in the Torah?" Rabbi Akiba cited the Golden Rule: "You shall love your neighbor as yourself" (Lev. 19:18). Ben Azzai, instead, proposed another verse: "This is the book of the generations of man; in the day that God created man, in

the image of God did He make him" (Gen. 5:1). Instead of relying on the
emotion of love to govern human conduct, Ben Azzai preferred to base
human behavior on two fundamental principles: the unity of the entire
race; and, consequently, the inalienable dignity of all its members, who
have been created in the image of God.

While some voices have argued that the enterprise is futile, the quest
for the essence of Judaism has had a long and respectable history. We
may hazard one more attempt in this direction. In the Middle Ages, the
Zohar declared, "God, Israel, and Torah are one," the classic statement
of the organic relationship uniting religion, culture, and peoplehood
in Judaism. Which of the three is *primus inter pares*? Parenthetically, it
has been suggested that the three principal trends in contemporary
Judaism—Orthodoxy, Conservatism, and Reform—have each made one
of the triad paramount: Reform stressing religion, Conservatism (and
its offshoot, Reconstructionism) peoplehood, and Orthodoxy Torah. Be
this as it may, it is possible to demonstrate the centrality of the Torah
through Talmudic reasoning, using two other passages in rabbinic literature. One, already cited in another connection, attributes to God the
statement "Would that men forsook Me, but kept my Torah" (P. *Hagigah*
1:7). The other emanates from Saadia, the tenth-century gaon, who declared, "Our people is a people only by virtue of the Torah." If we juxta-
pose the two passages we arrive at the conclusion that the Torah is the
most important member of the triad.

To be sure, the organic relationship of these three basic elements is
more important than their relative position on a theoretical scale. Without God there would be no Israel; without Israel there would be no
Torah; without the Torah mankind would be ignorant of the will of God.

That ritual is a means to an end is explicitly stated in the observation
of Rab, one of the creators of the Babylonian Talmud: "The ritual
mitzvot were given only for the purpose of refining human nature."[6]

The passages thus far cited to demonstrate the primacy of ethics are
drawn from the Aggadah, the nonlegal portions of rabbinic literature.
But the testimony of the Halakhah is equally conclusive. It emerges from
again juxtaposing two passages in the Talmud. One passage teaches
that the saving of one's life takes precedence over all other commandments of the Torah, including even the sabbath (B. *Ketubbot* 5a). The
other is concerned with the basic principles of Judaism for which a person must be ready to undergo martyrdom. It stipulates that the three
sins of idolatry, sexual immorality, and murder are forbidden even at
the risk of death. One of the Sages, Rabbi Ishmael, goes further and declares that a person may even practice idolatry in order to save his life,
except when the act is performed in public, where it may influence others to do likewise (B. *Sanhedrin* 7b). Thus only murder and sexual immorality are forbidden under all circumstances. It follows that in the

hierarchy of rabbinic values, ethical conduct rates higher than saving human life, which in turn takes precedence over the sabbath, the most exalted and fundamental of Jewish ritual *mitzvot*.

This conclusion is codified in a classical passage in the Mishnah:

> Sincere repentance on the Day of Atonement has the power to bring forgiveness for the sins which a person has committed against God. As for the sins committed against his fellow men, they cannot be forgiven by the Day of Atonement until one makes restitution to the victim [M. *Yoma* 8:9].

Clearly infractions of the ethical law are more severe than violations of ritual law. Clearly justice is the ultimate value to which God's will must conform.

In the nineteenth century, the Danish theologian Soren Kierkegaard enunciated his famous doctrine of the "teleological suspension of the ethical," according to which the highest rung of faith is reached at times by suspending ethical law. Kierkegaard offers as proof of his thesis the willingness of Abraham, "the knight of faith," to sacrifice his son Isaac, a manifestly immoral act, in obedience to the divine command. This idea has proved attractive to some twentieth-century theologians in Christianity and even in Judaism.

We have demonstrated elsewhere that this approach fails to reckon with the background of the episode, which has led to a total misunderstanding of biblical teaching. That God could command an immoral act is a notion completely unacceptable to Judaism.

In the elaborate liturgy of the Day of Atonement, the central feature, which is repeated eight times during the day, is the "Great Confession" (*al het*): "For the sin that we have committed before You." No fewer than 40 offenses are then listed; all are ethical sins, not one a ritual transgression—a fact that, unbelievably, has generally been overlooked.

Finally, there is no iron curtain between the Halakhah and the Aggadah; the same spirit underlies them both. The Aggadah, "The Telling," utilizes the characters and the events in the Bible to teach the fundamentals of faith and ethics. The Halakhah, "The Way," takes the laws of the Torah as its point of departure in order to develop its system of laws, practices, and institutions in the area of men's relationship both to God and to one's fellows.

Thus the Babylonian Talmud reports the incident of a learned wine merchant whose hired workers by their carelessness permitted the casks they were carrying to be broken, with a total loss of the contents. When the aggrieved employer hailed his workers before the rabbinical court, all his arguments proved in vain, and it was ruled that he could not collect any damages. As the merchant was leaving in high dudgeon, he was called back by the judge and ordered to pay the workers for their day's labor. "Where is it written?" he asked indignantly. "In the Torah," was the judge's answer, "in the Book of Deuteronomy. 'Ye shall do what is just and right in the eyes of the Lord'" [6:18]. Obviously the judge was not quoting a legal citation, but invoking a normative ethical principle, *lifnim mishurat hadin*, "beyond the strict letter of the law."[7]

The history of Jewish law, as will be indicated below, demonstrates how the ethical insight of one generation became the legal requirement of the next. The Halakhah is the prose of Judaism, the Aggadah its poetry. The Halakhah represents the bottom line below which no one may descend; the Aggadah the upper reaches to which everyone should aspire. The content of the Halakhah and the Aggadah and their interaction produce the Jewish tradition. It is to be hoped that the threadbare charges of "ritualism" and "legalism" will finally be consigned to the dustbin of history and that it will increasingly be recognized that in Jewish tradition and law the ethical is the highest rung on the ladder of faith.

This entire discussion of the primacy of ethics has concentrated on specific injunctions, positive or negative, and their relative position in the hierarchy of values. In this regard we have been true to the spirit of the great formative sources of Judaism, the Bible and rabbinic literature, which were rarely speculative and generally avoided abstractions. The Western theological tradition, on the other hand, following in the footsteps of the Greek philosophers, has developed a penchant for the theoretic approach toward ethics. The problem has been set forth lucidly by Jonathan Harrison:

> There are three ways in which God's command could be relevant to man's duties. The fact that God commands us to perform a certain kind of action might be what makes this kind of action right. On the other hand, it might be the fact that an action is right that causes God to command us to perform it. Finally, it might be the case that the fact that an action is right, and the fact that God commands it are one and the same fact; it might be that all we meant when we said that an action was right was that it was commanded by God.[8]

The debate between the advocates of a heteronomous ethics and an autonomous ethics is one of the long-standing issues in Western philosophy. It finds no echo in Jewish classical thought. In Genesis, when God informs Abraham of His decision to destroy the sinful cities of Sodom and Gommorah, Abraham counters, "Shall the Judge of all the earth not act justly?" (18:25). Clearly justice is the ultimate value to which God's will must conform; any dichotomy between them is unthinkable. The demand of ethics and the command of God are one.[9]

IV

REVELATION AND AUTHORITY

The postbiblical Jewish tradition is important on several counts. It represents a multiform, two-thousand-year-old endeavor to embody its basic ideals in a concrete legal system governing the practice of a living people. That these ethical standards were not universally observed goes without saying. Nevertheless, the enterprise achieved a substantial measure of success. As a massive social experiment, Jewish law is of interest to all who are concerned with human nature and human welfare.

Moreover, the fifteen million Jews alive in the world today still command attention and continue to exert influence to a degree far out of proportion to their numbers, as the newspapers and other media abundantly attest. Though most modern Jews no longer adhere to it totally, the Jewish tradition continues to play some role in the life of even the most alienated; for many more, it is highly significant and, indeed, is gaining importance today.

An understanding of the dynamics of Jewish law, the principles that govern it, the factors that helped determine its direction, and the procedures that it developed is important for two reasons: to clarify the character of the Jewish tradition and the Jewish people; and to make the products of Jewish insight and experience available to all those who must confront the same human problems in their own lives.

The first step is to investigate the origin and operation of the Halakhah. In general we know very little about origins, be it the origin of the universe, of life, or of humans; or about the genesis of language, art, or religion. Origins are nearly always veiled in darkness, because we cannot witness or repeat them. On the other hand, operations, which fall within the range of our experience, are given to us to observe, to classify, and to understand.

This elementary observation has one important implication for our theme: the history of Jewish law will not be apologetic or "denominational" in character. Its value will be determined by the same criteria that apply in all research—the accuracy of its data, the breadth and depth of its scholarship, and the balance and insight of its conclusions.

There can be neither privileged positions nor pariahs in the world of scholarship. The admonition of Maimonides must be heeded, "Accept the truth from whoever says it" (Introduction to the Commentary on *Abot*).

On the other hand, the claim that God is the source and the ultimate authority for Jewish law is not open to observation and therefore incapable of verification. It is necessarily a matter of faith and therefore belongs to the area of philosophy and theology. Hence there will be divergent views among the various schools of Jewish thought and even among individual members within the same school on the origin and nature of the Halakhah.

Historically, normative Judaism has always maintained that the Halakhah, the body of traditional Jewish law, is the product of divine revelation at its inception and of divine guidance throughout its history. With regard to the Aggadah, the nonlegal element in the Talmud, the tradition is more open-ended.

Since traditional Judaism had a strong penchant for the concrete and rarely engaged in exploring abstract categories of thought—in this respect it differed from Christianity—the Hebrew language has no term equivalent to "revelation"; its full dimensions are not covered by the rare rabbinic phrase *gilluy shekhinah*.[1] In view of the contribution that Judaism has made to its daughter faith, Jews should not hesitate to turn to Christian theology for the term!

A Literal View of Revelation

At the outset, we must recognize that there are two basic approaches in the Jewish tradition. One view regards the phenomenon as the literal disclosure of God's will for mankind, which He dictated to certain chosen messengers—Moses, the Prophets, and, later, the Sages, who transmitted His *ipsissima verba* to His people. These divine-human encounters, of which God's meeting with Moses on Mount Sinai was incomparably the greatest and the most significant, are obviously beyond the range of normal human experience and are, therefore, not subject to rational analysis or critique.

Revelation is then a mystery. The respective roles of the two participants, the mode of communication, and the psychological state of the human partner during the process are subjects that cannot be explicated in human terms. Indeed, they are best treated in silence, except in the case of chosen mystics and saints who may themselves aspire to an afflatus. However, we are not concerned with the encounter, which is beyond the range of normal human experience, but with the product of that meeting, the content of the revelation, the laws and teachings that God revealed to His children, the people of Israel, through His chosen messengers. It was they who set down the text of God's commands now to be found in the Torah and in the other books of Scripture. Such being their origin, they are eternal, immutable, and universally binding. Whether we call this concept literalistic revelation or verbal inspiration, biblical inerrancy or fundamentalism,[2] we are referring to a theory of revelation in which God is the active partner and the human role is essentially passive.

The Written Torah, however, did not constitute the total revelation of God's will. It was accompanied from the very beginning by another Torah, the Oral Law, which was also revealed to Moses. It was then transmitted through the generations to the elders and the Prophets of the First Temple, and after the Return, to Ezra and the *Sopherim* (usually rendered "scribes" but better "Masters of the Book"). From them, the Oral Law was handed down to the early Sages, who were the fathers of Pharisaic Judaism. Thus, both the Written Torah, which we call the Bible, and the Oral Torah, later put into writing in the Talmud, are transcriptions of God's revelation to Moses.

This concept of literal revelation finds abundant expression in Jewish tradition and can easily be documented in rabbinic and medieval sources, notably by Maimonides:

> All the commandments that were given to Moses on Sinai were given together with their explanation, as it is said, "And I shall give you tablets of stone, the Torah and the Commandments."
>
> "Torah" is the Written Torah and "the commandment" is its explanation, and He has commanded us to observe the Torah on the basis of the commandment. "The commandment" is called "the Oral Law." The entire Torah Moses our Teacher wrote before his death in his own hand, and he gave a copy to each of the tribes, and one copy he placed in the Ark forever. As it is said, "Take this book of the Torah and place it in the side of the Ark of the Covenant of the Lord your God and it shall be a witness against you" [Deut. 31:26].
>
> "The commandment," which is the explanation of the Torah, Moses did not write, but he commanded it to the elders, to Joshua and all the rest of Israel, as it is said, "Everything that I command you, you shall be careful to do; you shall not add to it or take from it" [Deut. 13:1, Hebrew]. For this reason it is called the Oral Law.
>
> Although the Oral Law was not written down Moses our teacher taught it all in his court of the seventy elders; Eleazar, Phineas, and Joshua, all three, received it from Moses. To Joshua, who was the disciple of Moses our teacher, he handed over the Oral Law and commanded him concerning it. Thus Joshua throughout the days of his life taught orally and many elders received it from Joshua. Eli received it from the elders and from Phineas. Samuel received it from Eli and his court and David received it from Samuel and his court. . . . Hosea received it from Zechariah and

his court, and Amos received it from Hosea and his court, and Isaiah received it from Amos and his court. . . Baruch ben Neriah received it from Jeremiah and his court, and Ezra and his court received it from Baruch ben Neriah and his court. The court of Ezra constituted "the men of the Great Assembly" . . . the last of them was Simeon the Righteous, who was one of the one hundred and twenty members. He received the Oral Law from them all, and he was the High Priest after Ezra.[3]

Maimonides then lists in the chain of tradition "the Fathers," as given in the first chapter of *Abot*, followed by the Catena of Sages in the Mishnah and the Gemara.

The Eighth Principle, as formulated in Maimonides' Commentary on the Mishnah (*Sanhedrin* 10) succinctly restates the concept, now formulated as a dogma:

> The Torah comes from God and we must believe that this entire Torah which was given through Moshe Rabbenu, peace to him, is all from the mouth of the Almighty. That is to say, all of it reached him from God, blessed be he, by means which may metaphorically be called "speech," but which was known only to Moshe, peace be to him, whom it reached. He was like a scribe taking dictation; he wrote down all the events, the narratives and the commandments, and was, therefore, called *mehoqeq*, "inscriber" [or "copyist"]. Hence, there is no difference [i.e., in sanctity] between the genealogy of the sons of Noah [Gen. 10:1ff.] and The Ten Commandments or the Shema.

Maimonides wished to have his *Thirteen Principles* (ʾani maʾmin) adopted as the test of adherence to Judaism. Though they exercised wide influence and are printed in the prayer book, neither they, nor any other set of dogmas, were ever adopted as obligatory.

It is often argued that this concept of verbal revelation is expressed in a famous passage in the Palestinian Talmud: "Whatever a conscientious student will one day teach in the presence of his master was already revealed to Moses on Sinai." (P. Peʾah 2, 4).

Today this interpretation of the passage is not altogether congenial even to the most fervent proponents of literalist revelation. This is clear from the treatment of the passage by an important contemporary scholar. He quotes the text, to sure, as a warrant for his own views. But it is most interesting that even he, in rendering his passage into English, paraphrases it as follows: "All of Halakhah is *inherent* in the original *revelation* at Mount Sinai"[4] (italics mine). He departs from the Hebrew text in two significant particulars. The reading in the Palestinian Talmud does not say *niglah*, "was revealed," but *neʾemar*, "was said." Thus even this right-wing spokesman finds it problematic to assume that every statement in rabbinic literature was *spoken* verbatim to Moses on Sinai. In addition, he abandons even this free rendition of "said" as "revealed" and speaks of the Halakhah as "inherent" in the original revelation at Sinai.

We may speak of an oak tree as inherent in an acorn, but an acorn and an oak tree are not identical. We may sit under an oak tree, but hardly under an acorn! We may regard an oak tree as "in the acorn" and, therefore, "inherent in it." Or more precisely, we may think of the tree as an outgrowth of the acorn, the fulfilment of its original potential, but we must also remember that the acorn is not the only determinant of the oak tree's growth. Its size and strength will also be affected by the character of the soil on which the acorn falls, the amount and distribution of rainfall, and the degree of access to sunlight. As in every living thing, nurture as well as nature play a basic role.

One may then consider the canons of interpretation in later generations as integral parts of the revelation itself, so that the Halakhist "merely" unravels the implicit meaning of the Torah for his time. But when—as is frequently the case—the explicit meaning of the text itself and the implicit meaning proposed by the later interpretation diverge substantially, it is obvious that the two are not identical. The history of the Halakhah is as important as its origins. To understand it truly, its growth is at least as significant as its birth.

Clearly the *Pe>ah* passage affirms that all of postbiblical Jewish law is inherent in the original Sinaitic revelation, partaking of its divine character. But it does not necessarily intend to make all of rabbinic Judaism a replay of an earlier biblical recording, as is attested by the thousands of differences of opinion and the hundreds of creative and innovative ideas found in the pages of the Talmud and the Midrash.

It is only to be expected that in ancient and medieval times, when an understanding of historical change and development had not yet emerged, the concept of an unchanged and unchangeable tradition was dominant. The opening statement of the Mishnah *Abot* declares, "Moses received the Torah on Sinai, transmitted it to Joshua, Joshua to the Elders, the Elders to the Prophets and the Prophets to the men of the Great Assembly."

Here an important parenthesis is in order. In recent times, two words from this last passage, *Torah missinai*, "the Torah from Sinai," have been lifted from the context and taken to imply that it is a dogma of traditional Judaism that the five books of the Torah were given verbatim to Moses on Sinai. Clearly the passage refers not to the Written Torah—the books of Genesis, Exodus, Leviticus, Numbers, and Deuteronomy—but to the Oral Law, the entire expanse of rabbinic literature embodied primarily in the Talmud and the Midrash. That the Pentateuch went back to Moses was not doubted in ancient times, and so the Talmudic rabbis never felt the need of making the belief in its Mosaic authorship a dogma of Judaism.

It should be added that the phrase *Torah missinai* never occurs in rabbinic literature as a concept. The lifting of the two words from the passage in *Abot* is a modern invention, an attempt to counter the higher criticism of the Bible. However, the question of the authorship of the biblical books is a literary and historical issue of great complexity and difficulty; it is not a religious dogma to be accepted on faith. Actually, the religious authority of the Torah does not rest upon any given theory of biblical authorship. As a Russian rabbi earlier in this century wrote in his Hebrew commentary on Isaiah with regard to the theory of a second Isaiah, "What real difference does it make to us whether God spoke to one or to two Prophets?"[5]

Returning to the theory of the literal revelation of the Oral Law, one can understand and sympathize with the effort to shore up fundamentalism by insisting that the Halakhah is absolute, monochromatic, and seamless. There is undoubtedly great attraction for some in an approach to the Torah as unchanged in the past and unchangeable in the future, exalted above time and impervious to circumstance. Such a view of the Torah has undeniable appeal to those unable or unwilling to wrestle with the uncertainties and problems of human existence. But this stance is possible only if one is capable of ignoring all the facts and their implications, accumulated by more than two centuries of research in biblical studies, comparative religion, anthropology, history, and sociology, as well as the insights of modern psychology and philosophy.

Today there are many men and women who are able to insulate their religious beliefs from the modern world. Some accomplish this by keeping themselves totally ignorant of it or uninvolved in it by their own volition or at the direction of their spiritual mentors. The sole exception is the occupation training they permit their young people to take in order to earn a livelihood.

Others, comfortable with a compartmentalized mind, keep the conclusions of modern science, philosophy, and thought hermetically sealed off from religious faith and practice. All too often these people become preoccupied with the minutiae of ritual and disregard ethics, both in theory and in practice. Moreover, these isolationist versions of Judaism being propagated so energetically today could spell the end of the process of creative interaction between the Jewish people and the world. That relationship produced the Bible and the Talmud as well as medieval and modern Jewish culture on the one hand, and the great contributions of individual Jews to civilization on the other.

This state of suspended animation is fragile and likely to collapse at any time. Modernism can penetrate the defenses of fundamentalism when it is least expected. One celebrated instance concerns Kaufmann Kohler, a disciple of the famous nineteenth-century German rabbi Samson Raphael Hirsch. Hirsch had taught the younger man that Hebrew was the oldest of all languages, since it was spoken in the Garden of Eden by Adam and Eve. When Kohler went on to study at a university, he learned that Hebrew was one of a group of Semitic languages and that structurally it represents a later stage than some others. His unquestioning faith in his beloved master was shaken; and Kohler broke away from Orthodoxy, eventually becoming a leading exponent of Reform Judaism in America.

A Dynamic Approach to Revelation

Fortunately we are not compelled to choose between a literalist view and a total denial of revelation. Modern Jewish scholarship has found in the history of the Halakhah evidence of the dialectic of continuity and change at every given point. This dynamic view of revelation, supported by authoritative research, offers a basis for maintaining the Halakhah as a vital and meaningful instrument for Jewish living.

Significant research in history and literature conducted during the last two centuries by Leopold Zunz, Nachman Krochmal, Solomon Judah Lob Rapoport, Samuel David Luzzato, Heinrich Graetz, and Harry A. Wolfson, as well as the studies in law and institutions by Zacharias Frankel, Abraham Geiger, Isaac Hirsch Weiss, Jacob Z. Lauterbach, Solomon Schechter, Louis Ginzberg, Chaim Tchernowitz, Solomon Zeitlin, and Saul Lieberman, together with their fellows and successors alive in our own day, have supplied abundant evidence of the mutual influence of the dominant cultures of each epoch and the Jewish tradition. They have demonstrated that the law of growth and development, which is universal throughout nature and society, applies to Judaism as well. The record is clear that Jewish law was never monolithic and unchanged in the past. There are, therefore, no grounds for decreeing that it must be motionless in the present and immovable in the future.

Modern research has laid the groundwork for a more-sophisticated and adequate understanding of the nature of revelation. In all true communication there are at least two participants. The one who speaks is obviously active, but the one who is silent is also contributing to the process—listening, striving to understand, and reacting by accepting, questioning, or even raising objections. Revelation is an act of communication between God and man, and the message is the product of this encounter. The human partner is important because if he is inactive there is no communication and, therefore, no revelation.

Moreover, the message is not what has been spoken at one end but what has been understood at the other. Hence, the written record of revelation always contains two elements: The divine factor, which is the source of its universal and eternal value, and the human component, which is the source of its time-bound and limited elements, reflect the flux of human events and the changing level of human understanding.

The human participants in revelation, the Prophets and the Sages, were no ordinary men. They were richly endowed with the attributes of mind and spirit described by Isaiah as "wisdom and understanding, counsel and courage, the knowledge and the fear of the Lord" (11:2). Hence the intersection of their lives with the divine produced a body of religious and ethical truth of enduring value. Although the message was first directed to their own time and place, their deep understanding of human nature, its needs and desires, its weaknesses and limitations, has given their words permanent relevance. The message also reflects the transitory and impermanent features in man's career on earth.

While the tradition claims that its authority derives from revelation, the determination of which aspects are permanent and which are subject to change and how that is to be achieved calls for the highest human wisdom, sensitivity, and integrity. The thousand Sages whose opinions and controversies fill the 3,000 pages of the Talmud testify to the legitimacy of differing views and the difficulties involved in reaching decisions.

To be sure, the dynamic concept of revelation lacks the cast-iron assurance of the static view, which has proved so attractive to those who have grown tired of uncertainty and have lost confidence in their own capacity to face their problems. They want the comfort of a snug harbor, where everything is settled for them, preferably by a father figure. To achieve this end, they are ready and willing to pay a high price; they dismiss—or better still, ignore—the incontrovertible evidence that makes their position intellectually untenable, and they deny the existence of problems in contemporary life that make it ethically intolerable.

Today, each individual must choose between these two conflicting concepts of the nature of revelation. How are they reflected in traditional literature? Do they both find expression, or is only one represented?

There is no doubt that the Talmudic Sages, by and large, viewed revelation as a phenomenon in which God is the active source and man the passive recipient. Thus when the Talmud discusses the closing verses of the Book of Deuteronomy, which describe the death of Moses, the obvious question arises as to how Moses could have written a section narrating his own demise. One answer—not the only one—declares, "The Holy One blessed be He, was speaking and Moses was writing with a tear in his eyes" (B. *Baba Batra* 15a). There is no need to multiply passages in which the literalistic concept of revelation is either explicit or implicit. The reasons for this approach to revelation are self-evident. The Sages rarely engaged in abstract theological inquiry, which might have led them to question this theory of revelation. Besides, living in periods when change was slow and often imperceptible, they were not confronted by the constant and rapid flux in all aspects of human experience and thought, so characteristic of modern life.

The Human Role in Revelation

Insight into the human role in revelation emerges from several profound Talmudic passages. The first, the implications of which have not been generally noted, discusses an incident recorded in I Kings 22. Jehoshaphat, king of Judah, has allied himself with the king of Israel for a war against Aram. Just before the battle, the Judean king asks that the prophetic oracle be consulted. Four hundred prophets appear and declare, "Go up, because the Lord will give the enemy into the king's hand." Far from being reassured by this unanimity, Jehoshaphat asks for an independent prophetic voice. A maverick prophet, Micaiah ben Imlah, is summoned, and he announces an impending defeat.

Why this distrust of the 400 optimistic prophets? The Talmud answers: "God's one watchword goes out to many prophets, but no two prophets prophesy with the same watchword" (B. *Sanhedrin* 89a). Rashi defines the word *signon*, "watchword," as "the poetic mode of expression *debhar melizot* of the Holy Spirit," and explains that "it enters into the heart of one Prophet in one form of expression, and into another in another, because no two Prophets speak in the same language."

It is often maintained by modern defenders of fundamentalism that the virtue of their position lies in its unanimity, its unshakeable certainty, and its total freedom from dissent or doubt. The Rabbis of the Talmud, on the contrary, believed that precisely because all 400 prophets spoke in identical language they were not divinely inspired! The absence of the human element of difference in their message was *prima facie* evidence that their oracle was a fraud and that they were not speaking in the name of God. Paradoxically, it is the variable human factor in revelation that is the warrant of its authenticity, because, as the Rabbis put it, the Torah was given not to angels but to human beings.

Recognizing a human role in revelation has another important consequence. It implies the existence of different levels of apperception of the divine message. In drawing this conclusion, the Rabbis stood on solid biblical ground. Chapter 12 of the Book of Numbers narrates an incident that occurred during the wilderness period. When Moses is slandered by his own brother and sister, God himself intervenes, chastises the pair, and sets forth the unique position that Moses occupies. In the process, a basic distinction is established between Moses and other Prophets:

> The Lord said, "Hear My words: If there is a prophet among you, I the Lord make Myself known to him in a vision; I speak with him in a dream. Not so with my servant Moses; he is entrusted with all My house. With him I speak mouth to mouth, clearly, and not in riddles; and he beholds the form of the Lord. Why then were you not afraid to speak against My servant Moses?" [Num. 12:6–8].

The Rabbis elaborate upon this difference, declaring that Moses saw reality through a clear telescope, while the other Prophets gazed through a clouded one (B. *Yebamot* 49b).

The Rabbis further distinguished levels of contact with the divine among the later Prophets themselves. The Prophet Isaiah offers a simple and majestic concept of God in his Inaugural Vision (chap. 6), while the Prophet Ezekiel presents a highly complicated and mysterious vision of the Godhead in his opening chapter. Obviously they were describing the same living God. The Rabbis reconcile the discrepancy by a parable. Isaiah was a city dweller who was accustomed to seeing the royal chariot riding through the streets, and so he described it in a few simple lines. But Ezekiel was a rustic coming to town, who was impressed by every detail of the royal entourage (B. *Hagigah* 13b). These two passages imply a difference in the degree of intimacy with God and the clarity of vision among the Prophets of Israel.

Since the biblical revelation is the product of the divine-human encounter, with both God and His chosen servants participating in the process, it follows that in the rabbinic legislation the human element will also be evident. This conclusion is clearly recognized by the Sages in a striking passage that is generally overlooked. The Midrash declares, *Devarim shelo> niglu lemoshe niglu lerabbi Akiba vetalmidav*, "Matters not revealed to Moses were revealed to Rabbi Akiba and his disciples" (Midrash Bemidbar Rabbah 19:6). The use of the verb *niglu*, "revealed," is highly significant.

That the entire Torah, Oral and Written, was given to Moses, was a basic dogma, inviolate and unquestioned. The Rabbis undoubtedly felt it essential to maintain the doctrine in order to buttress the authority of the Torah in the face of attacks by the Sadducees, who denied the validity of the Oral Law, and by the nascent Christian Church, which declared that the Torah had been superseded by the new dispensation. Nevertheless, in their debates in the academy and their day-to-day decisions in the law courts, the Rabbis do not give the impression that they are merely repeating verbatim what Moses had heard in Sinai. On the contrary, their discussions reflect a lively sense of recognition that human opinions and attitudes were at work in their deliberations.

Thus a difference emerged between Rabbi Akiba and Rabbi Ishmael as to the specific mode of execution that the Torah had prescribed for the married daughter of a priest who had yielded to immorality. To defend his opinion, Akiba said to his colleague, "Ishmael, my brother, I base my view on the superfluous letter *Vav* in the word *ubhat* [in Lev. 21:9]!" Rabbi Ishmael coolly responded, "Because you press the meaning of this one letter, shall this girl be punished by burning?" (B. *Sanhedrin* 51b).

Talmudic masters of the greatest eminence did not hesitate to view the Halakhah as the result of the interaction between a Torah divine in origin and its human interpreters, who are free to exercise their understanding and reason upon it. A striking case in point is afforded by the famous incident of the "Stove of ʿakhnai" (B. *Baba Mezia* 59b). Here the archconservative and highly respected Rabbi Eliezer ben Hyrcanus forcefully presented his view on the question under discussion, but none of his colleagues in the academy agreed. To justify his position, he called upon a series of three miracles, each of which duly took place. When his colleagues remained unconvinced, he asked that a *Bat kol*, "a heavenly voice," pronounce judgment on the issue. It was heard to say, "Who are you to differ with Rabbi Eliezer, for the law is according to his view on every question." Nothing daunted, Rabbi Joshua cited Deuteronomy 30:12, which declares, "'It is not in heaven.' This means that the Torah has already been given on Sinai. We pay no attention to heavenly voices, for You have already written at Sinai in the Torah that we must follow the majority." Rabbi Nathan then met the Prophet Elijah and asked, "What did God do in that hour?" Elijah answered, "He smiled and said, 'My children have overcome me!'"

Generally this passage is cited to focus attention on what the Sages were rejecting by their refusal to let a miracle influence their deliberative process. But even more significant is what they were affirming—not merely their right, but their duty to decide the law on the basis of their own understanding, as determined by majority vote.

This incident has another implication: Rabbi Eliezer was wont to boast, "I never taught anything that I did not learn from my teachers" (B. *Sukkah* 28a). As a staunch repository of past tradition, he was totally opposed to innovation. By overriding him so decisively, his colleagues were surely aware that their position represented a break with a hallowed past.

This is clear from a Talmudic legend, at once naive and profound, and not devoid of humor (B. *Menahot* 29b). According to this Aggadah, Moses in heaven found God adding decorative crowns to the letters of the Torah. When the lawgiver asked the reason, he was told: "In a future generation, a man named Akiba, son of Joseph, is destined to arise, who will derive multitudes of laws from each of these marks." Moses asked to see the scholar in action, and he was admitted to the rear of the academy where Akiba was lecturing. To his deep distress, Moses found that he could not understand what the scholars were saying, and his spirit grew faint within him. As the session drew to a close, Akiba concluded: "This ordinance which we have been discussing is a law derived from Moses on Sinai." When Moses heard this, his spirit revived.

The implications of this profound legend are far-reaching. For the Talmud, tradition is not static, it undergoes changes, so extensive at times as to seem unrecognizable. But this dynamic quality does not contravene either its divine origin or its organic continuity.

It is often maintained that the ancients did not have a sense of history. Hence it was possible for the Rabbis to conceive of Jacob studying the Torah with his ancestor Shem or of David and his warriors being members of a Sanhedrin and arguing points of Jewish law, or of the sinful King Menasseh disputing with God on theological doctrine.

But the Sages obviously recognized the great events that affected them fundamentally. The Babylonian Exile, the rebuilding of the Second Temple, the Maccabean revolt, the Hasmonean assumption of temporal and religious power, and the Roman destruction of the Second Temple all had a major impact on the Halakhah. The Sages were conscious not only of major events but also of slower and less-dramatic changes in the practice and the mores of the people. This led them to modify important aspects of biblical law.

What were the factors that permitted them to override the heavenly voice? They had to be relying only on their innate spiritual resources, on their reason and their moral conscience. Nor did they have any compunction about doing so, because they knew that these attributes were *ḥelek Eloah mimmaʿal*, "a portion from God from above." Nothing less could have induced them to set aside what they believed was a direct revelation from on high.

Throughout Jewish history these two great canons of reason and the moral conscience have been the means by which Jewish leadership received the traditional inheritance of the past and preserved it for the future. In the majority of instances, the tradition could be and was maintained with little or no change. But when change became necessary, the Rabbis did not hesitate to evaluate the tradition and modify it before handing it over to their successors. They recognized that successive generations of scholars were not merely repeating traditions and decisions from the past, but were revealing new and unfamiliar aspects of the Torah. It is not without interest that the comments of scholars on the work of their predecessors are called *ḥiddushim*, "novellae," "new interpretations."

Revelation as Process

If we turn from theology to law and examine the role of growth and change in specific provisions of the Halakhah, it is clear that the Rabbis were conscious of the role of innovation in the Halakhic process. The Mishnah (M. *Hagigah* 1:8) lists a series of basic elements of Jewish law, such as the annulment of vows, as "floating in the air" and having no real basis in the biblical text. Even the sabbath prohibitions, the laws of the Festivals, and the *Me<ilah* offerings are characterized as "mountains hanging by a hair."

It is sometimes maintained that interpretations by Talmudic Rabbis that departed from the letter of scripture were an unconscious process, and that the Rabbis believed that they were merely explicating the original meaning of the Torah, not introducing changes. This surely could not have been true of all the Rabbis. In the famous controversy on the biblical passage "An eye for an eye" (Exod. 21:24), the Rabbis interpreted the phrase to mean that *mammon*, "financial compensation," was the proper mode of payment for physical injury. The lone dissenter, Rabbi Eliezer, declared that the payment was to be *mammash*, "the removal of an eye of the perpetrator." It is impossible to believe that the Rabbis, who were unanimous in rejecting Rabbi Eliezer's literal view, failed to recognize that his interpretation was the literal meaning of the verse.

The same consideration applies to hundreds of rabbinic controversies in the pages of the Talmud. In these instances they had to be aware of the changes they were introducing into the *peshat*, the plain meaning of the text. For reasons they regarded as sufficient, they proceeded to interpret untold biblical passages freely; what is more, they defended their use of these texts against opponents within their own circle or in other competitive sects.

The Rabbis, totally committed to the faith that the Torah sets forth the word of God, were convinced that it embodies the highest spiritual and ethical values at every point. Therefore they did not hesitate to interpret the biblical texts freely, invoking one procedure in one case and a diametrically opposite one in another, depending on the goal they sought to achieve.

A case in point is afforded by the biblical law of the levirate, which ordains that if a married man dies without children his widow had to be taken in marriage by a brother of her deceased husband (Deut. 25:5–10). For valid social and ethical reasons, the Rabbis sought to limit the applicability of the biblical legislation. They therefore interpreted the scriptural words *ubhen >ein lo* (literally, "if he has no son") to mean, "if he has no offspring, either male of female" (B. *Baba Batra* 109a). In another connection, the word *ben*, "son," was interpreted in its strict sense: The Torah forbids cutting oneself as a mourning rite, because "you are the sons of the Lord your God" (Deut. 14:1). Here the word *banim*, "sons," is interpreted literally by Issi to mean that only males are forbidden to practice this rite, which evidently had a strong hold on the people (B. *Kiddushin* 35b).

From these specific instances we can draw an important general conclusion. In none of the hundreds of controversies in the Mishnah and the Talmud do we encounter a Sage saying to his opponent: "My view is a direct revelation of God, which I have received. Your position is therefore mistaken." On the contrary, in their debates the Rabbis argue vigorously for their particular standpoint, but they do not invoke any canons except those that are subject to rational argument and demonstration.

In sum, two distinct concepts of revelation may be discovered in rabbinic literature. The prevalent view conceived of revelation in simplistic terms as "the dictation of God" to Moses and the Prophets, whose task it was to transmit the message verbatim to their contemporaries. The other, more-sophisticated approach recognized the complex character of the process of communication on all levels and saw revelation as a meeting involving both God and man as active participants.

A New Doctrine of Infallibility

It is ironic that in our day when the doctrine of papal infallibility is being challenged even within the Catholic Church, a novel doctrine of rabbinic infallibility is being advanced in fundamentalist Jewish circles. In order to suppress any movement for change in the Halakhah, we are told that it is forbidden to question, let alone disagree with, the views of a given scholar or group of scholars, because they represent *da'at Torah*, "the true meaning of the Torah." This gift has been vouchsafed to them because they are the mystical embodiment of divine truth. Such a doctrine, designed to stifle discussion and controversy, was never advanced in the past by any of the thousands of Talmudic Sages, by Saadia or his adversaries in the tenth century, by the advocates and opponents of Maimonides in the thirteenth, or even by the adherents of the *Shulḥan Arukh* and its rabbinic opponents in the sixteenth and seventeenth centuries.

Nor are the advocates of this newly concocted doctrine of *da'at Torah* dissuaded by the fact that violent disagreement frequently exists among these *gedolei hatorah*, "great men of the Torah." The doctrine is designed to combat the growing divisions in the traditional Jewish community, but it has succeeded only in adding new fissures to the already weakened structure. Just as the institution of the Chief Rabbinate in Israel is a clear imitation of the hierarchical structure of the Christian Church, *da‹at Torah* is an unfortunate borrowing of the Catholic dogma of papal infallibility.

The Vital Role of the Conservative

Our concern thus far has been the evidence of the reality and legitimacy of growth and development in Jewish law. But change in the law is counterbalanced and often outweighed by static and conservative tendencies that are at least equally strong and, it should be added, equally indispensable.

We now turn to an analysis of the creative dynamism characteristic of Jewish tradition and law. Every legal system supports and in turn is supported by the dominant social, economic, and political powers. This innate tendency to protect one's interests is reinforced by psychological factors—loyalty to a revered, if mythical past; an attachment to familiar practices and institutions; and a sense of unease, which easily passes over into dislike, for new and unfamiliar ideas.

Moreover, the conservative bias for the law derives in large measure from its structure. Basically, law is embodied in precedents, taking the form of legislative enactment or juridical decision. As the term "precedent" itself indicates, the law enshrines the attitudes of thought and the patterns of behavior inherited from the past. Finally, the legal authorities win their bread and butter and acquire prestige in society by virtue of their familiarity with the "literature," the citations of earlier decisions and legislative enactments. It is no wonder that legal experts, whether they are lawyers or scholars, usually exhibit a conservative bias, since they are engaged—in both senses of the term—in the support of the old, established order.

The innate conservatism of the law is further strengthened when the society possesses a written constitution to which it accords absolute authority. Technically, a secular constitution can be amended, but it is a difficult and costly process resorted to only rarely. Thus the American people, after 200 years of eventful history and kaleidoscopic change, has adopted only 25 amendments in addition to the original Bill of Rights.

The power of the past is exponentially heightened when the basic document is not secular but religious in origin. Since the Bible is a sacred constitution, its text may not be modified by changes, deletions, or additions. To be sure, societies are not as immobile as this observation would suggest. Every community develops canons of reinterpretation that can radically alter and even nullify specific provisions in the sacred text in practice without tampering with it in theory.

Nevertheless, the existence of an authoritative constitution, be it sacred or secular, establishes broad parameters outside which society cannot go without destroying the entire social and political fabric. Thus, a hereditary monarchy cannot be squared with the American Constitution; a physical image of God is inconceivable in a synagogue. Reinterpretation is a potent instrument for flexibility; the written constitution or Torah serves as a safeguard for stability; the tension between the two is the seedbed for necessary growth.

The conservative tendency to resist change is not only deep-seated and ineradicable but also essential for the health of society. The vigor with which conservatives stand guard over the old challenges the thinking of the liberals and thereby reduces the danger of extreme innovation, especially when based on transitory phenomena. It compels the advocates of change to scrutinize their goals and make sure that they are not yielding to the whims of fashion masquerading as progress.

Moreover, the true conservative makes another necessary contribution to society—standing firm against the tyranny of the majority when it threatens to erode or subvert the protections extended to the minority by the sacred text. Despite mounting polarization among economic, religious, ethnic, and ideological groups in our own age, the Bill of Rights remains a bulwark for the protection of minorities. The rash of amendments currently being proposed to the United States Constitution are an expression of the frustration felt by those who are determined to suppress the rights of minorities they do not like. The true conservative in America performs a vital function in defending the provisions of the Bill of Rights.

There are, of course, those who try to minimize or ignore the injunctions of biblical teaching and postbiblical law on brotherhood and social justice. But in order to justify their defense of the *status quo*, with its blind eye toward violence and oppression and its indifference to the weak, the poor, and the stranger, they have no alternative but to dredge up isolated and obscure passages, often distorting their meaning. As is often the case, the reactionary is at the farthest possible remove from the true conservative, who seeks to preserve the humane ideals of the tradition.

To turn to our theme, in any functioning legal system, the conservative and the liberal, the advocate of stability and the protagonist of progress, are both indispensable. Together they constitute the systole and the diastole at the heart of the social and political process. Every period in the history of the Halakhah reveals the confrontation of those sensitive to new conditions and new needs and those concerned with the preservation of norms and practices hallowed by the past. Both groups have produced distinguished and venerated spokesmen for their respective positions.

Recognizing that the ultimate source of authority for the Halakhah lies in divine revelation, we have set forth a theory of revelation that is entirely compatible with the process of growth and development, in which the conservative, no less than the liberal, plays a vital role.[6]

V

THE HALAKHIC PROCESS
THE SCHOLARS' ROLE

The liberal and the conservative are both essential to any vital legal system, and the Halakhah is no exception. It is highly significant, however, that the outstanding exemplars of the Halakhah are creative and innovative figures. They represent the genius of Judaism at its highest, with careers that span twelve hundred years, from the Persian era to the early Middle Ages. They placed their stamp on the character of Jewish law and made it a viable system under radically changing social, economic, and political conditions. Their creative legal and intellectual activity enabled Judaism to function in the Hellenistic-Roman world, in the medieval Christian church-state, in the Islamic polity, and in the European feudal system. The Halakhah continued to operate in the early *laissez-faire* capitalist order and during the emergence of capitalist democracy, in the welfare state, and after the establishment of the state of Israel. Even Communist tyranny has not succeeded in obliterating loyalty to Jewish law. A vital Halakhah will have a significant role in the social and political order of the future.[1]

The Methods of Midrash and Mishnah

The origins of the Oral Law are to be found in the biblical period, for obviously no written law can operate without an oral tradition at its side to spell out its details and implications. The Halakhah became the basic spiritual enterprise in Judaism with Ezra (fifth century B.C.E.). His seminal influence is clear from the Talmudic statement "Ezra was worthy of having the Torah given through him, had not Moses preceded him" (B. *Sanhedrin* 21b). With Ezra's successors, the Sopherim (fifth to second century B.C.E.), the Pharisees (second century B.C.E. to first century C.E.), and the Tannaitic rabbis (first to third century C.E.), the two basic techniques of the Halakhah came into being.

One method, that of the Midrash, literally, "searching the scripture," is deductive; the other, that of the Mishnah, literally, "study," or the Halakhah, "the way," is inductive. The Midrashic method takes its point of departure from a painstaking study of the biblical text. Every passage, word, and letter is searched out and analyzed in order to deduce implications for contemporary life. The method of the Mishnah, on the other hand, originates in a life situation. When a problem or a controversy arises, the accepted authorities reach a decision on the basis of their religious and ethical perceptions. They may then seek to relate their ruling to a biblical text, which becomes its formal source and validation. Very often, the scriptural basis for the decision is left unexpressed.

While there is no iron curtain separating the two procedures, and the same scholars utilized both methods, two distinct types of literature emerged. The deductive method is embodied principally in the Halakhic Midrashim, the *Mekhilta, Sifra,* and *Sifre,* which reached their present form early in the third century C.E. The inductive method is embodied in the Mishnah, compiled by Rabbi Judah Hanasi at about the same time.

After the third century, the fortunes of the two techniques diverged radically. The method of Halakhic Midrash was virtually exhausted by the end of the Tannaitic age, and no significant Halakhic Midrashim emerged thereafter. The reason is not far to seek. While the Torah is, indeed, "longer than the earth in measure and broader than the sea," the legal passages in the Torah total only a few hundred verses. No matter how fruitful the text and how ingenious the interpreter, there are limits to the interpretations afforded by the text. On the other hand, changing conditions and new insights may need to go beyond the biblical text, even when it is homiletically expounded.

The inductive method of the Mishnah, on the other hand, is as unlimited as life itself, with each day creating new configurations. Hence, the Mishnah of Rabbi Judah Hanasi included only a portion, albeit the most significant one, of the material available to the redactor. Even the second compilation of Tannaitic material, the *Tosefta,* attributed to his contemporary Rabbi Hiyya, did not exhaust this material. Hundreds of *baraitot,* "external traditions," survived outside both collections as *disjecta membra* and have been preserved only because they were later cited in the Gemara.

The entire later development of the Halakhah followed the method of the Mishnah rather than that of the Midrash. Predominantly, the Halakhah began with life, which it sought to relate to the body of accumulated tradition. This is true of the Gemara of both Palestine and Babylonia.

The availability of this technique of the Mishnah, deriving its impetus from life, created the potential for a Halakhah that would be appropriate to all times and conditions. This potential was actualized because in each generation there were scholars of courage and insight who adapted the received Halakhah to the needs of the age—Ezra, Hillel, Rabban Johanan ben Zakkai, Rabban Gamaliel, Rabbi Akiba, Rabbi Judah the Patriarch, Rab, and Samuel, to cite only a few.

After it was consigned to writing, the Mishnah in turn became the subject of detailed analysis and extensive interpretation in the Gemara ("study") carried on by the *amoraim*, "expounders," in Palestine and in Babylonia.

After the sixth century the Mishnah and the Gemara, now constituting the Talmud, became a "canonical," or normative, Halakhah so that its text could not henceforth be altered. That all three terms—Mishnah, Gemara, and Talmud—literally mean "study" points to the importance that Judaism assigns to the study of the sacred texts as a cardinal commandment.

The Talmud, in turn, became the basis of minute analysis by later scholars, as had been the case with the Bible and the Mishnah centuries earlier. The interpretation of the hallowed text of the Talmud now became the activity of the Saboraim (sixth and seventh centuries C.E.) and the Geonim, the heads of the great Babylonian academies (seventh to eleventh century C.E.).

After the decline of Babylonia, a multiplicity of Jewish settlements arose in North Africa, Spain, Provence, Italy, Germany, and Poland. They created new literary forms in which the Halakhah continued to grow—legal treatises, commentaries, all-inclusive codes of law, and *responsa* by individual scholars on specific issues. *Responsa* have continued to augment the content of the Halakhah and show no signs of diminution even today, fifteen hundred years later. Every *Responsum* has two sections, the *she>elah*, "question," and the *teshuvah*, "answer." The question always arises out of a concrete situation encountered by the inquirer; the answer reflects the respondent's learning and sensitivity to the prevailing conditions.

Post-Talmudic Legislation

In theory, the Mishnah and the Gemara were the final authority, not to be added to or subtracted from. They were, however, subject to wide-ranging interpretation, and this process generally sufficed to meet most problems of Jewish life. But at times new important issues emerged that required different treatment. Rabbinic law made provisions for such radical steps, permitting the enactment by competent authorities of *taqqanot* "positive regulations" and *gezerot*, "negative ordinances." These legislative acts, which went beyond the bounds of the previously accepted Halakhah, were generally enacted for a fixed period and for a restricted territory.

Among the exceptions to these limitations was the *taqqanah* prohibiting polygamy. It was enacted by Rabbi Gershom of Mainz and his synod in the tenth century for the communities of what now constitute Germany, France, and Italy, to be valid for a period of one thousand years. Neither the time limit which has now expired nor the original territorial restriction has been invoked to abolish the ruling, which is permanent and universally observed by Jewry today. The same rabbinical synod enacted other significant *taqqanot*, including a major extension of the rights of women in divorce and the protection of the privacy of letters, which were generally sent by messengers.

The two techniques of *gezerah* and *taqqanah* are utilized infrequently in later periods, but they are still available as a last resort when the Halakhah is confronted by intractable problems.

Another far-reaching procedure used by rabbinic authorities has not been adequately noticed. When rabbinic leaders in medieval Jewry were confronted by a Halakhah they felt to be inappropriate to their situation, they sometimes adopted a strategy that can only be described as "tacit noncompliance." The problematic provision of the law was not rescinded, reinterpreted, or modified; it was simply ignored in practice and, where possible, passed over in silence in the literature. When the provision of the law could be reinterpreted, that was naturally preferred; if not, it was to all intents and purposes set aside for good and sufficient reasons.

Two major motivations were at work here. The first was the overriding desire to guarantee the physical survival of the Jewish people in the face of constant danger. The second was the wish to preserve traditional standards of family morality, for which, they believed, the subordinate position of women was essential. The following are a few instances of this practice:

1. A key element in biblical domestic law decreed that a father had the authority to give his daughter into marriage or sell her into slavery at will (Exod. 21:7). This absolute power was considerably abridged in the Mishnah by a process of interpretation. The Hebrew term *na‹arah*, "girl," which is used in several biblical texts, was given a technical meaning and was limited to females between twelve and twelve and a half years old. Before this period of "girlhood," the daughter was a *ketannah*, "a minor." During this period the father's right to marry her off was limited (B. *Ketubbot* 43b). The Babylonian Sage Rab went further and declared, "A man is morally forbidden to marry off his daughter while she is a *ketannah*" (B. *Kiddushin* 41a). After the age of twelve and a half, the girl assumed the status of a *bogeret*, "mature person,"

and her father no longer had legal authority over her. Thus in theory, the *patria potestas* was reduced to a six-month period. In practice, however, during medieval and even modern days, parents continued to marry off their daughters as they chose at almost any age, betrothals (*tenʾaim*) often taking place in the early teen years.

2. The early rabbinic schools of the house of Hillel and the house of Shammai were in agreement that the commandment "Be fruitful and multiply" was fulfilled by the birth of two children. The schools differed only as to whether two sons were required, as Shammai held, or whether a son and a daughter would suffice, as Hillel maintained. Both views were disregarded in practice. Ultratraditional Jewish couples continue to propagate large numbers of children to the present day.

3. A Tannaitic statement quoted six times in the Talmud discusses the use of an absorbent by three categories of women—a minor, a pregnant woman, and a nursing mother—in order to prevent conception. Classical interpreters differ as to whether these women are permitted (and other women are not) or whether they are required to practice birth control (and other women are permitted). That these three categories *must* and other women *may* practice contraception is the prevalent interpretation among the commentators.[2]

Obviously widespread family limitation would drastically affect the biological survival of Jews threatened by man-made perils like expulsion and massacre, as well as the "natural" dangers of disease and malnutrition. Here, two strategies were adopted. First, the statement was interpreted, at variance with well-known and common linguistic usage, to forbid the practice of contraception to all three classes of women.[3] Second, virtually none of the medieval law codes, not even the *Mishneh Torah* of Maimonides and the *Shulḥan Arukh* of Rabbi Joseph Karo, make any reference to the subject, thus the possibility of discussing the option of practicing birth control is completely eliminated.[4]

4. The Talmud cites two Tannaitic Sages on the subject of educating women in the Torah. The conservative Rabbi Eliezer ben Hyrcanus declares that teaching the Torah to women is tantamount to teaching obscenity (M. *Sotah* 3:4) and forbids it. He is contradicted by Ben Azzai, who makes teaching the Torah to women obligatory. As is noted at several points in the present volume, the law is rarely decided in accordance with Rabbi Eliezer's opinion. Nonetheless, during the greater portion of Diaspora history, his negative view on the education of women prevailed. The teaching of the Torah to women has been almost nonexistent in traditional Jewish communities until the present.

5. In the sixteenth century Rabbi Joseph Karo codified the practice of Sephardic communities in a work entitled *Shulḥan Arukh*, "The Prepared Table," to which Rabbi Moses Isserles added his *Mappah*, "Tablecloth," setting down the Ashkenazic practice in vogue among German

and Polish Jews. This supplement, which is always printed as part of the central text, was indispensable in making the *Shulḥan Arukh* normative for all traditional Jews.

On the subject of honors at the Torah reading, a statement in the *Shulḥan Arukh*, based on a ruling in the *Tosefta*, reads:

> All persons may be included in the number of *aliyot* [the seven honors at the sabbath Torah reading], but the Sages declared, "A woman should not read [i.e., receive an *aliyah*] because of the honor of the congregation [since it would suggest that the males are unlearned]."[5]

At this point, Rabbi Moses Isserles adds the crucial supplement: "What is meant is that women and minors may be added to other honorees at the Torah reading, but that not all the honors should be given to women or minors."[6] Clearly, this sixteenth-century ruling permits women to be called to the Torah, but it remained a dead letter until the middle of the twentieth century.

Obviously, every legal system must have a mechanism for deciding controversial issues, and the Halakhah is no exception. Interpreting the last three words of Exodus 23:2, *ʿaḥarei rabbim lehattot*, to mean "one must follow after the many," the Rabbis established the principle that the majority view should prevail (B. *Hullin* 11a), though there were many exceptions—because of the eminence of a particular scholar or for some other special reason. An ancient Mishnah then asks the pertinent question, Why record the views of scholars that are not adopted? The answer is highly significant: future authorities might discover grounds for finding the minority view more appropriate (M. *Eduyot* 1:4–6), thus laying the groundwork for a possible revision and even a reversal of the law under changed circumstances.

This open-mindedness toward nonauthoritative views derived not only from the pragmatic considerations already indicated, but from a profound theological conviction that all the views expressed in the Halakhah are "the words of the living God."

The fourth-century Palestinian scholar Ulla declared:

> When the Sages in Palestine adopted a restrictive enactment, they would not reveal the reason for twelve months, lest there be someone who would find the reasoning unconvincing and would therefore disregard the prohibition [B. *Abodah Zarah* 35a].

A well-known modern historian of the Halakhah finds a progressive principle in this apparently conservative procedure:

> But why did they announce the reason for their enactment after a year? So that coming generations, if they found that the reason was no longer operative, would be able to set aside the enactment.[7]

The Decline of the Creative Impulse

As the Middle Ages progressed, a tragic anomaly revealed itself—later generations proved less creative and courageous than their predecessors. The so-called Dark Ages—the earlier part of the medieval period, until the eleventh century—were by and large marked by favorable conditions for Jewish life. Jews enjoyed friendly relations with their Christian neighbors and were relatively free from persecution. On the other hand, the later Middle Ages, which saw expanding horizons for Christian Europe as a result of the Crusades, the Renaissance, the Reformation, and the voyages of discovery of the New World, was a period of constantly worsening conditions for Jews. The massacres of Jewish communities perpetrated by the Crusaders; the establishment of the ghetto as a universal phenomenon; the Black Death; the successive expulsions of the Jews from England, France, Spain, and Portugal; the ravages wrought by the Thirty Years War in Germany; the Chmielnicki massacres in Poland; and the tragic debacle of the false Messiah, Shabbetai Zevi, represented body blows to the vitality of Judaism and its creative élan. As cultural horizons were narrowed and fears for the future were intensified, the urge to hold fast to the old with ever-increasing fervor became the dominant mood in Jewish traditional life. During the previous three centuries, both the taste and the capacity for creative activity had been drastically reduced, precisely at a time when the need for creativity was greatest.

Biblical law, the foundations of which were laid in the periods of seminomadism and early rural and urban cultures, was successfully applied to the more-advanced agricultural and commercial conditions of the Greco-Roman era through the creative activity of the Rabbis. This corpus of the Halakhah was then put into operation during the feudal system, the age of the Industrial Revolution, and the various stages of capitalism. It continues to function in the world-girding conflict between democracy and communism in our day.

But in the last two hundred years traditional Judaism has faced massive and traumatic challenges, far greater than any of the past, perhaps less violent, but far more perilous. Only the Holocaust stands as a horrible "exception" that all but succeeded in destroying both Jews and Judaism. The political and civic Emancipation of the Jews, launched by the French Revolution, granted Jews as individuals political citizenship, economic opportunity, cultural equality, and a substantial measure of social integration. In return, the Emancipation in western and central Europe swept away the age-old structure of the Jewish community, with its power to tax and thus to govern its members. The parallel process of the Enlightenment, with its cargo of new philosophic and scientific ideas, undermined the authority of Jewish tradition and the validity of the Halakhah. In the last 150 years, the Emancipation and the Enlightenment moved inexorably from western and central Europe to the great mass settlements of East European Jewry. In the United States, Canada, and Latin America, no political emancipation was necessary, since Jews had never had a special status of inferiority. But neither was there a deeply entrenched tradition to withstand the onslaught of modernism. As wholesale defection from tradition became the rule, many observers were convinced that both Judaism and the Jewish people were in grave jeopardy in the modern age.

The natural reaction of the traditional rabbinate was to hold on to the old and reject the new. They intensified the demand for total adherence to the hallowed traditions and practices of the past, major or minor, appropriate or not, and gave no quarter to modern life and thought. The famous Hungarian rabbinic authority, the Hatam Sofer, borrowed a Talmudic dictum and coined a slogan designed to erect a dike against the floodwaters of the new age: *ḥadash ʾasur min hatorah*, "Anything new is forbidden by the Torah." That this pronouncement has proved counterproductive is clear from the wholesale defection of the vast majority of modern Jews from the Halakhah.

Suspicion of the contemporary world became the hallmark of Orthodoxy, and this suspicion turned to bitter hostility and scorn for modern ideas and ideals. This attitude, compounded of meticulous observance of all Halakhic minutiae and total rejection of the gentile world, is all too comprehensible. It produced the phenomenon of the *baʿalei teshuvah*, "penitents" or "returnees," who react violently to all manifestations of modern life and culture except for its economic opportunities. However understandable their position may be, it will prove less and less viable with the passing days. Its weakness lies in trying to turn the clock back to the sixteenth and seventeenth centuries. It is naive to imagine that a Western megalopolis can be transformed into an East European *shtetl*, which they regard as the only true model for the Jewish community.

As a minority within a minority in Western society, they cannot force the Jewish or the general majority to conform to their pattern. In increasing measure, therefore, they create their own enclaves in the larger cities or in independent suburban communities of their own. Their total self-assurance and fervent piety give more moderate elements in contemporary Orthodoxy a deep sense of inferiority and drive them inexorably to the right. Thus we have the paradox that the revival of Orthodoxy is an effective brake on Halakhic progress precisely when it is most needed.

Though creative Halakhic activity has been reduced, it never ceased completely because the pressures and demands of contemporary life cannot be ignored. Particularly in the state of Israel, where the Halakhah was declared operative in the areas of marriage, divorce, and personal status, new issues demanded solution. In all wings of modern Judaism scholars and thinkers are wrestling with the problems and working to restore the vital functioning of Jewish law in an age of rapid and dizzying change.

The long and fruitful history of Jewish law did not take place in isolation. Contrary to widespread impressions in some quarters today, the medieval ghetto and the modern *shtetl*, both of which were largely insulated from the world about them, represent only part of the varied Jewish experience through history. The ghetto and the *shtetl* possessed many positive qualities, but neither is a universal pattern or an ideal setting for a flourishing and creative Judaism. Nor do they offer a paradigm for a Jewish community in a free society. By and large, Jewish law, like all phases of Jewish culture, grew and developed most significantly in communities that existed in open societies and thus were able to respond without constraint to events in the world at large.

The process of reinterpretation and adjustment is only partially mirrored in the traditional Halakhic literature of the past two centuries. Much of the change in Jewish religious practice has taken place outside the limits set by the letter of the law. The formal content of the Halakhah has been the subject of passionate, indeed bitter, controversy; and the process of growth and adjustment has been neither easy nor systematic. Nevertheless, Jewish law has survived in the Diaspora in a variety of formulations. In the state of Israel, primarily for practical reasons, Jewish law has begun to undergo a renaissance, handicapped, to be sure, by the intellectual and ethical limitations of its official guardians in the present religious establishment.

Undoubtedly, the unyielding adherence to the letter of the law by its conservative partisans has played an important role in its preservation; but its vitality and its relevance to new conditions and problems are due to its protean capacity for adjustment upheld by its more-liberal expounders.

The Dynamics of the Halakhah

Jewish tradition is best compared to a flowing river that possesses a mainstream, but also side currents and even crosscurrents that affect its flow significantly. To be sure, it is not always easy to determine at any given point which is the dominant and which is the secondary stream. At the time that the issues were being debated, the rabbinic Sages were sure that the Sadducees were not in the mainstream of the tradition. But they had no such certainty at the time with regard to the controversies of Hillel and Shammai, Rabbi Akiba and Rabbi Ishmael, Rab and Samuel, Raba and Abaye. Even with the benefit of hindsight, we require considerable knowledge, insight, and intellectual integrity to recognize the difference between the normative tradition and aberrant groups in Judaism and to do justice to the contributions of both.

When the tradition is alive and well, there is a complex process of interaction between the past and the present. Each age receives a body of doctrine and law from the preceding period. As it comes into contact with contemporary conditions, problems, and insights, the spiritual and intellectual leadership in Judaism is called upon to evaluate these new elements, which are struggling to be admitted into the sanctuary of the tradition. The leadership will recognize some aspects as dangerous and ill-advised and will reject them *in toto*. Others it will deem ethically sound, religiously true, and pragmatically valuable, and these will be incorporated. Many, if not most, new phenomena will be judged to contain both positive and negative elements. The former will be accepted in greater or lesser degree, often after being modified so as to bring them into greater conformity with the spirit and form of the tradition. To utilize the familiar but useful terminology of Hegel, past tradition constitutes the thesis, contemporary life is the antithesis, and the resultant of these two factors becomes the new synthesis. The synthesis of one age then becomes the thesis of the next; the newly formulated content of tradition becomes the point of departure for the next stage.

This is not to suggest even remotely that tradition is bound to surrender to "the spirit of the age." It is always free, indeed commanded, to examine the demands and insights of each generation and to accept, modify, or reject them as it sees fit. But when the tradition is healthy or, more concretely, when its exemplars are true to their function, they will be sensitive to the age and respond to it. Often there will be sharp divergences of view as to the validity of these new factors and how the tradition should respond to them. Indeed, the issue may remain *in suspenso* for some time. Ultimately, however, life is the determining factor, and from its decision there is no appeal.

This dialectic process, which has operated throughout the history of Judaism and is the secret of its capacity to survive, can be documented in all areas—ritual, civil and criminal law, marriage, and divorce. It is most evident in the great creative eras of rabbinic Judaism—the Tannaitic and the Amoraic periods, which saw the creation of the Mishnah and the Talmud. This capacity never ceased, but it was weakened in the Middle Ages. The rabbinic leadership now brought about an ever-increasing ghettoization of the spirit and made Jewish group survival, rather than the needs, interest, and desires of the individual, their basic concern. The strength of their influence on the present state of the Halakhah can scarcely be exaggerated, since, for the bulk of East European Jewry, the Middle Ages continued until the twentieth century.

From this paradigm of the dynamic of the Halakhah, an important theoretical and pragmatic conclusion emerges: The Halakhah is not to be seen locked in mortal combat with the contemporary age, the demands of which are, therefore, to be resisted with every means at its disposal. The Halakhah itself comprises both elements in the dialectic; continuity with the past and growth induced by the present. History is neither inimical nor irrelevant to the Halakhah. It is the soil from which the Halakhah springs. Cut off from history, the arena in which men and women live and struggle, the Halakhah is doomed to sterility and death. Nor are the Halakhah and sociology mortal foes. Sociology supplies the data that the Halakhah must examine in order to determine how to deal with a new situation.

A statement about the United States Constitution by Chief Justice John Marshall in 1819 applies equally to the divine constitution of the Jewish people, which is the Torah and its embodiment in Jewish law: "The constitution is intended to endure for ages to come, and consequently, to be adapted to the various crises of human affairs." Described in these impersonal terms, the Halakhic process would seem to be a smooth, peaceful movement from one stage to another, but this is far from the truth. The agents of the process are human beings, with their individual attitudes, passions, prejudices, and interests, all of which come into play in evaluating contemporary conditions and the need to deal with them. The 3,000 pages of the Talmud are a monument to controversy, recording the debates by hundreds of rabbis, their arguments testifying to the vitality and creativity of the tradition.

A few instances of the struggles involved in reaching decisions will make the Halakhic process come alive. Parenthetically, these may help to reconcile the reader to some of the less-attractive features of current conflicts in rabbinic circles.

The Talmud reports that the school of Hillel and the school of Shammai were engaged in bitter controversy for many years. According to one report, physical violence broke out between them. Finally a heavenly voice proclaimed, "Both these and the others are the words of the Living God" (B. *Erubin* 13b), and the members of the two schools continued to intermarry, their differences notwithstanding (M. *Eduyot* 4:8).

Another far-reaching instance of the Halakhic struggle occurred in the year 70 c.e., when Jerusalem was being besieged by the Romans. Rabban Johanan ben Zakkai[8] saw that the imminent destruction of the Temple and the liquidation of the Sanhedrin, the supreme Jewish religious authority, would threaten the decimated and dispirited survivors with fragmentation, lack of leadership, and ultimate annihilation. He decided to transfer many of the functions of the Holy City of Jerusalem to the village of Jabneh. He set up his colleagues in his academy as a substitute Sanhedrin, with authority for the whole range of religious law, including civil and criminal jurisprudence. He also ordained younger scholars to serve as judges in the courts. Since the unity of the scattered Jewish people depended on their observing festivals on the same days, he arranged for the witnesses of the new moon to bring their testimony to Jabneh, as they had previously done with the High Court in Jerusalem. To build morale among the people, Rabban Johanan taught that even the destruction of the sacrificial system in the Temple, which had been the centerpiece of the Jewish religion, was not fatal to Judaism, because prayer and deeds of loving kindness were equally acceptable to God.

Most dramatic of all was the procedure he established with regard to the blowing of the shofar on the sabbath. Before the destruction of the Temple, when Rosh Hashanah fell on the sabbath the shofar was blown only in the Temple and in the Holy City. After the destruction of the Temple, Rabban Johanan boldly transferred this special prerogative of the Temple to the academy of Jabneh as part of his unremitting effort to endow it with central authority. When he proposed this radical break with tradition, conservative members of his court, the Bnei Bathyra, said, "Let us discuss the question." Johanan replied: "Let us blow the shofar and then we'll discuss the question." After the shofar was blown, they said to him: "Now let us discuss it." He responded, "We already have heard the shofar in Jabneh and the act cannot be withdrawn" (B. *Rosh Hashanah* 29b).

Undoubtedly, the heroic mass suicide of Jewish warriors and their families at Masada was more dramatic than the slow, patient labors of Johanan ben Zakkai at Jabneh. But it was Jabneh not Masada that preserved both Judaism and the Jewish people.

For many centuries, including our own, Judaism has been calumniated as primitive and cruel because of the famous passage in Exodus "An eye for an eye, a tooth for a tooth" (21:24). The history of ancient society demonstrates that *lex talionis*, the law of retaliation, is itself an ethical advance over the more-primitive doctrine that permitted any injury to be avenged without limit. Ancient societies regarded it as legitimate, indeed praiseworthy and heroic, to take a life for an injury. The biblical law restricts the punishment to the dimensions of the offense. The Talmud clearly recognized this in its comment "An eye for an eye," not "a life and an eye for an eye" (B. *Ketubbot* 38a).

Nevertheless, even this limitation came to be regarded as morally indefensible in the Mishnaic period, if not earlier. No scholar was more honored for his piety and learning than Rabbi Eliezer ben Hyrcanus,

the archconservative of his time, who was committed to the strict con-
struction of the text. Accordingly, he maintained that "an eye for an eye"
was to be taken literally (B. *Baba Kamma* 84a). Rabbi Eliezer's view was
duly recorded, but it was his opponents, who held that the verse meant
"monetary compensation," who prevailed. Their views proved both normative and decisive for the spirit of Jewish law.

Legal philosophers have long known that discovering the law is often
indistinguishable from creating the law. As Morris Raphael Cohen
pointed out, "The process of law-making is called finding the law." He
argues forcefully against regarding the process as "spurious interpretation," while noting that "it would be absurd to maintain that [legisla-
tors] are in no wise bound, and can make any law they please."

The United States Constitution possesses a quasi-sacred character in
the American ethos; thus an analogy between the American and the
Jewish systems of law may be fairly drawn. A proposal to establish a
monarchy in the United States would contradict the "clear intent" of
the fathers of the Constitution and would be unacceptable. On the other
hand, the call sounded in some circles today for returning to "the original intent" of the Constitution is often disingenuous, usually unattaina-
ble, and generally counterproductive. First of all, we lack access to the
mental processes of the original writers of the document. Second, various divergent views were reconciled in compromises and are reflected
in the final text adopted. Third, the American people is not governed
solely by the Constitution. In the past 200 years thousands of laws and
regulations adopted by local, state, and federal legislative bodies and
administrative agencies have defined the contours of American life. In
the process they have modified and reinterpreted the Constitution.
They have made it possible for a document created in a largely rural
society in the early stages of industrialization to serve as the basic law
of a technically advanced civilization.

The entire economic life of the nation would come to a virtual halt
if the "original intent" of the Fourteenth Amendment were taken to be
normative. When the statement "Nor shall any state deprive any person
of life, liberty and property without due process of law" was ratified in
1868 its purpose was to safeguard the rights of the newly enfranchised
slaves. Subsequently the word "person" was applied to the business cor-
poration, which was defined as a "legal person," and our entire economic structure now relies upon this concept. There is no word in the
Constitution about a presidential cabinet or political parties or judicial
review; yet without them the governmental structure would crumble.
The secret lies in finding the path between literalism and lawlessness.

A recent study of the late Chief Justice Earl Warren points out that
he was in fact an ethicist who saw his craft as "discovering ethical imperatives in a maze of confusion." According to his biographer, Warren

believed that "the rightness of results" was more important than "the doctrinal integrity of reasoning," but that "his results were not arbitrary." He believed that the Constitution of the United States embodied an ethical structure, and his job was to apply those standards. *Mutandis mutatis*, this was the role adopted by the Rabbis.

The function of the Rabbis in determining the growth of the Halakhah was clearly visible in every period. There was, however, another agent at work, unofficial and unacknowledged, which played a significant role in the development of Jewish tradition. In Judaism, the voice of the people is not the voice of God, but neither is it without influence.

VI

THE HALAKHIC PROCESS
RESPONSIVENESS TO
THE POPULAR WILL

In an age that loudly proclaims its allegiance to democracy, be it the substance or the shadow, insistent voices remind us that "Judaism is not a 'democratic' religion." The claim is formally true, but only formally—God commands, man is commanded.

Since its inception, Judaism has regarded the Torah, revealed by God to Moses on Sinai, as the highest and ultimate authority, but this revelation at Sinai did not take place in a vacuum; it was addressed to a people. It depended as much on acceptance by the hearers as the utterance of the speaker. The words of the Decalogue would have reverberated and been lost in outer space had there not been a response by the people, "Whatever the Lord has spoken, we shall do" (Exod. 19:8; 24:3,7). God's revelation of the Torah was an incomprehensible event that might be and was interpreted literally, philosophically, or mystically; but henceforth its growth and development were entrusted to human beings, for "the Torah was not given to angels" (B. *Yoma* 30a; B. *Kiddushin* 54a). In fact, it might take on forms that even Moses would not have understood (B. *Menahot* 29b). Later generations were guided by the rule of the majority; in support of this principle, the Rabbis cited the closing clause of Exodus 23:2, which they rendered "One must decide after the many." Thus there were limits to the power of the people to determine the direction and content of Jewish tradition, but they stemmed less from theological assumptions, which were always subject to interpretation, than from ethical, socioeconomic, and political factors.

After Moses, the divine will was not communicated to human beings directly, the only exception being the Prophets during the First Temple period. According to tradition, they numbered 50 men and women over a period of 500 years. This unpredictable and irregular mode of communication obviously could not suffice for a perdurable society; a steady and permanent source of guidance was required that would interpret the tradition and apply it to all aspects of life, both individual and collective, and would embrace belief, ethics, practice, ritual, and civil and criminal law.

The custodians of the Torah were the *kohanim*, a hereditary priesthood that traced its descent back to Aaron, the brother of Moses. They preserved the sacred texts, interpreted their meaning, and applied them to all situations in the life of the individual and the nation. These priests were the recognized and official religious authorities in ancient Israel. Their seat was the Temple in Jerusalem and the smaller, generally older, sanctuaries throughout the country. Their primary function was to officiate at the sacrifices, the basic form of religious observance. In return they received substantial dues and gifts in the form of agricultural products and animal offerings.

As was the case everywhere in the ancient world, the priests were the guardians of culture. The *kohanim* preserved the ancient traditions regarding the creation of the world, the Garden of Eden, Noah and the Flood, the Patriarchs—all serving as the prelude to the bondage in Egypt, the Exodus, the wandering in the wilderness, and the revelation at Sinai. Later historical accounts, such as the conquest of the Promised Land under Joshua, the exploits of the Judges, and the annals of the monarchy, probably fell within the purview of the priests as well. The preservation of these traditions did not arise from purely cultural concerns; it served to legitimize the priests' authority and validate the holiness of their particular sanctuaries.

The priests also performed other functions. They were the medical officers when contagious disease or ritual uncleanness were present. With the growth of royal power, secular judges were appointed, but the priests continued to adjudicate cases in civil and criminal law (Deut. 17:8–12), though the precise nature of the relationship of the two groups is not clear.

The post-exilic prophet Malachi, upbraiding the priests of his generation for their religious laxity and indifference, describes the ideal traditional role of the priest:

> The law of truth was in his mouth
> And unrighteousness was not found on his lips;
> He walked with Me in peace and uprightness,
> And turned many away from iniquity.
> For the priest's lips should keep knowledge,
> Men should seek the law from his mouth;
> For he is the messenger of the Lord of hosts.
>
> [Mal. 2:6–7]

After the return from the Babylonian Exile, an attempt was made to reestablish the *status quo ante* and restore priestly authority, but that proved impossible. While the sacerdotal functions of the priests in the sacrifices and at other rituals—and the emoluments—were safeguarded by the text of scripture, their role as religious authorities was effectively curtailed.

This process may have been begun by Ezra, who was both a priest by descent and a *sopher*, "a writer of the Book," in the Law of Moses, a term better rendered "Master of the Book." Standing at a turning point in history, Ezra chose to throw the weight of his influence behind his scholarly competence rather than his priestly descent. By this act, he placed a democratic stamp on the character of Judaism for all its subsequent history, in which the scholar and not the priest was the supreme authority.

While the Temple sacrifices and other rituals continued to be conducted by the priests as long as the sanctuary stood, the people—aside from some inevitable groups of dissidents—found their religious authority in the scholars, who interpreted the Torah and applied it to the problems of daily life.

The Synagogue

At some time during this period, the synagogue as an institution makes its appearance.[1] Since its origins are shrouded in obscurity, various theories have been proposed. The suggested dates range from the late biblical era (eighth to seventh century B.C.E.) through the period of the Babylonian Exile (sixth century B.C.E.) to the early Second Commonwealth period (fifth to third century B.C.E.).

By the time of the Greco-Roman era in Palestine, the synagogue was already a recognizable entity, with three names testifying to as many functions. The oldest term, *bet midrash*, "house of study," literally, "the house for searching out the meaning of scripture," occurs in the *Wisdom of Ben Sira*, written about 190 B.C.E. The second, *bet tefillah*, "house of prayer," occurs as a nontechnical term in Deutero-Isaiah (56:7); this use points to the rise of public prayer and the growth of a fixed liturgy, an ongoing activity to the present. The third name, which became dominant, *bet keneset*, "house of assembly," highlights its use as a community meeting-place for the discussion of issues of public concern. In addition, the synagogue served as the locale for several ancillary, relatively secular, activities: as a court; as a lodging for indigent wanderers, a hostel for traveling merchants, and, in the case of Jerusalem, a shelter for pilgrims coming to the Holy City; as a storehouse for communal funds; and at times as the residence for community officials. Intermittently, it served as the scene for sacred meals associated with Torah study and religious celebrations.

Unlike the Temple in Jerusalem, the synagogue was free of priestly control and unhampered by ritual restrictions. While there was only one Temple, the sanctuary in Jerusalem, there was no limit on the number of synagogues that could be created. The synagogue was seen as the literal fulfilment of the promise in scripture, "In every place where I cause my name to be remembered, I will come to you and bless you" (Exod. 20:24). The synagogue was not an edifice; it was the people's institution.

As the result of this democratic revolution, authority in the exposition of the Torah text and its embodiment in Jewish law, as well as its application to the settlement of disputes, was determined not by priestly lineage but by learning and character, qualities that could be found on every level of society. Indeed, long before the Freudian concept of sublimation, the Sages believed that scholarship was more likely to be found among children of the poor (B. *Nedarim* 81a), even among the offspring of the ignorant tillers of the soil (B. *Sanhedrin* 96b).

The growing body of law and lore in the "houses of study" required the stamp of legitimacy, no less than did the Torah of Moses. Hence the doctrine arose that the Oral Law, like the written law, was given on Sinai (*M. Abot* 1:1). It was imperative to buttress the authority of the Sages, particularly in the face of dissident sects, who accepted only the written law and developed their own oral tradition. Hence, the rabbis gave special emphasis and protection (*ḥizzuk*) to their own enactments, beyond the biblical laws (B. *Ketubbot* 82b and elsewhere).

The Pharisees and Their Opponents

In the decades before the destruction of the Temple (in 70 c.e.), the social and economic stratification of the people created two major parties: the upper classes, who generally became Sadducees; and the lower and middle classes and the poor, who gravitated to the Pharisees.[2] In addition, there were dissident sects that opposed the authority of both. Some, like the various groups of Essenes, which included the Dead Sea Sectarians, were apocalyptics who withdrew from the temptations of the world into communal settlements. They engaged in pious exercises, their goal being to hasten God's intervention into the world, destroy the evil power of Rome, and usher in the establishment of His kingdom. Others, like the Zealots, sought to rebel against Rome and throw off the yoke of the oppressor by military force. All these sects, which originally included the Judeo-Christians as well, were spiritually offshoots of the Pharisees, who carried various aspects of Pharisaism to extremes—or as they would insist, to their logical conclusion. As the history of sectarianism everywhere demonstrates, this basic similarity in outlook did not diminish the hostility that prevailed among the parties.[3]

The various sects received adherents from every social and economic stratum. However, the Pharisees and the Rabbis of the Mishnah were drawn principally but not exclusively from the lower and middle classes. Modern scholarship has documented the influence of these sectors on the Halakhah of the Rabbis, particularly on Hillel and his school, as against the more upper-class outlook of the School of Shammai.

In sum, during the creative period of rabbinic Judaism, which produced the Mishnah and other works, there was no sharp demarcation between the leadership and the masses, from whom many of the Sages were recruited. The Talmud reports that when pro-Sadducean rulers attempted to introduce their practices in the observance of *Succot* in the Temple, the common people compelled them to adhere to the Pharisaic ritual. The loyalty of the masses of the people to Pharisaic and rabbinic teaching remained firm and unbroken.

After the destruction of the Temple and the loss of Jewish independence, whatever distinctions had existed between the royal house and the nobility, on the one hand, and the commoners, on the other, disappeared in the common calamity. There remained, however, a measure of biological stratification on the basis of genealogy. The tradition speaks of ten categories of traced descent among the Jews returning from the Babylonian Exile; from the *kohanim* on the highest rung to the *ɔasufei*, the foundlings of unknown ancestry, on the lowest (M. *Kiddushin* 4:1). Eventually, some degree of social stratification set in, separating the *ḥaberim*, "colleagues," from the *ɔam haɔarez*, literally, "the people of the land," basically the farmers, who were regarded as ignorant and as lax in paying the priestly and levitical dues from their fruits and crops.

In later periods, the scholars constituted a specially favored class in society, enjoying some perquisites denied to others. Unofficial, but no less effective, on that account, was the opportunity for the scholars to marry into the more-affluent strata of society. These privileges, largely minor in character, apparently aroused little opposition, because of the universal honor in which the Torah was held and because the community felt a need for guidance by its scholars. By and large, the rabbinic leadership reflected the various social classes in society.

The major restriction on democracy in all periods of Jewish history, as in all other societies, derived from the divisions between the rich and the poor, and the greater power and influence enjoyed by the affluent. All these differences, however, should properly be viewed as limitations rather than as negations of the basic democratic impulse in Judaism, which was often submerged but was never destroyed.

The Rise and Growth of Custom

The power of the popular will, as distinct from the official Halakhah, is exemplified in the famous dictum "Custom sets the law aside" (P. *Yebamot* 12:1; B. *Baba Mezia* 7,1; B. *Sopherim*, 14).[4] Actually, as Alexander Guttmann has pointed out, the principle was not as far-reaching as it would appear to be on the surface.[5] It is cited only twice in the Palestinian Talmud and never in the Babylonian, though it was undoubtedly operative in both countries. In the Talmudic period, the doctrine was invoked when there was a difference of opinion among scholars regarding a law or when a set of exceptional circumstances prevailed.

Thus in connection with a borderline case of sabbath observance, the Talmud declares, "Let Israel alone [i.e., let them do as they please], for if they are not Prophets, they are the descendants of Prophets" (B. *Pesahim* 66b). Even more frequently, the Babylonian and the Palestinian Talmud invoked the principle "Go out and see how the people are acting" in order to determine the law (B. *Berakhot* 45a; B. *Erubin* 14b; B. *Pesahim* 24a; B. *Menahot* 38b; P. *Peˀah* 7:5; B. *Yebamot* 7:2).

When the scholars contemplated adding a new prohibition, a limited veto was accorded the people by the established rule "No prohibition is to be adopted if the majority of the community [*robh zibbur*] are unable to observe it."[6] Clearly, the Sages of the Talmud were very sensitive to the needs, the desires, and the capacities of the people they were called upon to lead.

Only at widely separated points in history were there instances of overt rebellion against rabbinical authority that took on the dimensions of a movement. The first took place in the eighth century, in Babylonia, where there arose a varied group of opponents of the Talmud called Karaites, "devotees of the scripture," who called for a return to scripture as the sole authority in Judaism. For several centuries Karaism was both a fructifying influence and a significant threat to rabbinism in Egypt, Palestine, and Babylonia. Ultimately Karaism lost its power; it has remained a tiny sect within the Jewish people.[7]

After the final redaction of the Babylonian and the Palestinian Talmuds, which was a consequence of the decline of the Babylonian and Palestinian centers, new Jewish settlements developed along the coast of North Africa and throughout southern Europe. Living under Christian and Muslim rule, these communities were exposed to varying cultural, economic, and political conditions. This far-flung and varied Diaspora accepted the authority of Talmudic law, which served as the bond of unity among them.

At the same time there grew up a substantial amount of variation in liturgy and ritual observance. Often the variation in custom extended to an entire culture sphere or country. The traditional prayer book, the basic form of which had been established in the period of the Mishnah, now underwent an elaborate development. Different *nusha>ot*, or prayer rites, came into being, the Sephardic (or Spanish-Portuguese) and the Ashkenazic (or German-Polish), as well as lesser variants like the Italian and the Provençal. Local holidays or fast days were observed to mark crises successfully surmounted or disasters averted.

In the Middle Ages, hundreds of new poems were added to the traditional liturgy, particularly for the High Holy days and the three Pilgrimage festivals. These additions to the body of accepted prayers were made without disturbing what was hallowed from the past, and thus they aroused relatively little opposition. Nonetheless, these *piyyutim*, "liturgical poems," were frequently complicated, obscure, and even ungrammatical. They evoked the objections of such radically different figures as the medieval grammarian and commentator Rabbi Abraham Ibn Ezra (1092–1167) and the Halakhic authority Rabbi Elijah, the Gaon of Vilna (1720–97).

The scholars often quoted chapter and verse against some innovations, but the popular will frequently overrode their objections, and official leaders proved powerless to prevent adoption of certain practices.

The many differences in local background and experience, coupled with the beliefs and desires of the common people, produced the phenomenon of *minhag*, "custom," as distinct from *din*, "law." These *minhagim* reflected every conceivable level of content and outlook and were marked by considerable power and persistence.

While most of the customs dealt with ritual practices, some manifested a fine ethical sensitivity. Many of them were expressions of folk belief, at times influenced by those of non-Jewish neighbors. Many *minhagim* had a brief life span, others lasted for centuries, and some became permanent elements in Judaism.

In general, *minhag* evoked radically different reactions from the rabbinate. On the one hand, it was maintained that *minhag mebhattel halakhah*, "custom sets the law aside" (P. *Yebamot* 12:1; B. *Baba Mezia* 7,1; B. *Sopherim* 14), a principle that frequently prevailed in practice. On the other hand, it was noted that a transposition of the consonants of *minhag* produces the vocable *gehinnom*, "Hell."[8]

Each custom might be praised or condemned, depending on its nature and on the personality and outlook of a particular rabbi. The ubiquity and the persistence of *minhag* testify to the power of the popular will in determining many elements in the practice and theory of the Halakhah. The impact of local *minhag* is far from spent, even in America today, as will be demonstrated below.

To appreciate the full significance of custom, two widespread misconceptions regarding medieval Jewry must be laid to rest. First, though the tempo of development in Jewish law was reduced after the periods of the Mishnah and the Talmud, medieval Judaism was by no means bereft of creativity and innovative vigor, as the activity of Rabbi Gershom of Mainz, "the Light of the Exile," and later scholars abundantly attest. But the achievements of the elitist leadership were far exceeded by the proliferation of *minhag* in all areas of life, largely as the expression of the people.

Second, the segregation of Jews and Christians in the Middle Ages was much less complete than is commonly believed, and personal contacts were not infrequent. Influences, spiritual and intellectual, percolated from one community to the other. It is hardly an accident that early German pietism was contemporaneous with Rabbi Judah the Saint of Regensburg, the author of the *Sefer Hasidim*, and his circle; or that the upheaval in seventeenth-century world Jewry caused by the pseudo-Messiah, Shabbetai Zevi, was contemporaneous with millenarian movements in seventeenth-century Christian Europe. Other examples might also be cited. Though the precise channels of transmission may elude us, it seems clear that some Christian beliefs and practices penetrated the Jewish community, though they were thoroughly Judaized in the process.

Generally, the popular will had a democratic thrust. It expressed itself in a pressure for greater participation in religious life by all the elements in the Jewish people, not merely its upper echelons. Since custom was often an expression of the religiosity of the masses, it did not always reflect the highest intellectual level. But because it rose from the depths of the human soul, it survived.

Mourning Practices

From German pietistic circles, in the early Middle Ages, Jews adopted the practice of the *Yizkor*, a memorial service during the festivals. The *Kaddish*, an ancient Aramaic prayer glorifying God's power, was recited by mourners during the first year following a death in the family. Thereafter, the anniversary was observed annually; its German name, *Yahrzeit*, testifies to its origins. These practices are still widely observed.

Rites of Atonement

Death and confession are perennial motifs of the religious consciousness. There is a hunger in the human spirit for divine forgiveness. This yearning to wipe the slate clean became particularly pronounced at *Rosh Hashanah*, the New Year, and at *Yom Kippur*, the Day of

Atonement. This impulse, clearly manifest in the Bible, produced a variety of practices that have maintained their hold to the present day. On the eve of *Yom Kippur*, the Jew is particularly conscious of the burden of sins accumulated during the previous year and feels a deep need to approach the throne of the heavenly judge in a state of purity.

The Scapegoat

The oldest example of this powerful desire lies behind the law of the "scapegoat," the central rite of the biblical observance of *Yom Kippur*. As ordained in Leviticus 16, two goats were chosen before this day. One was sacrificed on the temple altar as a sin offering. The other, bearing all the sins of the people, was marked "Azazel" and was sent out into the wilderness, where it was hurled to its death, thus freeing the people from the burden of its sins.

Kapparot

An analogous custom came into existence in medieval times. On the afternoon before *Yom Kippur*, one would wave a chicken over one's head seven times and recite the formula: "This be my atonement, this be my substitution." This practice of *kapparot* was opposed by authorities as eminent as Rabbi Solomon ibn Adret and Nahmanides.[9] Rabbi Joseph Karo, the author of the *Shulḥan Arukh*, called it *minhag shetut*, "a foolish, stupid custom."[10] Yet the practice persisted, and later editions of the *Shulḥan Arukh* deleted the passage. Today it is still observed by Hasidim and other right-wing groups. In many instances, the actual ritual is dispensed with and charity is given as a *kapparah*, "atonement." The ethical emphasis expressed in the tradition is the custom of asking one's family, friends, and acquaintances for forgiveness for any wrong committed against them during the past year.

Tashlikh

Another propitiatory rite designed to effect separation from sin may be documented from the fourteenth century onwards. On the afternoon of the first day of *Rosh Hashanah* people assemble at a body of running water and recite prayers based on a passage in Micah, "May you cast [*tashlikh*] into the depths of the sea all their sins" (7:19). Though the practices associated with *tashlikh* were questioned by some rabbinic authorities, it was endowed with special significance by the kabbalists and has retained its hold in modern Orthodoxy.[11]

Kol Nidre

Kol Nidre, perhaps the most solemn prayer in Jewish liturgy, which is recited on the eve of the Day of Atonement, derives from the same source. Standing before his maker on the holiest day of the year, the Jew was conscious of promises and vows he had made but not fulfilled. In the *Kol Nidre* formula, therefore, he prays that all such obligations made during the past or the coming year, or both, be null and void. It was not intended to invalidate undertakings and contracts entered into with one's fellow men but was designed to affect only promises made vis-à-vis God.

Nonetheless, the intent of the prayer was disregarded by anti-Jewish propagandists from the Middle Ages onward. In addition, from the standpoint of the Halakhah, there were legal difficulties with this blanket annulment, particularly with vows undertaken in the past year. Many distinguished authorities opposed the *Kol Nidre* and urged its elimination, but the prayer survived its detractors from within and its enemies from without, no doubt in large measure because of its deeply moving melody.

Simhat Torah, the People's Holiday

The popular will led to the creation of a major Jewish festival, unknown in the Bible or the Talmud—*Simhat Torah*, "Rejoicing in the Torah." Actually many elements of its observance contravened the accepted Halakhah and were originally opposed by the recognized rabbinic authorities.

In the land of Israel, the *Succot* festival concludes on the eighth day with a "holy convocation" called *Shemini Azeret*. Because of original uncertainties surrounding the calendar, Diaspora Jewry added an additional day to each of the Pilgrimage festivals, calling it "the Second Holiday of the Exile." Thus there emerged a couplet of *Shemini Azeret* that still bears this name in the prayer book. At the outset this additional day possessed little intrinsic meaning, and the Rabbis were compelled to create some touching parables to explain its existence.

The seed of the future development of *Simhat Torah* lay in the minor fact that, according to the Talmud (B. *Megillah* 31a), the Torah reading for the day was *Zot Haberakhah*, the closing section of the Torah (Deut. 33 and 34), which contains Moses' final blessing of the Israelites and the narrative of his death. In the fourteenth century the opening section of the Torah, describing Creation (Gen. 1:1–2:3), was added to the reading. The psychological motivation for this custom is expressed in characteristic medieval terms: "So that Satan might have no basis for accusing Israel by saying, 'They have finished the Torah and do not wish to read it any more.'"[12] Thus the fundamental character of the holiday as a festival of the Torah emerged, marking both the end and the beginning of the cycle and testifying to the indissoluble bond between Israel and its heritage.

So powerful was the hold of *Simhat Torah* on the people that the *Haftarah* ordained by the Talmud (B. *Megillah* 31a) for the day (I Kings 8:22ff.) was set aside and replaced by the opening chapter of Joshua, the logical continuation of Deuteronomy. Authorities like the Tosafists and Rabbi Isaac ben Moses of Vienna (thirteenth century) were at a loss to find a legal basis for the change,[13] but the new character of the day proved more powerful than legal precedents. Thus the *Shulḥan Arukh* codified the new practice, making no reference to the older Talmudic decision.[14]

Having virtually created a new festival, the people surrounded it with a large number of customs and observances, many of which have since disappeared. It is significant that their innovations often represented not merely an addition to the existing Halakhah, or even its modification, but a direct contradiction, or so it seemed to many scholars, who raised varied and weighty legal objections to them. Yet in practically every instance the people's will prevailed and the practices remained.

When Rab Hai Gaon (eleventh century) was asked about the custom of bringing incense to the synagogue and burning it before the scrolls, he decided, on the basis of the law (B. *Bezah* 22b), that it was forbidden. However, he felt able to permit decorating scrolls with women's veils, rings, and other ornaments, a practice that also raised some legal difficulties.[15] By the end of the fifteenth century, it was usual for children to tear down and burn the *Sukkah* on *Simhat Torah*; and, about the same time, dancing in the synagogues became widespread, a clear violation of the Talmudic prohibition "These acts are forbidden because of *shebhut* . . . dancing" (B. *Bezah* 36b). The widely diffused custom of carrying wax tapers in the *Simhat Torah* procession was strongly opposed by some authorities and equally staunchly defended by others. Characteristically enough, it created a serious controversy among the leaders of the Smyrna community.[16] In the eighteenth century, the custom of firing gunpowder salutes was introduced.

The development of the festival reveals not merely a flexibility inherent in Jewish tradition but also its democratic character. The people had created *Simhat Torah*, given it its character, and were determined to possess it as their own. The jovial *Hakkafot*, in which the poor as well as the rich, the unlearned no less than the scholars, shared the honor and joy of carrying the Torah scrolls in procession, are a case in point. Neither the Geonim nor the early Decisors (*Posekim*), as late as Rabbi Jacob ben Asher in the *Tur* (a fourteenth-century code), nor Rabbi Joseph Karo in the *Beth Joseph*, make any reference to the custom. The evening *Hakkafot* are first mentioned by Rabbi Isaac Tyrnau in his *Minhagim* (fourteenth and fifteenth centuries) and by Rabbi Moses Isserles.

In Bucharest it was the practice to take all the scrolls out for the *Hakkafot*. A newly elected rabbi felt "that they were not paying proper deference to the Torah, because the scrolls were being carried by the populace [*hamon ha‹am*] and the children," and so he wished to limit the practice to seven scrolls. The reply from an authority was that since the custom of taking out all the scrolls was mentioned in the decisions of Isserles, it was not to be set aside.[17] In a contest between dignity and enthusiasm, dignity came off second best—at least on *Simhat Torah*.

The most striking illustration of the strength of the democratic impulse is afforded by the reading of the Torah on *Simhat Torah*. According to the law, all the festivals have a fixed number of *keru›im*, men called up for the reading of the Torah. With regard to *Simhat Torah*, rabbinic authorities differed as to whether the proper number was five, six, or ten,[18] but these discussions became superfluous as the custom arose of calling all the men in the synagogue to the Torah. To make this possible, the Torah section was read again and again, and to expedite matters two men were called to the Torah simultaneously. Neither of these devices was free from Halakhic difficulties, but the principle that "all Israel share in the Torah" overrode all hesitations and became the accepted practice.[19]

Why did the Rabbis yield on all these issues and actually seek to find a legal basis for their leniency? Rabbi Joseph Colon (fifteenth century), in his *Responsa* (Root 9), lays down a fundamental principle: "A custom designed to honor the Torah sets aside even the prohibition of *shebhut*, such as dancing on a festival."[20]

The relevance of this principle for dealing with problems confronting the Halakhah today is obvious. It offers a fruitful distinction between types of innovation. On the one hand, there are new, non-Halakhic practices among the people that are designed to advance the vitality of Judaism and should therefore be welcomed and validated by rabbinic authority. This is the contention of those who advocate the *Bat Mitzvah* rite and the ordination of women to the rabbinate. On the other hand, in the Jewish community today there are many instances of attitudes and actions, both major and minor, that must be vigorously opposed. The growing disregard of the religious and indispensable character of the rite of circumcision and the vulgar ostentation at many *Bar Mitzvah* celebrations are a threat to the vitality of Judaism and the honor of the Jewish name.

In general, *minhag* evoked radically different reactions from the rabbinate. Some scholars were less than enthusiastic about the proliferation of these new practices. But a negative assessment of *minhag* is definitely a minority view. Thus the highly influential authority Rabbi Ezekiel Landau says, "No custom, no matter how baseless, may be abolished without the consent of the Sages." Even earlier, Rabbi Aryeh Yehudah Leib Hakohen (1658–1720) ruled "that a custom must not be abolished; we are not responsible for harmful consequences, even if it contradicts a law of Torah."[21] Even a rabbinic scholar as independent-minded as Rabbi Menashe of Ilya (1767–1831) declared, "Heaven forbid that I should change even one custom."[22]

The *Scheitel*

One of the unrecognized paradoxes in Jewish religious history originated in Europe in the seventeenth century. It was fashionable then for both women and men of high society to wear elaborate wigs. Jewish women in Germany were just as eager as their gentile counterparts to enhance their attractiveness and sought to justify the wearing of wigs as a fulfilment of rabbinic law. Among the rules of *zeni‹yut*, "modesty," that the Halakhah enjoined upon married women was one that forbade allowing their own hair to be seen by an outsider.[23] Some women covered their heads with a shawl, while others shaved their heads before their wedding day. In the eighteenth century the Jewish women who adopted the practice of wearing wigs (German *Scheitel*, "the crown of the head") found a happy solution—they were able to add to their attractiveness and at the same time satisfy the rabbinic law against showing their own hair.

However, some rabbinic leaders, Rabbi Jacob Emden among them, saw the solution as a subterfuge. They excoriated the practice as an observance of the letter of the law that actually defeated its spirit and purpose. The women were apparently not abashed, but persisted in the wearing of the *Scheitel*. By one of the ironies of history, this practice has become the hallmark of right-wing Orthodoxy today. The battle is not completely over. In Me›a She‹arim, the ultra-Orthodox quarter in Jerusalem, placards are frequently on view attacking women wearing the *Scheitel* as hypocritical, wanton, and impudent, violating the law while pretending to observe it (*zebhu‹ot, peruzot, hazufot*).

Minhag in the Modern Age

Following the Emancipation and the Enlightenment local *minhagim* tended to disappear, both in liturgy and in life. The city of Frankfurt-am-Main, which clung to its specific traditions until the Holocaust, is perhaps the only site where a local liturgy was maintained into modern times.

For many years after Karaism, rabbinic Judaism did not encounter a major challenge. In the seventeenth century and for decades to follow, the Jewish world was convulsed by Shabbetai Zevi (1626–76), "the false Messiah," and his adherents. While the movement spawned many changes in Jewish practice in its heyday, sabbatarianism left few permanent marks on the body of Jewish practice.

A far more significant attack on rabbinic leadership came in the eighteenth and nineteenth centuries, with the rise of the Hasidic movement in eastern Europe. Hasidism rated personal piety and emotional involvement far higher than abstract Talmudic learning, which the rabbinic Establishment placed at the apex of Jewish values.

Though the early controversies between the Hasidim and the Mitnaggedim, "opponents," were very bitter and even violent, ultimately the two factions made peace with each other, for two principal reasons. The first was the rise of a mediating group, the Habad, led by the rabbi of Lubavich. Under the slogan of *Hokhmah-Binah-De‹ah*, "wisdom, understanding, knowledge," the sect sought to combine the ideals of both contending groups, stressing fervent personal piety together with devotion to Talmud study as the heart and essence of Judaism.

The second factor was the powerful onslaught launched by modernism against all forms of traditionalism. The challenge came from inner Jewish movements, such as religious Reform, Haskalah ("the Enlightenment"), the science of Judaism, modern Hebrew and Yiddish literature, and Zionism. There were also pressures from without—the new secular scientific world view, the demand for new educational patterns, and the inroads of socialism among the Jewish masses, as industrialization came to eastern Europe. Though these trends often opposed each other, they were perceived as a menace to the survival of Jewish tradition. A new and militant Orthodoxy uniting Hasidim and Mitnaggedim now emerged to do battle against the common enemy.

The long-standing and deeply rooted regard for *minhag*, "established custom," was now invoked to stem the tide of Reform, which threatened to undermine the entire structure of Jewish practice. Very often *minhag* was to be maintained for its own sake, as a symbol of loyalty to Jewish tradition, even if the custom had no intrinsic merit or significant content. If it served to separate the Jews from general society and insulate them from the perils of modernity, it justified itself and was to be maintained with tenacity.

An effort to revive the practice of *minhag* in the modern era came from a rather unexpected quarter. Rabbi Isaac Mayer Wise, the architect of the basic institutions of Reform Judaism in America, labored to produce a prayer book that would reflect the ideology he believed appropriate to American Jewry. He called his prayer book *Minhag Amerika*, consciously patterning his usage on the names attached to the three major traditional rites, *nusaḥ Askenaz*, *nusaḥ Sephard*, and *nusaḥ Haᵓari*. Succeeding Reform prayer books were so far removed from the traditional pattern that the designation was dropped.

Seating in the Synagogue—Controversy and Convergence

Though the seating of women in the synagogue has been a source of heated controversy, very little is known about the background of this issue. It has generally been assumed that the seating of women in a special section of a house of worship is a unique Jewish practice. Actually, the segregation of the sexes at public worship was a widespread characteristic of Old World religion, Christian as well as Jewish. The famous sixth-century octagonal church of St. Theodotion in Ravenna has a gallery for women.

Nor has this segregation been limited to ancient times. Several years ago, Father John La Farge, a distinguished Jesuit leader in interracial justice, was sitting with me in the *Sukkah* of the Jewish Theological Seminary. In the course of our conversation, he asked me to describe the principal differences among the various Jewish religious movements. I mentioned among others, the family seating pattern in Reform and Conservatism, as against the separate seating in Orthodoxy. "I understand the situation you describe," he said, drawing a diagram on the paper tablecloth before us. "When I was a young priest, I was assigned to a Slavic community in eastern Maryland, most of the members of which were recent immigrants. In the church there were two sections. The boys sat on one side, with their fathers behind them to make sure that they behaved, while the girls sat on the other with their mothers behind them and for the same purpose. But in the rear of the church, the young, American-born adults sat without any segregation."

The separation of the sexes was apparently observed more rigorously in the Jewish than in the Christian community, though our information with regard to Jewish practice is far from complete. The Temple in Jerusalem, where, to be sure, sacrifice not prayer was the principal religious activity, had a special section, ᶜezrat nashim, "the court of women." We do not know its exact function or when it was used.

During the period of the Second Commonwealth a joyous holiday called *Simḥat Bet Ha-shoᵓebah*, "the festival of the drawing of the water," which preserved many ancient elements, was observed in the Temple in Jerusalem.[24] A third-century source (T. *Sukkah* 4) informs us:

> In the beginning when *Simḥat Bet Ha-shoᵓebah* was observed the men would look from within and the women would look from without. When the Court saw that they were approaching levity (*qallut rosh*), they built

three barriers in the Temple small court on three sides where the women
sat and saw the *Simhat Bet Ha-shoᵈebah* and they were not commingled,
while pious men would dance before them with torches and sing songs.

Here the participation of women at a festival ritual, albeit at a distance,
is clearly indicated.

The first-century philosopher Philo admiringly describes an ascetic
sect in Alexandria called Therapeutae[25] who celebrated a festival "after
seven sets of seven days" in which women participated. That seems also
to be the case with at least one group of Essenes in Palestine.[26] A frag-
mentary text from Qumran, recently published, describes a joyous ritual in which women were actively involved.[27]

It is difficult to believe that "mainstream Judaism" was stricter in en-
forcing the separation of the sexes than were the Essenes, who were revered for their deep piety. It may be that originally there was a mingling
of the sexes at worship services; the biblical Song of Songs testifies to
an easy relationship between men and women in the social sphere,
though that was in an earlier era. With the passing of time, however,
more-stringent attitudes developed in Pharisaic Judaism, so that the
mingling of the sexes survived only during special occasions, such as
Simhat Bet Ha-shoᵈebah in the Temple. The rise of ascetic tendencies in
rabbinic Judaism after the destruction of the Temple is well attested in
our sources.

Some ancient synagogues from early in the Common Era, recently excavated in Israel, seem to have made no provision at all for the presence
of women at services.[28] An intermingling of the sexes, as some have suggested, is hardly likely. It is more likely that women did not generally
attend public services. A parallel may perhaps be found in eastern Europe, where until almost our own day, they were not expected to go to
the synagogue, except for such special purposes as hearing the shofar
on *Rosh Hashanah*, celebrating *Simhat Torah*, and listening to the reading of the *Megillah* on *Purim*.

The practice of providing a special section for women in the synagogue evolved slowly and in a variety of patterns.[29] Their area might
be built under the men's synagogue, with a grille in the ceiling, so that
the women could hear the men's service, as in Avignon and Comtat
Venaissin; or they might be seated in the sexton's wine cellar. There
might be a ground-floor room set aside for them, as in Worms, or an
additional aisle, as in the Prague Pinkas synagogue. A women's annex
raised above the men's area at the side is found in synagogues from the
fourteenth century on. Beginning with the sixteenth century, a women's
gallery appears, and this became the dominant pattern in Europe until
the present.

The avowed purpose of these varied practices was to prevent the sexes from "seeing and being seen by each other" and thus being tempted to levity or worse. This goal was achieved either by seating men and women in different areas or by erecting a curtain or a grille around the women. This barrier was called the *mehizah*, literally, "division," "partition," a meaning that the term did not possess until the Middle Ages.

When the *mehizah* became an issue in the twentieth century, two striking aspects of the subject were overlooked. First, the separation of the sexes was universal in European synagogues of all denominations, including Reform. At the three rabbinical conferences at which the foundations of Reform Judaism were laid—Brunswick (1844), Frankfurt (1845), and Breslau (1846)—many radical changes in Jewish practice and belief were adopted, but the issue of the segregation of the sexes was never raised. The Reform movement introduced the organ, abbreviated and modified the text of the prayer book, and declared Hebrew not essential for Jewish worship; but Reform synagogues in Europe continued the separation of the sexes at services[30] as well as the time-hallowed practice of covering the head at worship. Contemporary historians have been unable to point to any discussion of mixed pews in the rich polemical literature engendered by Reform Judaism in Europe.[31]

Mixed pews are reported for a few small left-wing Reform synagogues in Cologne, Hamburg, and Berlin. The conclusion is inescapable that in this respect, the European synagogue was a reflection of European society as a whole. Women were generally relegated to a separate and inferior role in nearly all areas of life, and so the houses of worship followed suit. The change to family pews, which had not even been discussed in Europe, became the norm in America, again with no apparent attention being paid to the question at the annual gathering of the (Reform) Central Conference of American Rabbis.

Family seating in the synagogue had important ideological implications, but they were not recognized at the inception of the practice or for a long time thereafter. In fact, it is fair to say that the custom began accidentally in the first synagogues to introduce the practice, Anshe Emet in Albany in 1851 and Temple Emanuel in New York in 1854. It has been suggested that since both congregations had bought their houses of worship from churches with built-in enclosed family pews, it was cheaper to retain them than to rebuild, and the congregation voted for mixed pews. But, of course, there was nothing to prevent using those pews for separate seating. The innovation attracted little attention in the larger Jewish community at the time, neither among those who favored the innovation nor among those who did not.

Not until the closing decades of the nineteenth century, when mixed seating in the synagogue became a subject of controversy, were two religio-ethical motives articulated: first, that family pews further family unity, which was encapsulated in the popular American slogan "The family that prays together stays together"; and second, that unsegregated seating represents a significant step toward equalizing the status of women in Jewish religious life.

The family pew in the American synagogue was a direct consequence of the new American environment. The American frontier had been opened up through the cooperative labors and sacrifices of women as well as men. In all the major movements in American life—cultural, political, and religious—women played an important role and were pressing on to full equality. As a result, the frontier church was open to men and women on an equal basis.

The Jewish community had no such frontier tradition. Nor was the family pew, characteristic of Protestant churches, likely to serve as a model for the East European immigrants who began streaming into the United States after 1881. They naturally sought to replicate the synagogues they had known "at home"; they curtained women off from the main sanctuary or placed them in the gallery. As the process of American acculturation began to influence the immigrants and, even more, their sons and daughters, the physical separation of the sexes in the synagogue was abandoned by most groups. The main exceptions were among the right-wing Orthodox and the Hasidim, who set as their goal the reestablishment on American shores of what they believed was the ideal state of Judaism—the East European *shtetl* of the nineteenth century—and continued to maintain strict segregation of the sexes. The bulk of Orthodox synagogues, centrist and "modern," sought a symbolic practice that would signify "loyalty to tradition" and set them apart from non-Orthodox synagogues. This solution was found in the *meḥizah*, which was originally made of wood or cloth but is increasingly made of glass.

The practice of the total separation of the sexes, not only at worship in the synagogue but in all areas and activities, has been tacitly abandoned. Particularly as one moves away from the eastern seaboard, one encounters in Orthodox synagogues a variety of devices designed to pay tribute to the time-honored custom of segregated seating in theory, while surrendering it in practice. Some Orthodox synagogues place the women at the side of the main floor, slightly above the men's section. In others the women's area is separated by a token curtain, which affords total visibility. (Major battles have been fought over the requisite height of the *meḥizah* in order for the congregation to qualify as Orthodox.) In some synagogues the large central section is turned over to "mixed pews," while there are separate sections on the sides for men and for women.

The issue of mixed seating became a *cause célèbre* in Mount Clemens, Michigan, and in Cincinnati, Ohio. In each case a group of members of an Orthodox congregation sued to prevent the introduction of family pews in the synagogue. Their positions were upheld by the courts on the ground that the constitutions of the congregations established them as Orthodox.[32] The mass of oral and written testimony adduced in these cases shows that widespread as the traditional practice is, there are few explicit Halakhic sources for it, and that the arguments in its favor are primarily based on inference.[33] Thus a great contemporary Halakhic authority, Rabbi Aaron Kotler, who was strongly opposed to mixed seating, declared that segregated seating "would *seem to be* a biblical injunction" (italics mine).[34] Nineteenth-century European Halakhists had strongly objected to making a *meḥizah* of thin boards, as it would "permit the people to see and be seen"[35] and thus lead to frivolity. Several supported their position on the ground that separate seating is a *minhag* and therefore sacred and unchangeable.

The powerful impact of the American environment on the seating patterns of Orthodox synagogues is obliquely—and all the more impressively—attested by the *Responsa* of Rabbi Moshe Feinstein, a universally acknowledged Orthodox Halakhic authority.[36] He strongly urged that women be seated in the upper balcony of the synagogue. However, he was constrained by the prevalent conditions to accept the seating of men and women on the same level, provided that a suitable partition, high enough to cover the women's heads, be erected. In one instance he was compelled to go further and permit a lower partition, provided that most of the women's bodies remained out of sight and that the male worshippers refrained from looking in the direction of the women's seating. Even this concession was not the last. Where no partition existed, he ruled that separate sections might be maintained for men and women on the same level. All these variations fall within legitimate or at least tolerable traditional "limits," even for this most distinguished right-wing Halakhic authority.[37]

Another well-known rabbi called the partition "a symbol of loyalty to tradition," but did not offer a rationale for the inferior role of women at services.[38] That the sexes not commingle and "not see or be seen by each other" is scarcely a motive, since they sit side by side in the synagogue during lectures and on other occasions. A suburban synagogue carried a provision in its constitution that read, "This congregation shall be governed by the *Shulḥan Arukh* except on Rosh Hashanah and Yom Kippur, when mixed pews will be permitted." There are few, if any, large synagogues recently erected in the United States that have made provision for a women's gallery.

The present trend to the right in American religious life, both Christian and Jewish, may have slowed the process of integrating the sexes at services and strengthened the call for higher partitions in Orthodox synagogues. It is noteworthy, however, that Young Israel, which began as a liberal movement in traditional Judaism but has moved to the far right in Orthodoxy, has not forbidden its women worshippers to sing at services, Talmudic prohibition notwithstanding.

Clearly the various patterns of seating in the synagogue, all reflecting a surrender of the principle of segregation, constitute "the American custom." In the years ahead, the American environment and American cultural, ethical, and social attitudes will continue to affect various segments of American Jewry and have an impact on the content and spirit of Jewish law. Similarly, the new society in the state of Israel will undoubtedly produce a new *minhag Erez Yisrael*, rivaling the older body of custom in Talmudic and Gaonic times.

No Halakhist has thus far been able to validate the family pew from traditional sources. Nor has it ever been adopted as a *taqqanah*, a special ordinance by a recognized rabbinical body. The tacit surrender of the segregation of the sexes in synagogues of all tendencies like the other instances adduced in this chapter, is an example of *minhag* triumphing over accepted law. In this instance, it is *minhag America*.

New Days of Commemoration

A major sign of the spiritual impoverishment of modern life caused by secularization is the inability to lift certain days out of the ordinary routine and endow them with a unique atmosphere. Modern governments can establish holidays, but they cannot create holy days. In the United States virtually only Thanksgiving Day, among legal holidays, retains a timbre of its own, harking back to its religious beginnings. The other holidays, even Memorial Day and the Fourth of July, in spite of their patriotic origins, are at most occasions for staying away from work or extending the weekend. Only religion seems to possess the secret formula for infusing certain days with a unique spirit marking them off from all others.

The twentieth century has been the most momentous in the long history of the Jewish people, being indelibly stamped by two major events—the unspeakable horror of the Holocaust and the glory of the birth and growth of the state of Israel. Today's Jews are unwilling to permit either the catastrophe or the miracle to sink into the pages of history and leave no trace in the living experience of the people. On the contrary, it is only natural that a calendar that recalls the earlier agonies of destruction through fast days, such as the Fast of Gedalyah, the Tenth of Tebet, the Seventeenth of Tammuz, and the Ninth of Ab, should commemorate the catastrophe of our age in the *Yom Hashoᵓah*, "Holocaust Day," on the 27th of Nisan.

The traditional Jewish year celebrates major occasions of freedom and deliverance in the past through the festivals of *Hanukkah, Purim,* and *Pesah.* The calendar could scarcely ignore the burgeoning life of the state of Israel or fail to express thanksgiving for the miracle of its creation. Thus two new festivals came into existence, *Yom Ha‹atzma›ut,* "Independence Day," on the 18th of Iyyar; and *Yom Yerushalayim,* "The Day of Jerusalem," on the 30th of Nisan, marking the reunification of the Holy City.

Once again, the feeling that anything new is forbidden, a position reinforced in some cases by political attitudes, came into play. Some authorities in the religious establishment of Israel and in right-wing religious groups there and in the Diaspora, have opposed any celebratory additions to the liturgy, such as the *Hallel,* the Psalms of Praise recited on all the major festivals of thanksgiving. While they do not always oppose a prayer for the armed forces of Israel in synagogues throughout the world, these elements in the rabbinate refuse to permit the inclusion of a prayer for the state of Israel at sabbath services. Nonetheless, the observance of these days of joy and sorrow, both in the synagogue service and in the public arena, has become all but universal.

A people that lives remembers; a people that remembers lives.

VII

ABIDING PRINCIPLES AND CHANGING CONDITIONS

If the biblical period is regarded as the youth of the Jewish people, then the Talmudic era may be described as its coming of age. As we have seen, the three basic factors that endowed the Jewish tradition with its powerful ethical consciousness were the Egyptian experience of bondage and liberation; the nomadic period, both as an objective reality and as a subjective perception; and the extraordinary phenomenon of Hebrew prophecy.

It goes without saying that individual Jews and Jewish society did not always conduct their lives on the highest ethical plane. Human weakness and vice and the heavy burdens of exile and persecution conspired to limit the effectiveness of ethical concern. The inertia of the past and the body of legal precedents were powerful countervailing forces that limited growth and change in the Halakhah, but they were unable to prevent them. The emergence of new practices and institutions embodying the operation of ethical principles under changing conditions was not an unbroken linear process. There were periods of movement and stagnation, of advance and retreat. But the general direction was unmistakable. A new position once achieved was rarely abandoned; on the contrary, it proved the point of departure for another step forward toward the realization of the ideal.

The impact of ethical concerns on rabbinic law came in two stages: the first, formative, when a given provision was being promulgated; the second, operative, when it was felt that in a particular case the established norms did not sufficiently or effectively reflect currently accepted ethical standards, because of changed conditions or new insights.

Today, as religious loyalties have weakened, a countervailing tendency of considerable strength has made itself felt. It demands conformity to the law of God solely on the basis of its divine origin, which, it is argued, places it "beyond good and evil." It emphatically denies that ethical considerations or appeals to reason may be invoked as motives for religious obedience. Fundamentalism, which takes the form of "born-again Christians" and *ba‹alei teshuvah*, "returnees or penitents," in Judaism is today evident on every hand.¹ In the Catholic Church, Pope John Paul II has undertaken a campaign to suppress dissident voices by reaffirming and extending the boundaries of the doctrine of papal infallibility. In Judaism, with its thousand-year-old penchant for discussion and argument, such a stance would at first blush seem impossible; yet today, a parallel concept of rabbinic infallibility has arisen in right-wing circles. As already indicated, it has been formulated as *da‹at Torah*, "the will of the Torah"; God's command, it is contended, is embodied in the decision of the contemporary sages, who are the direct recipients of God's guidance. Hence, to differ with them, or even to ask for the grounds on which they have based their position, is heresy.

In more-sophisticated circles, it is argued on philosophical grounds that the divine character of the Halakhah frees it from the constraints of ethics or reason. Since the entire thrust of the Jewish tradition is against this approach, evidence for it is difficult to find. One erudite rabbinic scholar has adduced in its support the biblical provision "No bastard shall enter the assembly of the Lord; even to the tenth generation, none of his descendants shall enter the assembly of the Lord" (Deut. 23:2). Here, it is argued, is a law that does not accord with our sense of morality, yet it remains binding.²

That the severe provisions of this biblical law were not mitigated by the Halakhah constitutes a problem, particularly since the Rabbis had access to rich hermeneutic resources that they frequently employed elsewhere. Perhaps they were motivated by the desire to buttress the sanctity of the marriage bond, which they may have felt was threatened by the lax standards of Greco-Roman society.

In any event, the Rabbis were deeply sensitive to the injustice visited upon the innocent offspring of an adulterous or incestuous union. Their anguish is poignantly expressed in the Midrash (Leviticus Rabbah sec. 32:8):

> Ecclesiastes 4:1 reads: "I turned and saw all the oppressions under the sun." Daniel, the tailor, explained the verse as referring to bastards. "Here are the tears of the oppressed—their parents were transgressors, but they, poor wretches, what is their fault?" "They have no comforter, but power is in the hands of their oppressors"—"in the hand of the great Sanhedrin of Israel that penalizes them by the authority of the Torah and keeps them distant [from the community] because of the verse, 'A bastard shall not enter into the assembly of the Lord.'" "They have no comforter," said the Holy One blessed be He. "It is My duty to comfort them, because in this world there is a stigma upon them, but in the future, as Zechariah has said, 'I saw them seated on thrones made of pure gold.'"

We do not know the reason for the literal retention of the biblical law on illegitimacy. But to cite this case as proof that the Halakhah need not conform to ethical standards is to stand the evidence on its head and declare virtually the only exception to be the rule.

Uncompromising attachment to righteousness as the cornerstone of human conduct remains constant, as we have seen, beginning with the ringing challenge of Abraham, "Shall not the Judge of all the earth do justly?" It is explicit or implicit in every line of the Prophets and on every page of the Talmud.

One may accept the view of Rabbi Akiba that the Golden Rule, "You shall love your neighbor as yourself," is the great principle (*kelal gadol*). Or one may prefer the passage cited by Ben Azzai: "This is the book of the generations of Adam. When God created man he made him in the likeness of God; male and female He created them" (Gen. 5:1), a verse that underscores the brotherhood and equality of all mankind.[3] But there is no denying that "the great principle of the Torah" is ethical.

Since the Torah was the word of God, the Rabbis saw the Torah as both idealistic and realistic, though, to be sure, these terms were unknown to them. Hence, it was axiomatic that the Halakhah would always conform to the ethical ideal. At the same time, it would reckon with the limitations of human nature and the constraints on human behavior posed by objective conditions.

It has already been noted that the Hebraic tradition rarely enunciated abstract principles and preferred to embody its attitudes in concrete and specific form. This trait never disappeared, but as Jews came into contact with Greek thought, they could not resist the attractiveness of general principles. The Rabbis formulated a series of ethical norms that are embedded in the structure of Jewish law in the first stage. Since these doctrines entered the law at its inception, they manifestly did not require any changes in the law. Therefore they did not arouse any opposition and have remained normative throughout the history of the Halakhah.[4]

One of the most famous is the principle *mipnei darkhei shalom*, "because of the ways of peace, for the enhancement of goodwill in society."[5] It was applied to relations among various groups within the Jewish community, such as the priests and the laymen, as well as with gentiles. Thus, the Mishnah teaches, "Gentiles are to be greeted while they are working in the fields even during the sabbatical year [when Jews are forbidden to till the ground]" (M. *Shevi*it 4:3). Nor were indigent gentiles to be prevented from helping themselves to the produce that biblical law prescribed for the Jewish poor, *leket*, *shikhah*, and *pe>ah* (M. *Gittin* 5:8; B. *Gittin* 59b, 62a). Moreover, the Jewish community is obligated to feed the gentile poor along with the Jewish poor (P. *Demai* 4:6).

Undoubtedly, there were prudential considerations in the desire to maintain harmonious relations with the non-Jewish majority. As we have seen, prudence serves as a virtue in the ethics of biblical Wisdom as well. But this doctrine is distinct from the doctrine *mishum ,eibhah*, "to prevent enmity." The obligations "for the sake of peace" are basically ethical in motivation and surely in practice. Even more extensive in its implications is the doctrine *mipnei tikkun ha,olam*, "for the improvement of society," which is applied in various areas of Jewish law, such as divorce, inheritance, and social legislation (M. *Gittin* 4:2).

The Honor of God's Creatures

Deeply rooted in biblical thought was the concern for *kevod haberiyot*, "the honor of God's creatures, respect for the dignity of one's fellow human being." The effects of this principle are noticeable in various details of ritual as well as in major social institutions. Thus the traditional Grace after Meals ends with the citation of Psalms 37:25: "I was young and have grown old, but have not seen a righteous man forsaken or his children seeking bread." Since it is customary to invite poor people to the Passover *Seder*, the verse is omitted from the ritual on that occasion in deference to their feelings. In Jewish ethics, safeguarding the dignity of the poor was as important as meeting their physical needs.

An extreme instance may be cited from the Talmud (B. *Ketubbot* 67b). A beggar came for assistance. "What do you generally eat?" the rabbi asked him. "Stuffed fowl and old wine," was the answer. "Aren't you concerned about the expense to which you put the community?" The beggar calmly answered, "Am I eating what belongs to them? I am eating what belongs to God." And he proceeded to cite the verse in Psalms, "The eyes of all look to You and You give them their food in due season" (145:11).

In the rabbinic and medieval periods, Jewish communities established an elaborate system of charitable institutions to supply food and clothes to the poor, hostels for travelers, dowries for brides, support for widows and orphans, and shrouds and burial sites for the dead. In some communities the charity boxes were never locked, so that the needy might take what they required and the well-to-do contribute according to their means, without either the donor or the recipient being known to one another. The term applied to charity was *zedakah*, "righteousness." It was to be regarded not as an act of condescension and benevolence toward the poor, but as the performance of their duty by the rich.[6]

While many traditional virtues may have been attenuated among modern Jews, the practice of philanthropy has largely retained its hold. The first organization in the field, the Alliance Israélite Universelle, was founded in the middle of the nineteenth century by French Jews in order to defend the rights of Jews and protect them from intolerance, persecution, and discrimination. Since that time Jews in every land have created organizations for the defense of Jewish rights at home and abroad. They have also created exemplary institutions for the care of the needy, such as hospitals, orphanages, and homes for the aged and the destitute. They have established institutions for Jewish learning on every age level and have supported colleges and universities in the general community.

Great international organizations, such as the Joint Distribution Committee, have been established to gather and expend vast sums for the relief and rehabilitation of the remnants of European Jewry and for the rebuilding and development of the state of Israel. Throughout North America, Jewish Federations and welfare funds have aroused wide admiration for the advanced and comprehensive services they render in their communities irrespective of race, creed, and color.

Two other concepts that spanned the entire range of human experience, from the most mundane of money matters to the sublime act of martyrdom, were the ideal of *kiddush hashem*, "the sanctification of God's name," and its converse, the avoidance of *hillul hashem*, "the profanation of God's name." Jews were bidden to practice *kiddush hashem* and at all costs to avoid *hillul hashem*. The latter was applied particularly in connection with Jewish-gentile relationships. Being conscious of the fact that the non-Jewish world looked upon each Jew as a prototype of the entire people and a representative of his tradition, the Rabbis demanded the highest type of ethical conduct from individual Jews, particularly in their contacts with gentile society.

Though rabbinic sources contain some passages reflecting narrower perspectives on Jewish-gentile relationships, the ideal of *kiddush hashem* was invoked in the world of business against cheating or misrepresentation. The Talmud points out that ethical conduct is not limited to Jews. It cites the case of a gentile, Dama ben Netina, who suffered a major financial loss by foregoing a lucrative sale of jewels rather than wake his father from his sleep (B. *Kiddushin* 31a, b; *Abodah Zarah* 23b).

At its highest and most tragic level, *kiddush hashem* did not remain a pious exhortation but meant martyrdom. From the days of Hannah and her seven sons, who according to tradition suffered martyrdom during the Antiochian persecution in the second century B.C.E., through the Middle Ages, to the threshold of the modern era and beyond, thousands of Jews sacrificed their lives for their God and their Torah. The twentieth century has witnessed *kiddush hashem* on a colossal scale, as millions of men, women, and children whom the Nazis tortured and murdered refused to die as victims, but gave their lives as witnesses to their faith and people.

Concern for the Community

A juridical rule that deserves to be regarded as ethical as well as pragmatic is embodied in the principle *›Ein gozrin gezerah ›ela› ›im ken*
hazibbur yekholin la‹amod bah, "We do not enact an edict unless the
community can observe it."[7] The Sages, unlike many of their successors
in both the religious and the secular worlds, were keenly aware of the
limitations of human nature and, consequently, the problem of law enforcement. They did not shut their eyes to the damage inflicted on respect for the law and its authority when a particular ordinance is consistently flouted by the people.

The ethical principles and realistic insights we have adduced were
universally recognized and accepted in the Halakhah. When differences
arose it was only with regard to their proper application in a given situation. Basically, however, these ideas created no difficulties and encountered little opposition. Sharp differences arose when new circumstances made new demands, and Jewish law was called upon to serve
human needs and to function under untried and often difficult circumstances.

It was at this point that the liberal and the conservative parted company on particular issues. Many creative, courageous scholars felt it imperative to adjust the Halakhah to new conditions and bring it into harmony with newer insights. At times that was achieved by modifying the
law through legislation, the *taqqanah* and the *gezerah*, or—preferably
and far more frequently—through a fresh reinterpretation of traditional sources. On the other hand, the existing law, which had been formulated at an earlier period, had achieved a substantial measure of
sanctity and authority, and there were those who found a departure
from accepted norms of conduct intolerable. These conflicts, often
vigorous and at times even bitter, were by no means a total loss. On
some occasions one side or the other triumphed, but what frequently
emerged was a solution that encompassed the elements of strength in
the two opposing positions.

Practices

The twentieth century has witnessed far more rapid and fundamental change than did the past five hundred years. It is no wonder, therefore, that both the liberal and the conservative positions are being urged with greater intensity than ever before. Since we are confronted by revolutionary transformations of vast proportions and are being catapulted into an unknown and potentially dangerous world, it is argued that our generation needs stability above all else, and that it must, therefore, hold fast to the old and tried. At the opposite pole, it is maintained that if the entire tradition is not be disappear in the avalanche of change, it must follow the patterns of growth and development exemplified by its greatest spokesmen and teachers in the past.

Obviously both stability and flexibility are required for a living organism such as the Halakhah. Unfortunately, the importance of this balance is often lost sight of. Today there exists a widespread retreat into obscurantism that refuses to examine the evidence and prefers invective to evidence. There is a passionate insistence in many quarters that immobility is the touchstone of permanence and "tunnel vision" the only true light. It is, therefore, all the more important to point out that flexibility and the capacity for adjustment must be utilized to the full if the tradition is to bend and not break under the storms that threaten it from all sides.

To understand the Halakhah it is essential not to restrict ourselves to limited sections of time and space but to study its entire three-thousand-year history. Since our concern is not antiquarian but contemporary, we should not be content with a scholarly exploration of the past but should utilize all the insights achieved in order to illumine current issues that cry out for solution.

Both the leadership and the laity have had a role in the Halakhic process. Two major factors have been at work: The first consists of new ethical insights and attitudes *from within*; the second of the need to respond to new social, economic, political, or cultural conditions *from without*. These two factors are by no mean unrelated to each other, for new insights generally come to light from the stimulus of new conditions.

We shall examine the operation of Jewish law in the past and the problems it confronts in the present in the following categories: *social and economic factors* affecting debts, prices, and other issues; *new ethical insights* affecting laws of inheritance and criminal law; and *women's rights*, the most striking instance of new ethical attitudes molded by socioeconomic factors leading to legal change.

The struggle for women's rights has gone on for centuries, but it has reached its climax in our day. Here the Halakhah, contrary to widespread misconception, has been a respectable, if not a spectacular, force in the past; but it faces "unfinished business," as does modern society as a whole. The issue of women's status will be treated under four principal rubrics: marriage and divorce; the tragedy of the ʿ*agunah*, "the chained wife"; women's role in Jewish religion; and the ordination of women as rabbis. That women's issues require so much attention is not at all astonishing, for our century is witnessing the last great movement of liberation affecting more than half the human race.

In addition to the two prime causes for growth and development in Jewish law, the motive of Jewish survival, which is generally overlooked, plays an important, if somewhat lesser, role. This profound desire has beat powerfully in the Jewish breast from the days of the Babylonian Exile to the present. It is as significant an element in Jewish history as biblical prophecy, rabbinic law, medieval poetry and philosophy, modern Hebrew literature and culture, or Zionism—in fact it informs them all. The imperious desire for life of the Jewish people has produced a body of the Halakhah in areas as diverse as agriculture and the family.

Obviously the three major influences on Jewish law are not mutually exclusive, and in most instances, several motivations are present. In placing a given practice under one rubric rather than another, we have been governed by what appears to be the major or the most significant motive involved. The impact of these factors on the growth and development of Jewish law and practice constitutes the basic theme of the chapters that follow.

VIII

THE IMPACT OF NEW ECONOMIC
AND SOCIAL FACTORS

At this point it would be well to review the road we have traveled thus far. We began by calling attention to the historical experience of the Jewish people, which, on objective grounds and in no invidious sense, may fairly be described as unique. The secret of this attribute lies in its religious tradition. Many factors entered into the complex pattern of Jewish culture, all of which enriched the content of Jewish living, but it is the Halakhah, the system of Jewish law and practice, extending from the age of Moses to the present, that is the key to Jewish survival. Three factors early in the history of the Jews molded its psyche, the Egyptian experience of bondage and liberation, the period of the wandering in the wilderness following the Exodus, and the centuries-old exposure to the teaching of the Prophets. They placed a permanent stamp upon Jews and their tradition—an insistence upon righteousness as part of their covenant with their God and as the moving principle in the history of men and nations.

Throughout the development of Jewish law, from its simple beginnings in the biblical era to its incredibly complex forms in the Talmudic and medieval periods, this ideal of justice and mercy was never lost sight of. We then traced the workings of this Halakhic process through its recognized leadership on the one hand, and the will of the masses on the other. We noted how the structure of Jewish law was erected on principles that were imbedded in its foundations.

Mere adherence to the tradition, however, would have been powerless to preserve it in the face of the radical vicissitudes to which the Jewish people was exposed. Jewish national independence lasted some 500 years during the First Temple (ca. twelfth century–586 B.C.E.) and less than a century during the Second (142–63 B.C.E.). At least two thousand years, about three times as long, were spent in exile, under foreign domination. Over the centuries the socioeconomic structure has undergone radical changes, and new ethical insights have emerged. A primitive nomadic society developed into an early rural-urban economy, which froze into the feudal system. Finally the Industrial Revolution ushered in the era of capitalism. Both capitalism and the Jewish people have gone through several stages in their vastly different struggles for survival in the modern world.

Jewish law, which has been contemporaneous with the entire history of Western civilization, obviously required stability to survive, but equally important was its flexibility, a sensitivity to new conditions, and an openness to new ethical ideas. The interplay between the forces of conservation and the factors making for change produced a tradition both firm and flexible. We shall now turn to an examination of the external, material conditions and the inner spiritual attitudes they engendered that changed the contours of the Halakhah, a process that will continue as long as the Halakhah itself.

Religion is a human concern, and the injunctions it promulgates are directed to men and women. It therefore follows that Jewish tradition and law will reveal many instances of the effect of new social and economic conditions upon the content of Jewish law. Conversely, ethical norms help to shape economic precedents and social realities. The interplay of cause and effect may be complex, indirect, and reciprocal. Since it is rarely possible to give due weight to each of the several elements present in a given situation, the various factors are not to be regarded as mutually exclusive.

New Economic Practices

Our first instance of a Jewish practice being modified by new economic realities is prerabbinic in origin. The ancient Hebrews had a national calendar, from which the names of several months—Abib, Bul, Ethanim, and Ziv—have survived in biblical texts.[1] This calendar, which is distinct from specialized month lists like the agricultural calendar found at Gezer by R. A. S. Macalister,[2] was in use until the destruction of the First Temple. The Babylonian Exile, followed by the Return during the fifth and sixth centuries B.C.E., left large Jewish communities living, working, and often thriving in the Diaspora. Convenience, perhaps even necessity, dictated that Jewish merchants conform to the practices of their gentile associates in dating documents and signing contracts.

With no echo of opposition, the old Hebrew calendar was eliminated and the names of the Babylonian months were adopted. Nor was the Jewish community given pause by the fact that at least one of the months, Tammuz, carries the name of a pagan deity, a key figure in the widespread oriental myth of the death and rebirth of the gods. The felt need of Jews to participate fully and conveniently in the economic life of their region proved more powerful than the natural desire to cleave to traditional ways or the fear of assimilating to the ways of the gentiles.

The change in the calendar left no mark in the literature, but a much more significant accommodation is discussed in the Talmud. Ezra is credited with having replaced the ancient Hebrew script by the square Aramaic script, not only for secular purposes but even for the writing of Torah scrolls and other sacred documents.[3] Obviously, conforming to the style of writing that was universal in the Middle East had major economic advantages.

Emanating from a later period, and thus documented in Tannaitic sources, are several other accommodations to non-Jewish usage. Thus the Mishnah prescribes the inclusion of the name of the Roman emperor in dating a bill of divorce, a practice some groups saw as demeaning if not down right irreverent. This usage seems to parallel the introduction of Roman weights and measures, a standardization that undoubtedly facilitated business relationships.

A classic instance of the Halakhah responding to new economic conditions is Hillel's famous *taqqanah* of the *Prosbul*. Out of its deep solicitude for the well-being of those in need, the Torah lays down the principle that a debt that has remained unpaid for six years is to be cancelled on the seventh, "the year of release."[4] This norm operated to the advantage of the underprivileged in the primitive economy of the First Temple. In a simple, rural-urban society, a farmer would borrow money only when some disaster, such as sickness or drought, had left him and his family destitute. Hence, virtually all lending of money was a form of charity or, in economic terms, "consumer credit."

However, in the more-advanced agri-urban economy of the Greco-Roman world, the cancellation of unpaid debts in the seventh year proved to be a major obstacle to securing the credit necessary for buying merchandise or for investment, "producer's credit." Here the charitable motivation played little or no part. The prospect of having debts wiped out at the end of six years served to "shut the door against borrowers," as the Talmud observes.[5] Accordingly, Hillel established a far-reaching *taqqanah*. Falling back on the biblical text "The creditor shall release his hand on the seventh year from the debt he sought to collect from the borrower," Hillel declared that the Torah forbade the creditor, but not the courts, to collect the debt in the seventh year, so that if a man transferred the debt to the court, it would be collectable after "the year of release."

Superficially viewed, Hillel's *taqqanah* would seem to represent a total abrogation of the law. Actually, both the Torah and Hillel had the same objective—to make economic help available to those in need. New conditions required radically different, even apparently contrary, procedures for achieving the same goal.

As the relatively simple economy of the First Temple days was transformed into the more complex socioeconomic order of the Roman and Parthian empires, the biblical prohibition against taking interest posed a major obstacle to the free flow of credit. The Talmud was clearly aware of the problem and permitted a variety of practices bordering on the direct taking of interest (*abhak ribbit*, "dust of usury"). As the economic order became increasingly complex, loans and interest became the lifeblood of commerce and industry. In the Middle Ages, the use of a legal fiction became widespread. In a document "permitting a business transaction" (*shtar heter ʿisqa*), the lender became a partner *pro forma* in the business enterprise of the borrower, thereby protecting the lender against any loss and guaranteeing him a minimum fixed "profit."[6]

Preserving a Jewish Presence in the Land of Israel

In the centuries following Ezra and Nehemiah, the Persian rulers of Palestine were succeeded by the Ptolemies of Egypt and the Seleucids of Syria. Then followed a brief period of Jewish independence (142–63 B.C.E.), which was ended decisively by the Romans. The Rabbis of the Mishnah saw Jewish survival in constant peril, on both the spiritual and the economic level, and so they adopted various measures to meet the threat.

The ongoing challenge to Jewish spiritual integrity, stemming from close contact with pagans, was a source of perpetual concern. Among the eighteen *gezerot*, "prohibitions," that the school of Shammai succeeded in adopting over the objections of the school of Hillel, shortly before the destruction of the Second Temple, were provisions forbidding Jews to eat the bread of pagans, drink their oil and wine, or marry their daughters.[7]

To preserve the integrity and the economic viability of the Jewish community in Roman Palestine was a difficult task, in view of the heavy taxation and other forms of oppression practiced by the Romans. Increasingly Jews were tempted to leave the land of Israel for more favorable centers of settlement elsewhere—Babylonia, North Africa, and Europe. The Pharisees and the Rabbis after them sought to stem this emigration by enacting a *gezerah*, "restrictive decree," declaring territory outside the land of Israel "unclean" and by adopting other regulations.[8]

However, the efficacy of these measures was probably limited. It was not easy for the Jewish farmer to maintain his precarious foothold in the Holy Land. There was the burden of the various "gifts" due to the priesthood: the firstborn of animals, the first crops, the heave offering, and the Levitical tithes.[9] In addition, he was obligated to let his land lie fallow every seventh year, the year of release prescribed in the Torah.[10]

The Rabbis sought to solve the last problem by establishing a principle that, they declared, emanated from the Men of the Great Assembly: The land conquered by Joshua after the Exodus, "the first entrance," become holy only temporarily, (*kedushah rishonah*), while Jews lived on it, but not for the future.[11] Only the land acquired after the Return from the Babylonian Exile, "the second entrance," attained a permanent sanctity (*kedushah sheniyah*). Since the second Jewish settlement was much smaller than the first, considerable portions of the country were free from these priestly and Levitical dues. Measures such as this undoubtedly helped to prolong the existence of a Jewish presence in Palestine.

That these biblical precepts concerning tithes and produce were seriously observed by the Jewish community was demonstrated by the discovery in 1959 of a mosaic inscription in the floor of a synagogue at Rehov, some seven miles south of the present settlement of Beth Shean.[12] The 29-line inscription gives a detailed list of 90 cities and agricultural settlements and 30 kinds of fruit and vegetables that were either "released" or "forbidden" by rabbinic authorities. While the material is to be found in the Palestinian Talmud, the presence of these detailed lists on the floor of a synagogue frequented by the people indicates the practical importance of the exemptions the Rabbis afforded the sorely tried farmers.

To help them in their plight, Rabbi Judah the Patriarch (c. 200 C.E.), the compiler and redactor of the Mishnah, used his considerable power to free Caesarea, Beth Guvrin, and Beth Shean from the payment of tithes. He stood his ground in spite of the argument of his opponents: "A thing which your fathers and forefathers said was forbidden—how can you declare it permitted?"[13] But he proved less successful in promulgating a more far-reaching change. Because of steadily worsening economic conditions, Judah proposed the total abrogation of the biblical law that ordained leaving the land lie fallow every seventh year as a "Sabbath to the Lord." Here Rabbi Phineas ben Yair and his colleagues, who opposed this radical change, carried the day.[14]

Some efforts were also made in the late Middle Ages to create industries for Jewish employment. The village of Pekiin boasts that it has been inhabited uninterruptedly by Jews from ancient times to the present. However, it was the Zionist movement that effectively brought back large masses of Jews to the land and ultimately established the independent state of Israel.

The rabbinic concept of different categories of sanctity in the Holy Land has significant implications for dealing with the difficult problem of "trading territory for peace" in contemporary Israel. However, this emotion-laden issue is not our concern here.

The modern historian Gedalya Alon describes the first half of the second century C.E., when the Tannaitic sources were collected and edited, as

> especially prolific in measures enacted by the Jewish authorities to meet the social and economic circumstances of the times. The leaders of the day, especially the Patriarchs, show themselves responsive to the needs of the people, and display the courage to discard time-hallowed traditions when that was what had to be done.[15]

In the case of the *Prosbul* and the taking of interest, the new stage in economic development was permanent. In other instances, the changed conditions were of limited scope, either in time or space. Even here, the Rabbis did not hesitate to make the Halakhah responsive to felt needs by drastically modifying the law. Two instances in the area of ritual may be cited. According to biblical law, a woman was obligated to bring an offering of two doves or pigeons to the sanctuary each time she gave birth.[16] Since a family did not make the pilgrimage to Jerusalem each year, a woman who had borne several children since her last visit might require four, six, or eight birds for the offering. One year, the merchants took advantage of the heavy demand for the fowl and asked an excessive price. Rabbi Simeon ben Gamaliel thereupon ordained that a woman was required to bring only one pair of birds to the Temple even after bearing several children. As a result the price quickly reverted to normal.[17]

The second instance occurred in the Amoraic period in Babylonia, where people were accustomed to discarding their ordinary earthen pots before Passover, thus creating a high demand for new crockery after the holiday. The hardware merchants took advantage of the increased demand and raised their prices exorbitantly. The Amora Samuel threatened to accept and proclaim Rabbi Simeon's view that the *hamez* pots, having been used for leavened food and therefore unusable during Passover, did not need to be broken before Passover, but could be saved and used after the festival. The threat was sufficient to bring down the price.[18]

These two instances reveal the ethical sensitivity of the Sages and their responsiveness to contemporary conditions. They did not hesitate to set aside what they understood to be Torah law. But the situations they sought to meet affected only one locality at one specific period. Their morally courageous actions did not spring from any change in accepted ethical attitudes. Fleecing the poor for personal gain is as old as human society, and the denunciations of this evil fill the pages of the Prophets.[19]

Changing Behavior Patterns

Observers of the contemporary scene are wont to lament the erosion of ethical standards and the corruption of human behavior both in society as a whole and among its individual members. The Rabbis of the Greco-Roman era were confronted by a similar breakdown of accepted norms of behavior. In several striking cases they responded to the challenge by abrogating ancient laws laid down in the Torah that no longer served their original purpose.

One such practice was the public expiation of an unsolved murder through the breaking of the neck of a calf, accompanied by a litany of atonement pronounced by the elders of the nearest city (*eglah 'aruphah*) (Deut. 21:1–7). Another was an ordeal in which a woman suspected by her husband of infidelity (*sotah*) had to drink "bitter waters" (Num. 5:11–31). These antique biblical rites were no longer considered adequate in rabbinic times. The motivation for the change was explicitly recognized in the Mishnah, *Sotah* 9:9:

> When the murderers increased, the rite of the *eglah 'aruphah* was given up [*batlah*]. . . . When adulterers increased, the bitter waters ceased to be employed [*pasku*]. It was Rabbi Johanan ben Zakkai who abrogated the practice, for it is said: "I will not punish their daughters for playing the harlot nor their daughters-in-law for committing adultery. For the men indulge their lust with harlots and feast with prostitutes" [Hos. 4:14].

The Prophet Hosea's words are the oldest extant protest against the double standard of sexual morality, which has prevailed down to our own day. It is equally significant that Rabban Johanan ben Zakkai finds a warrant in the Prophet's words for dispensing with a Torahitic ordinance, in spite of a well-established principle to the contrary.[20]

In suspending the operation of the laws of the undiscovered murderer and the suspected wife, Rabban Johanan ben Zakkai was obviously responding to changes in the *objective* conditions prevailing in Jewish society. He might also have been moved by a *subjective*, even unconscious, attitude that the retention of these primitive rites, particularly in a more-sophisticated society, was not likely to achieve the desired results. Measuring the distance between a corpse found in the open field and the nearest settlement did not necessarily demonstrate the guilt of its inhabitants. Drinking the "bitter waters" might not be an infallible guide to the guilt or innocence of an accused woman. These speculations aside, Rabban Johanan ben Zakkai's sensitivity to social realities was equaled by his boldness in dealing with them.

Sexual Laxity in the Middle Ages

Another extraordinary instance of the ability of the Jewish leadership to face unwelcome situations and deal with them courageously occurred in medieval Spain. As Jews acculturated to the dominant groups in Spanish society, some members of the upper classes imitated their Muslim prototypes by establishing liaisons with women outside of marriage.[21] We may be certain that the rabbinical leadership of Spain did not favor these extramarital arrangements; many of them translated their opposition into stringent prohibitions and anathemas. But the liaisons did not abate, even in the face of rabbinic opposition:

> In vain did the great Maimonides try to prohibit concubinage: not only did the practice continue but most contemporary and later rabbinical authorities . . . accepted it. Acceptance, of course, did not mean approval.[22]

In the light of their inability to eliminate the practice through social and religious pressures, religious leaders sought to meet the situation by reviving the biblical concept of the *pilegesh*, "concubine" or "secondary wife," thereby conferring a measure of legitimacy. Thus, Nahmanides (1194–1270) declared that if the relationship was with an unmarried woman and was not temporary or promiscuous but, on the contrary, permanent and exclusive, it was permissible. He and other like-minded authorities applied to the practice the biblical status of concubinage, which had been practiced by the patriarchs Abraham and Jacob as well as other biblical figures. Rabbi Abraham ben David of Posquières, the great commentator and critic of Maimonides' code, *Mishneh Torah*, declared that there is no negative precept or prohibition involved in such an arrangement.[23]

Such leniency was naturally not universally accepted. Rabbi Isaac bar Sheshet Perfet (1326–1408), for instance, was far stricter. He decried the popular saying "An unmarried woman is not forbidden."[24] Yet even he saw other and greater threats to traditional standards of personal morality in his time.[25] Apparently, the practice was not prevalent in Ashkenazi Jewry, yet the great German authority Rabbi Jacob Emden adopted a very lenient view toward the practice.[26]

Liaisons of the kind we have described ended with the tragic destruction of Spanish Jewry during the expulsion from Spain in 1492 and from Portugal in 1497. Thereafter, the earlier and stricter traditional standards became all but universal again, and there no longer was a need to find even a quasi-legal basis for extramarital relations.

IX

NEW ETHICAL ATTITUDES AND INSIGHTS

As we have seen, the Sages were sensitive to the specific conditions of their age and showed concern for the weaker members of society—the poor, the women, the children, and strangers. When the necessity arose the Sages even took steps to abrogate earlier law, either temporarily or permanently. Possessing an incomparable knowledge of the text of the Torah, with all its minutiae, and armed with the canons of interpretation set down by Hillel and his successors, they were able to find a formal basis in the biblical text for their most far-reaching decisions.[1] In setting aside a particular provision in the Halakhah, they were safeguarding its basic objective, the practice of justice and mercy. With the passing of time and the accumulation of experience, undoubtedly refined by contact with other cultures and creeds, new ethical attitudes sought and found expression in the Halakhah.

Family-Law—Inheritance and Disobedience

In the following instances rabbinic leadership went beyond local or temporary ordinances and established new legal norms that were universally and permanently binding. They testify to the evolving ethical consciousness of the Sages and to their unremitting effort to interpret the Torah in the light of these ethical insights. Both cases are derived from the same biblical passage, Deuteronomy 21:15–21:

> If a man have two wives, the one beloved, and the other unloved, and both the loved and the unloved have borne him sons, and if the first-born son be hers that was unloved, then on the day that he wills his property to his son, he may not treat the son of the beloved as his first-born in preference to the son of the unloved wife, who is the first-born. He shall acknowledge the position of the first-born, the son of the unloved wife by giving him a double portion of all he owns, for he is the first-fruits of his strength; the birthright is his.

> If a man have a stubborn and rebellious son, who does not heed his father or his mother, and though they chasten him, will not obey them, his father and mother shall take hold of him, and bring him out to the elders of his city, at the gate of his place. They shall say to the elders of his city; "This, our son, is stubborn and rebellious, he does not heed us; he is a glutton, and a drunkard." Then all the men of his city shall stone him to death. Thus you will uproot the evil from your midst; and all Israel shall hear and be afraid.

Here the lawgiver sets down, side-by-side, two provisions of family law. Both paragraphs are expressed in the same casuistic style:[2] "If a man have two wives" and "If a man have a stubborn and rebellious son." Both were obviously meant to be regarded as operative law. Yet these two similarly formulated provisions sustained radically different treatment in rabbinic Judaism, neither being treated literally.

The Torah ordains that the eldest son in the family must receive as his inheritance *pi shenayim bekol ›asher yimmaze› lo*. In biblical Hebrew this idiom means "two parts [out of three]," that is, two-thirds of the entire estate. Thus, at the ascent of Elijah to heaven, when the young Elisha asks that *viyehi na› pi shenayim beruhakha ›eylai*, "a double portion of thy spirit be upon me" (II Kings 2:9), he is not demanding that he receive double the divine spirit granted to his master but, more properly, only two-thirds. The meaning is even more explicit in Zechariah 13:8; "In the whole land, says the Lord, two-thirds [*pi shenayim*] shall be cut off and perish, and one-third [*hashlishit*] shall be left alive."

The Rabbis, with their knowledge of the most minute detail of the biblical text, were adept in invoking a *gezerah shavah*, a comparison of two similar or identical usages in language, however remote from one another in location or in theme. Although the text of Deuteronomy 21:15–17 is clear, and the passages in Kings and Zechariah remove any possible question about the meaning of the idiom, the Rabbis do not invoke these parallel usages. Instead, they engage in a casuistic discussion that reveals that they were well aware of the original meaning of the phrase.

> Does the Torah mean double any other brother's share, or two parts (out of three) of all his possessions? You may argue it as follows: Since the eldest son inherits at times with one other brother, getting twice as much means he receives double any other portion even if there are five. Or follow another line of reasoning and conclude that he receives two parts of the entire estate when there are five! The verse instructs us: "In the day that he gives an inheritance to his sons." The verse has added *to his sons* (and made the sons the measure of the inheritance).[3]

Other biblical verses that are unclear are then cited[4] to support the conclusion that the firstborn receives twice the share of any other brother and not two-thirds, but the unambiguous passages in Kings and Zechariah, where the identical phrase is used, are not mentioned.

The reason is clear. The Rabbis sought to limit the prerogatives of the firstborn, so that in a family of five sons, for example, he would receive two-sixths and not two-thirds of the patrimony. In this moderate form, the Rabbis found the verse in conformity with their standards of equity, or at least not in violent conflict with them. They never doubted that the Torah, being the word of God, embodied the highest level of justice; anything else would have been unthinkable.

The fate of the following provision in the Torah dealing with "the stubborn and rebellious son" was quite different. The requirement in Deuteronomy that the son be tried before the elders of the city represents a great step forward in the protection of the young. In other cultures, the *patria potestas* was virtually unlimited, so that a father could beat or even kill his child without being answerable for the act. The Torah denies to the father the right to take the law into his own hands, and insists upon a trial of the alleged culprit. However, in Talmudic times, the literal meaning of the text, while more moderate, was no longer in harmony with the moral sensitivity of the Rabbis. Obviously, the law of God could not be inferior to the conscience of men.

The Halakhah, therefore, proceeded to apply a series of casuistic limitations to the text in Deuteronomy, making the law inoperative in practice. In one set of restrictions (out of many), if either parent was deaf, mute, or blind, crippled or a dwarf, the law did not apply. Perhaps the most remarkable statement is the *Baraita*: "Rabbi Judah says, If his father and his mother are not identical *in voice, appearance and height*, he cannot be treated as a stubborn and rebellious son."[5] The end result of the process was the declaration by the Rabbis that the biblical ordinance regarding "the stubborn and rebellious son" never was and never was destined to be put into practice. They explained that the law was placed in the Torah merely to stimulate the hermeneutical skill of the Sages and to serve as a warning to possible youthful offenders.[6]

Here we can see the Halakhic process at work. In one case, the law was modified to meet the demands of justice, as the Sages understood it. In the other, the law was completely set aside, because the Rabbis could not reconcile it with their ethical stance and their fundamental conviction that the Torah was designed to teach men to practice justice and mercy. In both instances, as in many other provisions in the Mishnah and the Talmud, the dynamic of the Halakhah is clearly evident. What remains constant from the Bible to the Talmud and beyond is the ethical goal of "righteousness and justice, loving kindness and mercy."[7]

Criminal Law

In the area of criminal law, the best-known instance of the Halakhah responding to deepening ethical insights is to be found in the Rabbis' attitude toward capital punishment. While biblical legislation prescribed the death penalty for many crimes and religious offenses, the Halakhah interposed a large variety of safeguards before such a sentence could be carried out. The most notable was *hatraʾah*, "warning," the requirement that two adult male witnesses expressly inform the sinner of the gravity of his contemplated crime and of the specific penalty that it entails. This must be followed by his explicit admission that he is aware of both the crime and the penalty.[8]

Undoubtedly, a good deal of the Halakhah in the area of criminal jurisprudence is utopian in character, deriving from the period of Roman hegemony, when the Jewish courts no longer had jurisdiction in capital cases. Nevertheless, the spirit of Jewish law is clear from the famous statement that a Sanhedrin that had convicted a criminal once in seven (or 70) years was called a "murderous Sanhedrin."[9] Equally eloquent is the appended statement of Rabbi Tarphon and Rabbi Akiba that had they been members of that court, even the single execution would not have taken place.

Here, too, viewed externally, these provisions of the Halakhah would seem to make biblical law inoperative in practice. In a deeper sense, however, the Rabbis were fulfilling the implications of the biblical world view. One of its pillars is the sanctity of human life, which goes back to the covenant with Noah. Thus the ingestion of the lifeblood of any living creature is forbidden and is linked to the prohibition of murder, which is a desecration of the divine image in which man is created.[10] The Rabbis felt that before a human agency could take a life, there must not be the slightest doubt of the culpability of the accused. Since the imposition of a death penalty by the court would be a fully conscious and completely premeditated act, its guilt would exceed that of the criminal if there were any uncertainty regarding the conscious and willful character of the crime. A death sentence would, therefore, be a violation of the principle of equity expressed by God in the doctrine of *middah keneged middah*, "measure for measure."[11]

This principle is the key to the Jewish understanding of a frequently repeated principle in biblical law, "An eye for an eye, a tooth for a tooth."[12] We have already seen that the primitive doctrine of *lex talionis*, which was all but universal in ancient society, was mitigated by a more-sophisticated and more-merciful interpretation[13] that took it to mean *mammon*, "financial compensation for the injury."[14] Only in this way

was it possible to make sure that the punishment would fit the crime
and not exceed the damage sustained.

In another striking, though less-familiar, instance from the area of
criminal law the Halakhah drastically limited the application of the
death penalty. The Book of Deuteronomy deals with the all-too-
common phenomenon of a perjured witness falsely charging the accused with guilt.

> If a man appears against another to testify maliciously and give false tes-
> timony against him . . . the magistrate shall make a thorough investiga-
> tion. If the man who testified is a false witness, if he has testified falsely
> against his fellow man, you shall do to him as he schemed to do to his
> fellow. Thus you will sweep out evil from your midst. . . . Nor must you
> show pity; life for life, eye for eye, tooth for tooth, hand for hand, foot
> for foot [19:16–21].

The Sadducees interpreted this passage to mean that if false testimony had led to the execution of an innocent party, the false witness
would suffer the same fate. The Pharisees, followed by the Tannaim, restricted the provisions of the law to one rare situation. They applied it
only to the case where two witnesses (not one) had charged the accused
with a crime and then two other witnesses accused the original ones
of lying, by declaring: "You were with us at that time at another place
[so that your testimony is false]."[15] If the secondary witnesses were then
discovered to be false, the Rabbis ruled, *they* fell under the provisions
of the biblical law.

This was not all. The death penalty was to be meted out to the lying
witnesses only if the execution of the original group of innocent witnesses had *not* been carried out. If the primary witnesses had already
been executed, the lying secondary witnesses would not be killed. This
latter ruling, which ran counter to the Sadducean practice, was derived
by the Rabbis from the biblical phrase, "You shall do to him as he had
plotted to do to his neighbor," which they interpreted "as he had
schemed to do, not as he had actually *done*."[16] Although false testimony
in civil lawsuits and in criminal proceedings was apparently rife in ancient times, the Halakhah drastically limited the practice of judicial execution by imposing these two limitations.

The intent and the content of the Halakhah here should be clearly understood. We have discussed above the establishment by the Halakhah
of the general principle of *hatraʾah*, "warning," as a prerequisite for conviction in capital cases. In these instances, the goal of the Halakhah may
be construed as the desire to fulfil the inner intent of the Torah by proving the wilful character of the crime beyond the shadow of a doubt. In
the case of the biblical provision regarding a perjured witness, the
Halakhah goes beyond this purpose and radically restricts its applica-

tion to a set of circumstances so rare and complicated as to be virtually nonexistent. It is interpretation carried so far as to become legislation, to all intents and purposes.[17]

As has already been noted, the creative vigor of the Halakhah beat most powerfully in the Mishnah and the Gemara, but became weaker in the post-Talmudic period. Like all generalizations, even true ones, the exceptions are important and must not be overlooked.[18]

The Prohibition of Polygamy

One of the most notable examples of the dynamism of the Halakhah in post-Talmudic times is a famous *taqqanah*, "ordinance," prohibiting polygamy. It was adopted by Rabbi Gershom ("the Light of the Exile") and his synod about 1000 c.e. Although this ordinance represented a radical departure from both biblical prototypes and Talmudic law, it did not introduce a totally new custom. Monogamy had been the prevailing practice since the inception of the Jewish people, for self-evident reasons. The biological ratio of the sexes, as well as economic considerations, made polygamy virtually impossible for anyone except the royal dynasty and the aristocracy.[19] The Adam and Eve narrative in Genesis obviously pictures a monogamous family, as do Psalm 128 and other biblical sources. No instance of polygamy is recorded among the 3,000 Sages named in the Talmud. Nevertheless, when the *taqqanah* of Rabbi Gershom forbidding polygamy was adopted, it was valid only for 1,000 years and was applicable only to Jews living in Christian lands.[20] In Islamic lands, polygamy remained both lawful and operative until very recently.[21]

What explains the divergence? It would be fatuous to deny the impact of the Christian environment on Rabbi Gershom and his colleagues. They found it intolerable for Jews to maintain an attitude toward marriage—in theory, if not in practice—that set women on a lower social and ethical plane than did their monogamous Christian neighbors.[22] For polygamy is obviously based on the inferiority of women, with the male being dominant and free to have more than one spouse, but not the female.

Today, of course, the original limitations of this *taqqanah* with regard to time and country have fallen away, and monogamy is universally observed in Jewry. But the impact of cultural influences from without is clear both in the *taqqanah* and in the formal limits on its operation.

These instances, drawn from the diverse areas of inheritance, family law, and criminal law, are significant in revealing the techniques by which the Halakhah grew. Although today many of the specific provisions are merely of historical interest, they remain significant for the light they shed on the techniques the Halakhah adopted to meet new challenges, both external and internal. Most important of all is the spirit revealed in Jewish law—its insight into human nature and its concern for human well-being, qualities that each generation must exhibit in relation to its own time and place.

Since the loss of self-government by the Jewish community during almost 2,000 years of exile, considerable sections of the Halakhah have lost their practical importance and are studied only as a form of religious and intellectual activity, a not unimportant function. Even the state of Israel has not made the civil and criminal laws of rabbinic Judaism the basis of its jurisprudence, though the ancient and medieval sources are consulted for background and guidance.

The one major area in Jewish law that continued to function through the Middle Ages and into the modern period are those relating to family law and the status of women. It is precisely here that our times are proving a battleground between contending forces, in which the virtues of the Halakhah at its best are most insistently called for.

X

WOMEN'S STATUS IN MARRIAGE AND DIVORCE

The Challenge of the Feminist Revolution

Revolutions are never neat and rarely bloodless. Even when they are successful they never completely cure the ills they came to remedy, and they frequently create new problems. Future historians may well decide that the greatest revolution of modern times was not the disappearance of the old colonial empires, or the Communist challenge to the democratic order, or the Nazi onslaught on civilization, or even the advent of the technological age, but the radical transformation in the status of women.

The movement is by no means clear and united in its objectives, as can be seen from the variety of names it bears, each highlighting one or another aspect of its goals: "feminism," "women's rights," "women's liberation," "the equality of women," "the sexual revolution," "the new morality." This revolution has spread in varying degrees to every continent and culture, including the Soviet bloc and the "Third World."

That the women's revolution has spawned a host of new problems in human relations goes without saying. But it is equally clear that it is irreversible. The task facing our age is not to reenact the role of King Canute and command the tide to roll back, but to deal with the revolution wisely and sympathetically, utilizing all its positive achievements, attempting to overcome or correct its errors, and trying to solve the new problems that have come in its wake. In a word, women's liberation must be an instrument for the enhancement of human life. That Judaism must be involved in this process has become evident very quickly.

As the women's movement gained momentum, its partisans found themselves confronted by ideas and patterns inherited from the past. It was not long before the Jewish tradition was singled out as a prime obstacle to progress.[1] One writer, bearing the unimpeachable authority of best-sellerdom, informed her readers that Judaism forbids sexual intercourse except for the purpose of producing male children. Another found in a delicate lyric in The Song of Songs, which, incidentally, she amputated in the middle of the passage, "the origin of the disgraceful tradition of the sexual abuse of children."[2]

Most of the challenges hurled at the Jewish tradition were more restrained and more significant. By and large the critics pointed to the major liabilities under which women labor in Jewish law, citing evidence from the Bible, the Talmud, and later rabbinic sources. The defense was not slow in coming to the rescue. When it could not ignore the evidence, it sought to explain it away or reinterpret it in symbolic terms or in some other fashion. Above all, the defenders of tradition called attention to the fact that women had lived under the aegis of the Halakhah tolerably well for centuries, and that even today there were many women who are happily governed by its ordinances. Actually, both the opponents and the proponents of tradition were right, except that each group looked at only part of the evidence.

Woman's Position in the Biblical Era

The Bible makes it clear that women in ancient Israel were regarded as persons and not as mere chattel. Beginning with Mother Eve, whose fateful act determined the destiny of all her children, and the wives of the Patriarchs, whose will prevailed over that of their husbands, the Bible offers an unforgettable portrait gallery of strong-willed women who knew what they wanted and got it. Three Prophets—Miriam, Deborah, and Hulda—played decisive roles at critical hours in their people's history. As for the mass of mothers who remained anonymous, the Torah exhorted that they be honored on a par with their husbands. This injunction was derived by the Rabbis from the Decalogue "Honor your father and your mother" (Exod. 20:12; Deut. 5:16) and the Holiness Code, "Each one of you shall revere his mother and his father" (Lev. 19:3). The reversal in the order suggested to the Rabbis that both parents are to be honored equally.[3]

Psalm 128 offers a beautiful portrait of an ancient Jewish family:

> Blessed is every one who fears the Lord,
> who walks in his ways;
> You shall be happy,
> and it shall be well with you.
> Your wife will be like a fruitful vine
> within your house;
> Your children will be like olive shoots
> around your table.
> Lo, thus shall the man be blessed

who fears the Lord.
The Lord bless you from Zion:
May you live to see your children's children;
Peace be upon Israel!

Most famous of all is the song of praise addressed to "the Woman of Valor" in Proverbs 31:10–31. The opening phrase is rendered more prosaically, but more accurately, in various modern versions of the Bible as "a good wife," "a capable wife," and "a worthy wife."[4] She is praised by her husband and children for her ability, industry, and enterprise; her charity, insight, and piety—a formidable collection of virtues indeed!

> What a rare find is a capable wife!
> Her worth is far beyond that of rubies. . . .
> Her husband safely trusts in her
> And he has no lack of gain.
> She does him good and not harm
> all the days of her life. . . .
> She rises while it is yet night
> and gives food to her household
> and the allotted fare for her maidservants:
> She sets her mind to consider a field and she buys it:
> With her own earnings she plants a vineyard. . . .
> She stretches out her hand to the poor;
> She reaches out her hands to the needy. . . .
> She opens her mouth with wisdom
> And the teaching of kindness is on her tongue. . . .
> Charm is deceptive, and beauty is fleeting,
> But a woman who fears the Lord is worthy of praise.
>
> [Prov. 31:10, 11, 12, 15, 16, 20, 26, 30][5]

This picture of the wife's happy estate has its counterpart in the even more blessed leisure enjoyed by her husband:

> Her husband is known in the gates,
> When he sits among the elders of the land.
>
> [Prov. 31:23]

In this panegyric, beauty is decried and love is not mentioned. The omission is not due to any indifference in Israel to beauty or to love; the poet has in mind a family with grown children (v. 28), with a wife weighed down by responsibilities and with little time or taste for the passions of youth. This lack of praise for love and beauty in Proverbs is magnificently atoned for in the Song of Songs; here the ecstasy and passionate love of man and woman are those of equals.

To be sure, women were physically weaker than men and legally subordinate to them, but they were far from helpless. As the Talmud sagely observes, "A woman carries her weapons in her own person."[6] As for the physical abuse of women, centuries later the medieval work *Sepher Hasidim* declared as a matter of fact, "We Jews do not beat our wives, as do the gentiles."

To evaluate the status of Jewish women fairly, it should be added that there was no exploitation of women in Jewish society. There was no institution like that of the Greek Hetaerai, a special class of women, cultivated in the arts, set aside to serve the sexual and cultural needs of the patricians, who kept their wives at home for household duties and child-bearing. Classical Judaism, like every other ancient culture, was male-dominated. It cannot be denied that women were isolated from the centers of power and authority and were consigned to a position of social, cultural, and economic inferiority. But in both ancient and medieval times, Jewish women enjoyed a position of relative dignity and security within a male-centered society. Their life can be fairly described as a state of benevolent subordination.

Masculine preference was much more than a grammatical usage. It emerged in countless forms, both obvious and subtle. There are such devastating judgments as the Talmudic statement, *nashim da‹atan kallah ‹aleihen* (B. *Shabbat*; B. *Kiddushin* 80b), which is variously understood and cited to mean, "Women are light-headed, frivolous, prone to temptation, intellectually vacuous." On the other hand, women are praised for being merciful (B. *Megillah* 14b) and more sensitive to spiritual concerns, so that Moses at Sinai addresses the women before the men (B. *Mekhilta* on Exod. 19:3).

Various subtle indications in both biblical and rabbinic sources testify to the fact that women's inferior status was taken for granted as "natural." Before the revelation at Sinai, the Bible tells us, "He said to the people, 'Be ready the the third day, do not go near a woman'" (Exod. 12:15). The distinction between "the people" and "a woman" speaks for itself.

The Talmudic Sages, concerned with safeguarding purity of thought, declare, "A woman's hair and her voice are sources of sexual temptation."[7] Such an attitude has its analogs in other cultures and is understandable for societies in which a woman was sequestered and had no contact with males outside her immediate family. On the other hand, there is no corresponding statement, "A man's hair and voice are sexually seductive (to a woman)." But if the first statement is true, so is the second. The various restrictions designed to safeguard *zeni‹yut* "modesty," relate in overwhelming measure to female behavior, yet the virtue should be equally applicable to males. These instances could easily be multiplied. Apologetics designed to explain, or explain away, the male-centered character of biblical and rabbinic law are no service to the truth or the tradition.

On the other hand, attacking the classical tradition on the score of its being male-centered is a flagrant anachronism; it means demanding of an ancient society the egalitarian ideals that are barely emerging in the twentieth century. The fair evaluation of any phenomenon in history requires not a dot but a line on a graph; we must know not only its position but also its direction. It is not strange that women began with many disabilities. What is remarkable is the ongoing effort in Judaism to enlarge their rights and opportunities and to limit the powers and prerogatives of men, a pattern that may be traced from the biblical and rabbinic periods to the present.

The earliest biblical law indicates the existence of *patria potestas*, "the father's unlimited power." A girl could be sold into bond service or marriage by her father solely at his will (Exod. 21:7). If she made a vow, it could be annulled by her father before she was married and by her husband afterward (Num. 30:2–17).

The rape of an unmarried girl was regarded as damage to her father's property, and the father was compensated by the offender, who was compelled to marry her (Deut. 22:29). A seduction was also considered an offense against his property, for which the father had to be compensated; unless the father refused, the seducer was compelled to marry the daughter (Exod. 22:15–16). In either case, the girl's wishes played no part in the decision.

The feeling that women are inferior to men in intelligence or responsibility lay at the root of the Talmudic law that women are ineligible as witnesses in court.[8] Based on a dubious interpretation of the biblical text, even by their own canons, as Maimonides recognizes, the Talmudic Rabbis declared women incompetent to testify in lawsuits except in a few, very special cases. By that token they could not serve as judges, the biblical example of Deborah notwithstanding. They were thus consigned to a legal position on a level with that of minors, deaf-mutes, and the mentally incompetent (M. *Rosh Hashanah* 1:8). This ruling has important consequences today, often being cited in connection with the issue of women as rabbis.

Originally, inheritance was the prerogative of sons. After the protests by the five daughters of Zelophehad, who were perhaps the first feminists in history, the law was modified to allow daughters to inherit, but only in the absence of male issue (Num. 27:1–11, 36:1–13).

In the area of divorce, women labored under a major disability. Deuteronomy 24:1–3 was interpreted by the Rabbis to mean that the husband possesses the sole power to initiate a divorce, which his wife is then compelled to accept. They render it, "When a man takes a wife and marries her, if she then finds no favor in his eyes, because he has found some indecency in her, he shall write her a bill of divorce and shall put it in her hand, and he shall send her out of his house."[9]

The most fundamental mark of women's inferiority was polygamy, which was lawful throughout the biblical and Talmudic periods and beyond. It was practiced only rarely, however, primarily by the royal house and the upper echelons of society. The ideal image of the Jewish family was monogamy.

The Levirate

Perhaps the most striking evidence of the inferiority of women throughout primitive and ancient society is the institution of the levirate (from the Latin *levir*, "brother-in-law"), the obligation of a man to marry the childless widow of a close male relative.[10] On the one hand, the power of the levirate at its inception is limitless. On the other, the later history of the institution in Israel illustrates the development of the Halakhah in its efforts to protect women—and men as well—from enforced marriage.

The practice of the levirate virtually girds the globe, having been found among the Indians of North and South America; in Indonesia, Australia, and the Middle East; and in all parts of Africa. In most religions, the death of a man who had no offspring was regarded as the direst of calamities. In addition, there was a desire to preserve for the family the property rights of the deceased, which included those of his widow. Hence, the practice arose that when a man died without issue, his wife was taken in marriage by his brother or another close relative, so that the first child born of the new union would carry the name of the deceased and thus perpetuate his memory. The combined power of the religious and economic motives was enormous; hence the levirate rite could not be set aside by the dead man's male relation or by his widow, whether because of personal feelings between the principals or for other reasons.

It is rare for institutions or practices to exhibit a virtually unilinear process of development; the Hebrew *yibbum*, "levirate," is therefore particularly interesting because we can trace the process of change."[11] The first instance of *yibbum* in the Bible occurs in Genesis 38, where Tamar is married successively to two of Judah's sons, Er and Onan, both of whom died without issue. Understandably, Judah holds off giving his third son, Shelah, in marriage to a woman who had already lost two husbands. Tamar concludes that Judah has no intention of fulfilling the duty of the levirate. She disguises herself as a harlot, entices Judah to have relations with her, and becomes pregnant. When she is about to be executed for immorality, Tamar reveals to Judah that he is the father of her twin sons, and he declares, "She is more righteous than I, for I did not give her to my son Shelah," and her life is spared.

In this period, the power of the levirate is so pervasive that even the extreme measure adopted by Tamar is considered justified. Moreover, while the obligation to marry the widow falls most naturally on a brother, who is more likely to be close to her own age, in special cases, as here, the dead man's father is not ineligible. Thus there is no hint of incest in the relationship of Judah and Tamar or of illegitimacy in the status of the children, Perez and Zerah. On the contrary, Perez is the honored ancestor of King David (Ruth 9:18–22).

The next stage in the levirate is set forth in the legislation in Deuteronomy:

> If brothers dwell together, and one of them dies, and has no son, the wife of the dead man shall not be married outside the family to a stranger; her husband's brother shall go in to her, and take her as his wife, and perform the duty of a husband's brother to her. And the first son whom she bears shall succeed to the name of his brother who is dead that his name may not be blotted out of Israel.
>
> But if the man does not wish to take his brother's wife, then his brother's wife shall go up to the gate to the elders, and say, "My husband's brother refuses to perpetuate his brother's name in Israel; he will not perform the duty of a husband's brother to me." Then the elders of his city shall call him and speak to him; and if he persists, saying, "I do not wish to take her," then his brother's wife shall go up to him in the presence of the elders and pull his sandal off his foot and spit in his face, and make this declaration: This shall be done to the man who will not build up his brother's house and his house shall be called in Israel, "the house of the unsandaled one" [25:5–10].

The rite has here been considerably constricted. It is now limited to "brothers dwelling together," with no indication that the obligation also falls upon more-distant relatives. Moreover, even for the brothers, *yibbum* is no longer obligatory, though it is clearly the preferred procedure. A brother may avoid the duty of marrying his brother's widow if he is willing to be exposed to public indignity and have his family carry some stigma, the severity of which we cannot judge.[12]

For rabbinic Judaism *yibbum* proved increasingly problematic. In the first instance, a man's cohabitation with his brother's wife seemed to be categorically forbidden by a passage in Leviticus, "You shall not uncover the nakedness of your brother's wife; she is your brother's nakedness" (18:16). The Rabbis met this contradiction by declaring that the prohibition in Leviticus and the injunction in Deuteronomy were both pronounced simultaneously (on Sinai).[13] Both were equally binding, the prohibition in Leviticus referring to the lifetime of the brother, the levirate obligation in Deuteronomy being operative after his death.[14]

Moreover, the Rabbis became increasingly aware of the role of personal desire and the play of human likes and dislikes affecting both the brother-in-law and the widow. One classic statement declares:

> *Yibbum* took precedence over *haliẓah* [casting off the sandals, a symbolic divorce of the widow] in earlier times, when people were concerned with fulfilling the divine commandment. But now that people are not concerned with fulfilling the divine commandment, *haliẓah* takes precedence over *yibbum*.[15]

Another statement, also Tannaitic, reads:

> Abba Saul says: "He who marries his sister-in-law for the sake of her beauty or because of desire, or any other ulterior motive [the *Tosefta* reads, "for the sake of her property"] is guilty of incest, and I am inclined to regard the offspring as illegitimate." The Sages say: "The biblical statement 'her brother-in-law shall come in to her' means that *yibbum* takes place no matter what the circumstances or the motives."[16]

Measures taken by the Rabbis to restrict the levirate were motivated by their concern for the moral stance of the brother-in-law rather than for the widow's wishes. In a male-centered society this is entirely to be expected. Nevertheless the limitation and ultimately the virtual elimination of *yibbum* had the effect of freeing the woman (as well as the man) from the misery of an unwanted marriage.

All the resources of rabbinic hermeneutics were mobilized to limit and, where possible, prevent the consummation of the levirate. On the basis of the phrase "when brothers dwell together" (Deut. 25:5), the Talmud excludes half-brothers on the mother's side as well as a younger brother born subsequent to the death of the husband. Even more revelatory of the rabbinic attitude is the broad interpretation given the biblical phrase *ubhen ʾein lo* (Deut. 25:8). Quite at variance with the general practice in rabbinic exegesis, *ben* is construed broadly to mean "child" and not merely "son," and the phrase is understood as "if he left no offspring." Hence, if the dead man has a daughter or a grandchild, or even an illegitimate child, the brother-in-law is forbidden to marry the widow.[17]

Undoubtedly, the rarity of polygamy, even in Talmudic times, also militated strongly against the practice of *yibbum*, since most adult men were married. When in the tenth century, the *taqqanah* of Rabbi Gershom ben Judah of Mainz and his synod forbade polygamy for European Jewry, *haliẓah* became the only permissible procedure.[18] *Yibbum* continued to be practiced only in Muslim countries until the liquidation of all Jewish communities in the Arab world and their ingathering in the state of Israel in our day.

Polygamy is no longer a live option in Judaism; monogamy is now universal. The religious and economic motives for *yibbum* are not operative, and the rights and predilections of the individual men and women involved are recognized. The levirate is a striking illustration of an institution that can be traced from its earliest stage, when it was compulsory, to the present, when it is forbidden.

The Extension of Women's Rights

In other areas, the dual process of extending the rights of women, on the one hand, and limiting the powers of men, on the other, is less clear-cut and consistent, but the general trend is unmistakable. As we have noted above, the right conferred by the Bible on the father to marry off his daughter at will was considerably restricted by the rabbinic interpretation of the word *naʿarah*, taken to refer to a girl between the ages of twelve and twelve and a half. For the father to marry off his daughter before that age was morally reprehensible; above the age limit, he was legally forbidden to do so (B. *Kiddushin* 4a).

With regard to the dissolution of marriage, various significant steps were taken. In ancient and medieval society, a divorced woman had no alternative but to go back to her father's house, if he was still alive, or to the home of her brother and sister-in-law, where an uncertain reception might await her. A gainful occupation or "living alone" was, of course, not dreamt of.

Obviously, the woman needed protection. Tradition ascribes to Rabbi Simeon ben Shetah the provision that while the husband could utilize the wife's marriage gift for his business, it had to be available to her in cash if the marriage was dissolved by death or divorce (P. *Ketubbot* 8:11; 32c). Henceforth, the *ketubbah*, "marriage agreement," was obligatory in all Jewish marriages.[19] Since cash was rare in earlier periods, this requirement would serve to prevent a divorce out of pique or momentary anger, "so that it would not be easy for him to divorce her."

While the power to issue a divorce remained in the hands of the husband, the Mishnah granted women a substantial measure of initiative. On a variety of grounds, a woman might sue for a divorce before the rabbinic court (M. *Ketubbot* 5:6; 7:2–9). A far-reaching principle was established, *kofin ʾoto ʿad sheyomar rozeh ʾani*, "the court pressures him until he says, 'I am willing'" (B. *Yebamot* 106a; B. *Kiddushin* 50a; B. *Baba Batra* 48a). The Rabbis justified this substantial limitation on the husband's powers by a subtle psychological argument. They were convinced that the husband's consent under duress was genuine, because fundamentally all people are decent and law-abiding, so that his deepest wish, even though temporarily submerged, is to obey the teaching of the Sages!

In addition, the writing of a *get*, "bill of divorce," was surrounded by many technical requirements, and the delivery of the document had to follow strict rules—all this was designed to discourage quick divorce.

A major step in curtailing the husband's powers and extending the wife's rights was taken by Rabbi Gershom of Mainz and his synod in the tenth century. In addition to the prohibition of polygamy, they adopted a *taqqanah* making it mandatory to obtain the wife's consent before a divorce issued by the husband became valid (*Shulḥan Arukh, Eben Haᶜezev*, 119:6, 7, Rama). In point of fact, however, ways were often found to circumvent the *taqqanah*, sometimes for justifiable reasons, at others for more unsavory motives. In any event, though the effectiveness of the ordinance has remained less than complete, its intent is clear.

The most important factor protecting women against arbitrary divorce by their husbands was extralegal. It lay in the spiritual climate of the Jewish community. From the days of the Prophet Malachi (fifth century B.C.E.), who had denounced the practice (Mal. 2:16), divorce was considered a disgrace and a calamity for all concerned and was frowned upon by the community except under dire necessity.

The fact remains, however, that the legal disabilities of women with regard to the marital state, and particularly in the area of divorce, have always been a source of misery, and the situation has been immeasurably aggravated in modern times.

Our survey of the status of women has thus far been concerned with the provisions of normative law, based on the biblical legislation as interpreted and amplified by the Rabbis of the Talmud and embodied in legal decisions by their successors in the *Responsa* and the Codes. However, this body of codified law does not represent the totality of the Jewish legal tradition. Evidence is accumulating, both for the biblical and even more for the postbiblical periods, that a secondary body of legal precedent has functioned. By and large, the provisions of this customary law has tended to mitigate the stringencies in the codified law with regard to the rights of women. Only a few instances have survived in our sources; many more have undoubtedly been forgotten.

The first example concerns remarriage after adultery. Adultery is regarded as a major infraction of the moral law, being forbidden in the Decalogue. While the Code of Hammurabi permits a husband who finds his wife *in flagrante delicto* to accept compensation from the offending paramour and to take her back (sec. 129), biblical law has no such provision. In Deuteronomy the act is punishable by death of the partners (22:23–24). Such a reconciliation is expressly forbidden in rabbinic law: In the language of the Talmud, "Just as she is forbidden to her lover, so she is forever forbidden to her husband" (M. *Sotah* 5:1).[20]

The opposite approach is presented in the Book of Hosea. At the core of the Prophet's activity (eighth century B.C.E.) was the tragedy of discovering that his wife had been committing adultery with many lovers.[21] His first reaction was one of anger, and he drove her from his home. But later his love triumphed over his indignation, and after a period of separation, a reconciliation took place and she came back to his home. In this personal experience, Hosea saw a paradigm of God's relationship to his wayward people—Israel too had gone whoring after strange gods, arousing the wrath of its God, but through repentance, Israel could reestablish her relationship of loyalty and love with its maker.

Scholars have propounded various views of the event described in the first three chapters of Hosea.[22] I believe that this deeply moving, enigmatic text is best explained by the assumption that Hosea was originally a Prophet who underwent the soul-shattering experience of betrayal by his wife. From his own reactions, which went from heartbreak to wrath to forgiveness, he derived an insight into the divine-human relationship. But even if the episode is understood as a vision, an allegory, or a dream, as some scholars believe, one conclusion is inescapable—the reclamation of a sinful wife and her restoration to her husband is praiseworthy, or at least legitimate. Whether the procedure recounted in Hosea is laxer or more humane than that of the codified law depends on one's point of view, but clearly it is different.

Another instance is to be found in the laws of inheritance. In biblical and postbiblical law, as we have seen, a woman could not inherit her father's estate unless there were no sons in the family. But the Book of Job explicitly indicates that Job gave his daughters an inheritance "along with his sons" (42:25).

The codified Halakhah has no provision for a widow to inherit her husband's property. In the absence of children, his brothers and their progeny take precedence over her. However, customary law affords many instances, deriving from different periods and societies, of widows who succeeded to their husbands' possessions. In the maneuvers accompanying the transaction described in the Book of Ruth, Boaz announces before the elders of the city, "Naomi, now returned from the country of Moab, is selling the parcel of land that belonged to our kinsman Elimelech" (4:3), and, a little later, "You are witnesses today that I have acquired from Naomi all that belonged to Elimelech and all that belonged to Mahlon and Chilion" (4:9). There are major difficulties and various views about her selling land belonging to her dead husband and their sons,[23] but clearly Naomi is the legally recognized heir. In the documents from the Jewish military colony at Elephantine in southern Egypt during the fifth century B.C.E. we read of widows inheriting the property of their husbands. In the Apocryphal Book of Judith we are informed that the beautiful and pious heroine, whose husband, Manasses, had died suddenly, had been left "gold and silver, male and female slaves, livestock and land, and she lived on her estate" (8:11). That she had complete title to this property is clear from provisions she made at the end of her life: "Before her death she divided her property among all those who were most closely related to her husband, Manasses, and among her own nearest relations" (16:24).

The male prerogative in the areas of marriage and divorce is unlimited in the biblical legislation. The power to give a child in marriage is reserved to the father, as both biblical narrative and law indicate. In the Apocryphal Book of Tobit, when Raguel arranges for the marriage of his daughter Sarah to Tobias, he tells her mother to "bring the book and write an instrument of cohabitation" (7:14). This was probably an early form of the traditional *ketubbah*, other examples of which have been found at Elephantine in Egypt and elsewhere.[24]

The most radical extension of women's rights in customary law, and incidentally the best attested in our sources, is the power of the wife to initiate a divorce, which has not yet become normative in traditional Judaism.

The ʿAgunah—Problem and Tragedy

The most agonizing moral challenge confronting Jewish law in modern times is the plight of the ʿagunah, "the chained wife," which has troubled Jewish consciences through the centuries. No one who has read Chaim Grade's powerful novel, *The Agunah*, will soon forget its tragic heroine, who can never remarry because her husband has left her and refuses to give her a *get*.[25] Actually, the novel describes only one of several categories of ʿagunah. The pathetic situation of these women stems from the rabbinic interpretation of Deuteronomy 24:1ff., which places the initiative for the issuance of a *get* solely in the hands of the husband. The tragedy was immeasurably compounded in modern times by the erosion of authority in the Jewish community, so that today it is powerless to compel the husband to obey.

Ancient and medieval rabbis were highly sensitive to the woman's undeserved suffering and sought every conceivable method of freeing the ʿagunah from her chains.[26] The Talmud went so far as to.rule that if the woman herself had evidence that her husband had died, her unsubstantiated testimony would be acceptable, and she would be declared a widow, free to remarry.[27] This radical decision set aside three fundamental principles in the Halakhah: the rabbinic rule that a woman is ineligible to testify as a witness (see below, p. 182); the biblical law that two witnesses are required to establish valid evidence (Deut. 19:15); and the rabbinic principle ꜣadam karobh ꜣetzel ʿatzmo, "every person is close [i.e., partial] to himself," and therefore his testimony on a case in which he is involved is invalid.[28] Other rulings designed to help the woman were adopted, and rabbis in medieval and modern times have been persistent in searching for a missing husband and persuading him to issue a Jewish divorce.

Customary law, as practiced over a period of a thousand years in Egypt and Palestine, utilized far-reaching procedures to compensate for a woman's legal inability to dissolve a marriage. These provisions made it possible for the woman to demand and receive a divorce when she found her marriage intolerable. In fact, surviving documents indicate that in some cases it was sufficient for her to come to the court and declare, *lo> >erḥemeh*, "I do not love him," for the judges to compel the husband to issue a divorce.

The problem of the ʿagunah was relatively soluble as long as Jewish tradition retained its authority and the Jewish community had the power to enforce its decisions. This condition prevailed everywhere during the Middle Ages and, until our own century, in eastern Europe. During this period, nonlegal procedures were available to secure the husband's compliance, such as public opinion and social ostracism. In addition, the court could impose a *ḥerem*, "excommunication," which meant total isolation for the offender. Generally, the threat sufficed to bring the husband into line. Nevertheless, the *Responsa*, or legal decisions of the great rabbinic authorities of the Middle Ages, contain many cases of unfortunate women chained to a recalcitrant or nonexistent spouse.

The breakdown of the Babylonian center about the year 1000 C.E. and its replacement by a multiplicity of independent communities in North Africa, Spain, France, Germany, Italy, and eastern Europe led to a general fragmentation of authority. With many areas of local jurisdiction, the power of individual rabbinic leaders was now reduced. The frequent uprooting of Jewish communities, the mass migrations, and the transplantations of individuals, as well as deaths caused by natural disaster, famine, or massacre substantially increased the number of ʿagunot. In spite of all ameliorative efforts, the lot of the ʿagunah remained an unhappy one.

Beginning with the second half of the eighteenth century, the Enlightenment and the Emancipation wreaked havoc with the traditional pattern of Jewish life. The attainment by Jews of political citizenship, civic equality, and economic opportunity was directly and explicitly linked to the surrender of the authority of Jewish traditional law and to the loss of legal status by the Jewish community, which now became a voluntary association with no coercive power.

In some quarters today both the Emancipation and the Enlightenment are decried as totally evil, though one sees little evidence of a wholesale stampede to turn in citizenship papers and return to the ghetto (with the possible exceptions of some Hasidic groups that had never left it). Both the Emancipation and the Enlightenment brought substantial benefits to Jews and Judaism, but they exacted a heavy price in the form of assimilation and alienation, first in western and central Europe and now in the Western Hemisphere as well. With the rapid growth of secularism, civil marriage and divorce were established in nearly all Western countries.

Three principal categories of ʿagunah have emerged in modern times and are on the increase (and women loyal to the Jewish tradition are the chief victims):

1. A man divorces his wife in the civil courts and may even remarry, but refuses to give his wife a *get* because of malice or greed. All too often the husband tries to extort money from his wife in exchange for the *get*.

2. A man disappears without leaving a trace, so that he is not available to issue the divorce demanded by the Halakhah. During the early decades of the twentieth century, when Jewish emigration to the United States from eastern Europe reached its height, Yiddish newspapers published a regular feature, "The Gallery of Missing Husbands," asking readers to help locate errant spouses. Together with the photographs, there would appear pathetic pleas for help from deserted wives. Today this category of missing husband is more prevalent than ever. Since thousands of Americans drop out of sight every year, it is a safe assumption that there are Jewish married men among them.

3. A man is lost in military action or dies in a widespread disaster, and his body is not found or is not identifiable. When there is no hard evidence that the soldier is dead, the wife becomes an ʿagunah, since the Halakhah has no such category as "declared or legally" dead.

During the Russo-Japanese War of 1905 some great Russian rabbis visited the troops before they left for the front and persuaded the Jewish soldiers to issue a *get ʿal tnai*, "conditional divorce," so as to free their wives from the status of ʿagunah, should they fail to return. But this temporary procedure, however helpful in individual cases, did not meet the growing problem.

Beyond these three categories, there are the following less-common instances of ʿagunah:

4. Not strictly a case of "desertion" but similar to it is the rarer predicament of a childless widow who, according to the Halakhah, requires *ḥalizah* from her husband's brother before she can remarry. This situation has also served as an occasion for extortion.

5. A particularly heart-rending situation is that of a woman whose husband has gone insane. Since he is legally incompetent, he cannot issue a divorce, and she remains "chained" to him as long as they both

live. However, when a woman becomes insane, her husband is not left without remedy under the Halakhah. Since polygamy is prohibited, not by the Bible or the Talmud but by the enactment of Rabbi Gershom and his synod in the early Middle Ages, a special procedure called *heter meʾah rabbanim*, "the permission of one hundred rabbis," is available to the husband. The signatures of 100 rabbis are solicited, generally through the mail, to set aside the prohibition of polygamy in his case. With the understanding that he will support his insane wife throughout her lifetime, he is granted permission to remarry. While one may be grateful that a measure of relief in this domestic tragedy is available for the husband, the inequality and the inequity of the sexes under the Halakhah still exists.

The chained wife faces an agonizing dilemma. If she remains obedient to Jewish law, she is doomed to a life without marriage. If she remarries, she is committing adultery in the eyes of Jewish law, and her children carry the taint of illegitimacy. Although the Orthodox rabbinate has been aware of the problem and is deeply sympathetic, it has done little to improve the situation. A few individual scholars, including some Sephardic authorities, proposed solutions that were compatible with Jewish law, but they were voices crying in the wilderness. The problem of the ʿagunah is especially agonizing in the state of Israel, where secular divorce does not exist, and the rabbinate is not known for its flexibility and compassion.[29]

Since Reform Judaism has abandoned the authority of Jewish law, the ʿagunah is no longer a problem for it. Only the Conservative rabbinate has sought to translate its concern into action, through a variety of approaches. In 1930, after many years of study, Rabbi Louis M. Epstein of Boston presented a plan for dealing with the problem. Leading rabbinic scholars agreed that it was in total conformity with the Halakhah. Epstein proposed that before his marriage, the groom name specific individuals as his agents for the issuance of a *get* (*minnui shelihut*), if, at some future date a civil divorce were to be issued; or the husband disappeared; or he was lost in an accident or in military action with no witnesses; or he wished to remarry.

The (Conservative) Rabbinical Assembly adopted the Epstein plan in 1935 and used it many times when soldiers were going into action, but it proved cumbersome and unwieldy in practice. Though Halakhically sound, it was subjected to a barrage of misrepresentation and finally fell into disuse. Ironically, virtually the same procedure was adopted by the Orthodox Rabbinical Council.

A more-comprehensive approach to the problem was taken in 1953, when the Rabbinical Assembly's Committee on Law adopted the "Lieberman Ketubbah."[30] The text was the work of one of the most eminent modern rabbinic scholars, Saul Lieberman. He was universally recognized as a Gaon, a luminary of the Torah whose credentials in piety and learning could not be challenged.

Lieberman added a clause to the traditional marriage contract in which the husband and wife agreed that in their life together they would be governed by Jewish law. Thus if the marriage was subsequently dissolved and the husband refused to issue a *get*, the wife could request that the civil courts order his compliance with the terms of the contract, which called for obedience to Jewish law, including the issuance of a *get*.

The theory underlying the Lieberman *ketubbah* is that the courts would not be intervening in a religious issue. They would merely be called on to require "specific performance," as promised in the original marriage agreement. In the one case that has come to trial, the woman's suit was supported by several organizations, including Orthodox as well as Conservative legal groups. By a vote of 4–3, the New York Court upheld the wife's right to bring suit. A majority of the justices declared that church-state relations were not involved; what was at issue was the husband's failure to perform an act that had been stipulated at the time of the marriage. Accordingly, the court returned the case for retrial in the lower court.

Unquestionably, this decision is a gratifying development. It offers hope that women who have been divorced under civil law will no longer be easy victims of malice and greed. It is doubtful, however, that the ruling represents a total or even a major solution to the problem of the ᶜagunah, on either pragmatic or theoretic grounds. Even in the New York case, there could be a long delay before the *get* is issued. And not every ᶜagunah is able to undertake extended and costly litigation.

Not only was the decision in the New York Court of Appeals very close, but there is no assurance that it will be followed by other courts in other states. In general, judges prefer to settle cases on the narrowest possible legal basis. It is also possible that other judges would view such a suit as an example of the state intervening in a religious issue and declare it outside their jurisdiction.

A variant of the Lieberman plan, proposed by some individual Orthodox rabbis, takes the form of a prenuptial agreement. The husband stipulates that in the event of a civil divorce he would issue a *get* to his wife. Should he fail to fulfil his obligation, she could sue for "specific performance," as in the Lieberman plan. Some individual rabbis may have put the plan into operation, but there has been no public announcement and surely no collective action by any Orthodox rabbinic body. Subsequently, it was announced by the Rabbinical Council of America that all "research" on this approach had been terminated.

Unable or unwilling to deal creatively with the rabbinic law of divorce, some Orthodox Jewish leaders, both lay and rabbinic, came up with another proposal. They persuaded the New York Legislature to pass a law that no civil divorce would be issued if "there were any impediment to the remarriage of either partner." This euphemism was designed to avoid the charge that the provision represented state interference in religion. Governor Mario Cuomo, facing the same pressures as the legislators, signed the bill but expressed grave doubts as to its constitutionality. It has not yet been tested in the courts. Attempts to pass similar legislation in Connecticut, Pennsylvania, and California have failed.

To justify the involvement of the civil courts with the issuance of *gittin*, it has been argued that the issuance of a *get* is not a religious act but a civil procedure. But most experts, both in the civil law and in the Halakhah, would maintain that the issuance of a *get* is definitely a religious act.

A more-fundamental objection to these approaches is that procedures that rely on the state to enforce the issuance of a Jewish divorce are—or should be—unacceptable, not only from the standpoint of the American polity but from the purview of Judaism. Today a determined and many-pronged assault on the basic American concept of the separation of church and state is under way, taking on a variety of shapes, from "ancillary" government aid to religious schools to the campaign to declare the United States a "Christian nation." Jewish citizens should be in the forefront in the defense—not the erosion—of this fundamental principle of separation.

Moreover, the Halakhah, the Jewish system of jurisprudence, has for centuries been an autonomous and independent system of law, no matter under what social and political system Jews lived. To rely on civil courts to execute provisions of the Halakhah means to subject Jewish law to 50 different and sometimes contradictory jurisdictions in the United States alone. It means undermining its unity and universality, its applicability everywhere and always. Nor would it meet the problem of the ʿagunah outside the United States, thus fragmentizing Jewish law even further.

Finally, this effort to rely on secular government to right the wrongs that arise from the observance of the Halakhah is—or should be—intolerable on religious grounds. It is a confession that the Halakhah, which derives its authority from God on Sinai and is intended for all times and places, lacks the resources to do justice, enforce equity, and relieve human misery. It is a denial of the basic goal of the Halakhah and its claim to be a *Torat ḥayyim*, "a Torah of life and compassion." For this writer, the practical difficulties of this unholy marriage between the Halakhah and the secular state are less important than the affront to the dignity and honor of Jewish law.

Another approach, universal in applicability and ethically unobjectionable, was adopted in 1966 by the Rabbinical Assembly, which authorized its Beth Din (rabbinical court) in New York and other cities to deal with cases of the ʿagunah. The Beth Din based its operation on a far-reaching Talmudic principle in the laws of marriage that had been invoked earlier by some individual, primarily Sephardic, rabbis. The doctrine declares that "whoever enters into Jewish marriage does so by the authority of the Rabbis" (ʾadaʿata derabbanan).[31] Hence, if the need arises, the "Rabbis have the power to annul the marriage retroactively" (ʾafkeʿinho rabbanan lekiddushei minneh), so that no divorce by the husband would be necessary. It should be understood that though the marriage may be annulled, the legitimacy of the children of the marriage is not in question.

A highly interesting parallel exists in the Halakhah of the Karaite sect, who reject the authority of the Talmud. Several thousand Karaites now live in the state of Israel. Some Karaite authorities have ruled that when a woman petitions the court for a divorce on justifiable grounds and her husband refuses to issue the document, the marriage can be dissolved by the court. A case was reported of a Karaite who beat his wife because she refused to have marital relations on the sabbath, an act forbidden in Karaite law. When he refused to divorce his wife, the Karaite court issued a get without his consent.[32] Whether the rabbinite Halakhah affected the Karaites in this instance is difficult to determine.

Actually, the Beth Din of the Conservative Rabbinical Assembly in New York and similar rabbinical courts elsewhere have found it necessary to invoke the principle of annulment (hafkaʿat kiddushin) in only a limited number of cases.[33] When a civil divorce has taken place but the woman finds it impossible to secure a get, the Beth Din tries to persuade the husband to act ethically and to dissolve the marriage in Jewish fashion. If he remains obdurate, he is reminded that he will no longer be able to vent his anger or indulge his greed by refusing the get, since the Beth Din stands ready to annul the marriage legally and free his wife.

Unlike other, more-limited techniques, the procedure of hafkaʿat kiddushin solves the problem for all categories of the ʿagunah: those involving a recalcitrant husband, one who has disappeared, and one who has been lost in a military action or some other disaster. It also addresses the situation of the childless widow, who requires a "release" (ḥalizah) from her dead husband's brother; and of the wife whose husband is not legally competent to issue a get.

In addition to its practical advantages, this annulment procedure underscores the power of the community and places the authority once more where it belongs—in the collective rabbinate as the representative of the Jewish community.

At long last, the resources of the Halakhah are being utilized to relieve the suffering of the ʿagunah. The procedure of *hafkaʿat kiddushin* should be more widely known and more generally adopted, for it offers a workable plan for healing an ancient wound, indeed righting an ancient wrong. If Jewish women continue to languish in the loneliness of the ʿagunah state, their unnecessary suffering will not be chargeable to Jewish law but to its latter-day defenders, who invoke the memory of the great Sages of the past but lack the courage and the compassion to follow their example.

The significant steps taken in both the codified and the customary law of traditional Judaism to restrict the powers of the man and extend the rights of the woman must not be overlooked or discounted. It would be fatuous, however, to deny the persistence of substantial elements of inequality in the status of women. Perhaps they can be explained or justified for earlier periods, when women were excluded from the larger concerns of society—though this condition itself is in need of justification.

XI

WOMEN'S ROLE IN RELIGIOUS LIFE

The High Place of Women

As the pattern of Jewish traditional life took shape, it was the woman who was charged with its implementation in the home. The preparation of food according to the laws of *kashrut*, the kindling of the lights on the sabbath and the festival eve, the observance of the rules for sexual abstinence before, during, and after the menstrual period—all were the responsibility of the woman. The importance attached to woman's role is highlighted by the Mishnaic statement, "For three transgressions women may die in childbirth, because they have been negligent with regard to the periods of separation, the setting aside of *ḥallah* [the first cake of the dough] and the lighting of the sabbath lamp" (M. *Shabbat* 2:6). The care and nurture of the children, indeed, the conduct and supervision of the Jewish home in its physical and spiritual aspects—all this constituted the woman's domain, her responsibility, and her glory. It was no idle flattery that called her ʿakeret habayit, "the root and foundation of the home."

Important as this role was, it must be qualified in at least three respects. The woman's sphere of activity was entirely private. The Rabbis interpreted Psalm 45:14 to mean, "All the glory of the king's daughter lies within [the home]." The woman had no voice in community decisions, except to the extent that she could influence her husband. She had no active role in the synagogue, where all the functions were conducted by men; and she was not even expected to attend public services in the synagogue.

Jewish women had no obligation and no opportunity to engage in the study of the Torah, which rabbinic Judaism regarded as the highest of all human activities. To be sure, a few isolated instances of learned women are recorded in the sources. The most famous was Beruriah, the daughter of Rabbi Hananya ben Teradyon, who educated her in the Oral and the Written Torah. As the wife of Rabbi Meir and his equal in learning and brilliance, her opinion was sought by scholars, and in at least one case her view carried the day.[1]

Nonetheless, she clearly chafed at the inferiority to which her sex consigned her. When Rabbi Jose the Galilean asked her, "*>eizeh haderekh haholekh lelud?*" (Which is the road leading to Lydda?), she answered, "Foolish Galilean, have you forgotten the rabbinic injunction, 'Don't talk overmuch with women?' You should have said, '*>eizeh lelud*' [Which to Lydda?], using only two words!" (B. *Kiddushin* 80b).

The Rabbis were clearly uncomfortable with her vigorous and independent personality. They reported that her later years were filled with calamity; her mother suffered a violent death, and her sister was carried off to Rome to lead a life of shame (B. *Abodah Zarah* 18a). Indeed, a later legend declared that she permitted herself to be seduced and then committed suicide (Rashi, on *Abodah Zarah* 18b). The names of very few other learned women from the next fifteen hundred years have been preserved.

The stringent opinion of Rabbi Eliezer forbidding the teaching of the Torah to women prevailed, rather than the more-liberal ruling of Ben Azzai. While the building of schools, elementary and advanced, for the instruction of males was the first priority in any community, there were no schools for women, who were expected to learn from their mothers the basic observances they were called upon to maintain.

Next to the study of the Torah, the basic Jewish observance was prayer; from this obligation (*hiyyub*) and privilege women were declared exempt. The exemption was buttressed by the Talmudic principle that "women are free from commandments that must be traditionally performed at specific times" (*mitzvat <aseh shehazman gerama*). Neither the rule nor its rationale was questioned in ancient and medieval times.

Of course, women frequently had recourse to prayer, but the act was entirely private, individual, and voluntary. Archaeological excavations have revealed that in some cases no provision was made for women in the synagogue structure.[2] Generally, however, a curtained-off area was provided, where they could not be seen or heard by the male congregation.

The inferior status in religious life, to which the Jewish tradition seemed to assign women, became an issue primarily in the twentieth century. For Reform Judaism, the procedure was easy—the segregation of sexes at services, the inadmissibility of women to serve as witnesses, and the weightier problem of the *<agunah* were all "solved" by Reform's surrender of the entire Halakhic system.

In Orthodox circles, the various legal disabilities of women remained intact. The break with patterns of the past took place primarily in the field of education. Schools for girls, like the Beth Yaakov network in Poland, and later in the United States and elsewhere, were established, often in the face of strong opposition. Ultimately even day schools were created under Orthodox auspices; some were limited to girls, others segregated male and female pupils, and nearly all gave girls an "easier" curriculum from which the study of the Talmud and other advanced texts were generally excluded. Very recently a few pioneers in the "modern Orthodox" community have established facilities for advanced Jewish studies for women, notably Stern College of Yeshiva University and the Drisha Institute founded by Rabbi David Silber in New York.

In several communities, Orthodox women, seeking to participate more fully in Jewish religious life, have organized women's *minyanim*, "prayer groups" for sabbath services. They take care not to infringe on any of the prohibitions against women reciting certain prayers or performing certain rituals. In the spring of 1985, the entire concept was strongly denounced and forbidden by a group of Talmud teachers at Yeshiva University. But the movement is not likely to disband on that account, though its growth is problematic.[3] Right-wing Orthodox circles, both Hasidic and non-Hasidic, committed to a perception of Jewish law and practice as immutable, naturally have had no traffic with these or other innovations.

It is Conservative Judaism that is challenged by the growing call for the equality of women. The majority of its leaders, inspired by the authority of the Halakhah and its capacity for growth and development, felt the need to restore the dynamism inherent in the Jewish tradition. As the eminent historian Salo W. Baron wrote:

> Neo-Orthodoxy, equally with Reform, is a deviation from historical Judaism. No less than Reform, it abandoned Judaism's self-rejuvenating historical dynamism. For this reason we may say that . . . the "positive-historical" Judaism of Zacharias Frankel and Michael Sachs and the "Conservative" Judaism of America have been much truer to the spirit of traditional Judaism. By maintaining the general validity of Jewish law and combining with it freedom of personal interpretation of the Jewish past and creed, Frankel and his successors hoped to preserve historical continuity. . . . It is Conservative Judaism which seems to show the greatest similarities with the method and substance of teaching of the popular leaders during the declining Second Commonwealth, inasmuch as, clinging to the traditional mode of life, it nevertheless allows for the adaptation of basic theological concepts to the changing social and environmental needs.

As happened in the Tannaitic period, the twentieth century saw the adoption of a series of steps to enlarge the sphere of women's participation, often independently from one another, yet reflecting the general trend. Once again, as in the period of the Mishnah, there were strong divisions of opinion as to the propriety and wisdom of each new practice.

The first great step toward the equalization of women in religious life took place decades before the emergence of the feminist movement. The segregation of the sexes in public worship had been rigorously maintained in Old World synagogues of all denominations. But as the process of acculturation set in for American Jews, the practice of separate seating for women began to erode in American synagogues of every type. The full significance of family pews was largely ignored or minimized at the outset, even its proponents often defending it on other, extraneous grounds, primarily as a means of keeping family members together. Because this major change is a striking illustration of another factor in the development of Jewish law, the power of the popular will, this subject has been treated above under another rubric.

The subordinate position of women is expressed in the Preliminary Blessings of the traditional Morning Service. The second, third, and fourth benedictions read: "Blessed are You, O Lord our God, King of the Universe, who has not made me a non-Jew [*goy*], a slave, a woman." For the last blessing, women were taught to substitute "who made me according to His will."

The phrase "who has not made me a *goy*" created considerable difficulty in the Middle Ages, when censors, disputants, and other enemies pointed to it as evidence that Jews were hostile to outsiders. The explanation offered was that these three blessings carry no negative meaning, but are intended to express the sense of privilege that the male Jew feels in being able to fulfil the Torah and the *mitzvot*, "blessings," many of which are not obligatory for non-Jews, slaves, and women. One witty rejoinder declared: "That the blessing is phrased in the negative proves nothing. We certainly love our wives, and yet we say 'who did not make me a woman.'"

The medieval censor had already ordered a change in the printed editions of the Talmud (B. *Menahot* 43b), which read *she‹asani yisra›el*, "who made me a Jew," instead of *shelo ‹asani goy*. Earlier editions and commentators, like *Asheri* and *Tur*, still read the blessing in the negative form, which is undoubtedly the original. Yet it is noteworthy that the Gaon of Vilna accepted this altered reading.

Similarly, the blessing "who did not make me a slave" has a unique Jewish variant, *shelo› ‹asani bor*, "who did not make me an ignoramus." Thus there was warrant in the tradition for a change in the text.[4]

Nor can it be gainsaid that for the masses of the people, at least, the Preliminary Blessings were regarded as establishing an invidious contrast, validating a sense of innate superiority by the Jew over the gentile, the free man over the slave, and the man over the woman. Admittedly, the negative form in which these blessings are couched has been unfortunate. The sense of joy in Judaism is far more beautifully expressed at many other points in the liturgy, as in the affirmation, "Happy are we. How goodly is our portion, how pleasant our lot. How beautiful is our heritage."

The traditional concept of the election of Israel also is frequently expressed in positive terms. It is generally linked with the gift of the Torah and the *mitzvot* in such prayers as *ahavah rabbah* and in the blessings at the reading of the Torah.

How were these blessings to be treated in the first official prayer book of the Conservative movement, *The Sabbath and Festival Prayer Book*, which appeared in 1946? The omission of the three Preliminary Blessings posed no problem for Reform Judaism, which worshipped in a drastically curtailed liturgy. For Orthodoxy, at least for the present, any deviation from the traditional text was unthinkable. In Conservative Judaism, the general bias in favor of tradition was reinforced by a feeling that deleting the three Preliminary Blessings would be an unsatisfactory procedure, since they contain religious values worthy of preservation. The solution was to rephrase two of the three blessings in the positive rather than the negative. One had only to adopt *she‹asani yisra›el*, "who made me a Jew," for the first and to formulate the second as *she‹asani ben-*[or *bat-*]*horin*, "who made me free."

In its new form, the blessing "who made me free" expresses the basic conviction that freedom is not a gift conferred upon human beings by governmental fiat and therefore liable to restriction or removal at the pleasure of the ruler or the desire of the majority. Freedom is thus affirmed as the inalienable right of every human being, deriving from his estate as a creature fashioned in the image of God. Thus the Jew begins the day with two reasons for thanksgiving appropriate to his condition or his aspirations.

With regard to the remaining benediction, a simple, yet brilliant suggestion by Rabbi Max Gelb was adopted; the blessing was formulated as *she‹asani bezalmo*, "who has made me in His image." For all its novelty, the new blessing has a basis in tradition; it occurs virtually verbatim in a liturgical fragment in the Cairo Geniza, emanating from the early Middle Ages. It is to be hoped that with time the new formulation of all three Preliminary Blessings will become part of the liturgy of all traditionally oriented Jews.[5]

It is noteworthy that these new Preliminary Blessings parallel the categories of the noble statement in *Yalkut Shime‹oni* (Judges 42): "I call heaven and earth to witness that whether one be gentile or Jew, man or woman, slave or free, the divine spirit rests on each in accordance with his deeds."

By replacing the blessing "who did not make me a woman" by "who created me in His image" more was achieved than the deletion of an embarrassing passage. It introduces into the rubric of prayer a fundamental Jewish idea that inexplicably finds little expression elsewhere in the traditional liturgy—the sanctity and the dignity of the human person.[6] This concept of the creation of man and woman in the divine image and of their equal dignity, recognized today as a fundamental insight of Judaism,[7] is expressed twice in Genesis: "God created man in His own image, in the image of God created He him; male and female created He them" (1:27) and "This is the book of the generations of Adam. In the day that God created man, in the likeness of God He made him; male and female created He them" (5:7).[8] The theme finds magnificent expression in Psalm 8:

> When I look at Your heavens, the work of your fingers,
> the moon and the stars which You have established;
> What is man that You are mindful of him,
> and the son of man that You care for him?
> Yet You have made him little less than God,
> and have crowned him with glory and honor.
> You have given him dominion over the works of Your hands;
> You have put all things under his feet.

This doctrine was a cardinal belief of Rabbi Akiba, who declared, "Beloved is man who was created in the image of God. Special love was granted him by man's being made aware that he was created in the image of God" (M. *Abot* 3:14).[9]

Through the new form of the Preliminary Blessings, the Jew, male and female, expresses gratitude for having been made human, a sentient and conscious being, endowed with reason and freedom of will, and thankful to be alive, in spite of the tragedies and frustrations inherent in the human condition.

Bar Mitzvah and Bat Mitzvah

The first new ritual was the *Bat Mitzvah*, introduced in 1922 by Mordecai M. Kaplan for his daughter, Judith. In the fourteenth century the practice of calling a boy to the Torah immediately after his thirteenth birthday came into vogue. This public act signified his assuming the religious obligations of Jewish manhood as a *Bar Mitzvah*, "son of commandment." For centuries the *Bar Mitzvah* rite remained a relatively minor event in traditional Jewish communities. It gained enormously in importance in modern Jewish life, not merely as the rite of passage from childhood to adolescence but as a mark of a boy's formal acceptance of Judaism and his affiliation with the Jewish community.

As the family structure has weakened in the twentieth century, the *Bar Mitzvah* rite has become an instrument for celebrating and cementing family ties. Moreover, it comes at a point in life when the parents are in their prime. Unlike a wedding ceremony, the *Bar Mitzvah* does not represent a separation of parent and offspring. All these factors have conspired to give the rite major significance in America and Western Europe.

However, the *Bar Mitzvah* has all too often become an occasion for vulgarity and ostentation, bordering on the obscene, and it has accordingly been criticized and satirized unmercifully. There is a great need to restore emphasis where it belongs, on the religious ceremony, and make the social function subordinate. But abolishing the rite would mean throwing out the baby with the bathwater. For all its excrescences, the *Bar Mitzvah* remains a valuable resource for Jewish living.

Throughout the five hundred years of the *Bar Mitzvah* rite, there was no corresponding ceremony for girls until the introduction of the *Bat Mitzvah*. Reform Judaism, which originally sought to eliminate the *Bar Mitzvah* ceremony, had created a Confirmation Service, usually conducted on *Shavuot* for both boys and girls, a practice that was subsequently adopted by many Conservative congregations. But the Confirmation ceremony was a group function and did not revolve around the individual child. It did not succeed in displacing the *Bar Mitzvah* even in Reform congregations, and it did not meet the need of individual recognition for girls, which the *Bat Mitzvah* fills admirably.

Primarily because it is of recent origin, the *Bat Mitzvah* rite has not been standardized. Its central feature is the calling of the girl for an honor (ᶜaliyah) at the Torah, with the traditional blessings, generally followed by her chanting the *Haftarah*, or Prophetic section, also with the appropriate benedictions. She usually delivers a talk at the occasion. In many instances, the girl also conducts part of the service, chanting portions of the liturgy. The *Bat Mitzvah* now almost rivals the *Bar Mitzvah* in popularity. It represents a formal recognition of the equality of the sexes in transmitting and safeguarding the tradition.

Pressures for such a rite have also been felt in the American Orthodox community. Unwilling to concede a debt to another movement, many Orthodox rabbis have introduced a similar ceremony, giving it another name. It is often conducted on a Sunday or other weekday, thus bypassing any problem for the Orthodox Halakhah by the girl's being called to the Torah or leading the congregation in prayer. These variations aside, what is significant is that for the first time in history the entrance of women into Judaism receives public recognition. Whether this type of ceremony will suffice remains to be seen.

In 1955, the Committee on Jewish Law and Standards of the Rabbinical Assembly authorized the calling of women for honors (ᶜaliyot) at the Torah. As has already been pointed out in another connection, this practice was explicitly permitted by Rabbi Moses Isserles in his authoritative gloss on the *Shulḥan Arukh* (*Oraḥ ḥayyim* 282, 3), but it was not observed.

One major virtue of the new ruling was that it gave meaning to the *Bat Mitzvah* rite. Hitherto a girl was called to the Torah at her *Bat Mitzvah*, but never afterward, so that the rite was meaningless. Now a *Bat Mitzvah* could look forward to an honor at the Torah throughout her lifetime. The ruling of the Law Committee was permissive not obligatory. It evoked opposition in some quarters, but more and more congregations are introducing the practice.

Women in the *Minyan*

In 1973 another step was taken when the Committee on Law and Standards permitted counting women in the *minyan*, the quorum of ten that is required for public worship. For this change, there was no direct support in traditional sources. It was, however, warranted on two grounds: the irrationality of counting a boy in the *minyan* but excluding a grown woman; and the illogic of permitting a woman to be called to the Torah but refusing to count her in the quorum for prayer. Here again there was disagreement with the decision, among both the rabbis and the laity. Although many synagogues did not adopt the practice, the ruling is steadily gaining acceptance.

While these steps have substantially advanced the cause of equal rights for women, no significant progress has been registered in connection with the ineligibility of women as witnesses. The issue had appeared to be entirely theoretic, but it assumed greater relevance and importance when the next step was proposed, the ordination of women.

The Ordination of Women

The struggle for women's rights in Judaism reaches its culmination, though not its end, in the ordination of women as rabbis. The history of the issue sheds light on the dialectic of change in Judaism. Since the issue came to a head in our own time, it allows us to observe at close range the tensions and conflicts that undoubtedly have accompanied every significant step in the history of the Halakhah.

The ordination of women as rabbis has been a problem primarily for Conservative Judaism. Reform Judaism, though increasingly sympathetic in recent years to Jewish tradition, continues to reject the authority of the Halakhah. Whatever problems Reform encounters with regard to women's ordination are entirely practical—overcoming innate prejudices against women in new areas of activity. Hence, women are being ordained in growing numbers by seminaries that reflect the Reform attitude. In the felicitous words of a distinguished Reform leader, Jewish law is a source of guidance not of governance.

Orthodox Judaism, thus far, has encountered no problem in this area, since it rejects the idea completely. Orthodox dogma maintains in theory—though often not in practice—that the Halakhah is an immutable manifestation of the divine will. Since women have not been rabbis in the past, they should not be rabbis in the future. Rabbinic texts are then searched for sources from which a prohibition of women's ordination can be extracted.

The problem has been acute for Conservative Judaism, whose basic doctrine has been the concept of the dynamic nature of Jewish tradition. On the basis of nearly 200 years of historical and critical scholarship, Conservative Judaism regards Jewish tradition as the product of a dialectic between God and the people of Israel. Hence, in every age, the body of Jewish tradition is the result of the law and lore received from the past coming into contact with new conditions and new religious, philosophic, and ethical insights. The same process comes into play with each succeeding generation. That this creates major theological and philosophic problems is self-evident, but the reality of the dialectic process is undeniable.

Though the issue surfaced in Conservative Judaism only during the last two decades, there were earlier adumbrations. In 1902, Henrietta Szold, daughter of Rabbi Benjamin Szold of Baltimore and secretary and editor of the Jewish Publication Society, moved to New York. She continued her advanced Jewish studies by taking courses in Hebrew, the Bible, and the Talmud at the Jewish Theological Seminary, though there is no evidence that she was interested in a rabbinical degree.

In this area, as in so many others, German Jewry has been both a prototype and a laboratory for American Jewry. The first modern female rabbi was Regina Jonas, who was admitted to the Hochschule für die Wissenschaft des Judentums in Berlin in the mid-1930s. This rabbinical seminary for German-style Reform Judaism was probably closer in spirit and outlook to American Conservatism than to American Reform. But when Jonas completed the course, the professors refused to grant her ordination. She then secured private ordination from a rabbi in Offenbach and served as rabbi in several social service agencies until 1940, when she was sent to the Nazi concentration camp in Theresienstadt, where she died.

A few years later a similar problem of ordination arose in the United States. Helen Levinthal Lyons, daughter of one of the most distinguished rabbis in Conservative Judaism, Israel H. Levinthal of the Brooklyn Jewish Center, decided to seek ordination, which was impossible at the Jewish Theological Seminary. She took the entire rabbinical course at the Jewish Institute of Religion in New York, which had been founded by Rabbi Stephen S. Wise as a "nondenominational" seminary to train rabbis for all branches of American Judaism. This variety was reflected in the composition of its faculty and of its student body. (After Wise's death it became the New York school of Hebrew Union College, the Reform Seminary in Cincinnati.)

When Lyons completed her course, the majority of the faculty, including the great historian of the Halakhah, Chaim Tchernowitz, known as Rav Zacir, favored her ordination, but others, notably Henry Slonimsky, opposed it. On May 28, 1939 she was awarded the academic degree of M.H.L. (Master of Hebrew Literature), with diplomas in both Hebrew and English, but was denied ordination.

In the 1960s the Reform Hebrew Union College—Jewish Institute of Religion in Cincinnati and New York, and the Reconstructionist Rabbinical College in Philadelphia began to admit women to the rabbinical course. On June 3, 1972, nearly thirty years after the ordination of Regina Jonas in Germany, Sally J. Priesand was ordained in Cincinnati, the first woman rabbi in the United States. Since then, the number of female rabbinical students has continued to rise dramatically; women now constitute approximately one-third of the students in all three schools.

Meanwhile, pressure for the admission of women to the Conservative rabbinate was mounting. The constitution of the Rabbinical Assembly, the international organization of the Conservative rabbinate, was amended to admit to membership "any person possessing the requisite qualifications of character, learning and commitment."

At the annual convention of the Rabbinical Assembly in the spring of 1977, a motion was presented asking the faculty of the Jewish Theological Seminary to admit women to the rabbinical course. There was a marked division of opinion in the membership, and at a heated session, which lasted beyond midnight, the Chancellor of the Seminary, Gerson D. Cohen, requested that the resolution be held in abeyance. The commission he appointed to study the question in all its aspects took its assignment very seriously. It examined the theoretical as well as the practical aspects of the issue and conducted interviews and surveys throughout the American continent. The majority report, presented to the Assembly in January 1979, recommended the admission of women to the rabbinical course, concluding,

> There is no direct Halakhic objection to the acts of training and ordaining a woman to be a rabbi, preacher and teacher in Israel. The problems associated with ancillary functions were deemed by the Commission to be insufficient grounds for denying a considerable and growing group of

highly talented and committed Jewish women the access they desire to
the roles of spiritual and community leaders.

Cohen requested that each member of the Seminary faculty prepare
a position paper by May 30, 1979, in advance of the vote on the question.
By the stipulated date, only a few such papers were in his hands.[10] It
became clear that a group in the faculty, spearheaded by members of
the Talmud department, was strongly opposed to the ordination of
women and was determined to block consideration of the issue. When
various efforts to resolve the situation failed, a vote to table the question
was adopted at a faculty meeting.

Chancellor Cohen, who had frequently expressed his strong commitment to women's ordination, now made a new proposal. His plan was
to train women who wanted to become rabbis in a separate curriculum,
equal in content and quality to that pursued by male students. He presented the idea to six women who were already enrolled in the graduate
program at the Seminary and were hoping to be admitted to the rabbinical course. The women themselves were divided as to whether this version of "the separate but equal doctrine" should be accepted as a step
toward their ultimate goal or rejected as a diversionary tactic, even
though it had been proposed by the Chancellor in good faith. He announced that the Religious Ministry Program would be launched at the
opening of the 1980 academic year.

At meetings with members of the administrative staff of the Seminary
who were charged with implementing this new program, the women
were warned against becoming "overeducated" and were informed that
the plan was intended to train "paraprofessionals" or "quasi-rabbis."
Consequently, the proposed curriculum would stress "practical training" rather than "academic concerns." The representations and objections of the women were fruitless, and ultimately they turned to other
careers.[11]

In the Rabbinical Assembly a substantial militant minority organized
to combat the proposal for ordination. This group, calling itself, with
unconscious irony, "The Committee for the Halakhic Process," carried
on a vigorous campaign for the *status quo*, using the mail, interviews,
and announcements in the press and other media. The group later
changed its name to "The Committee for Traditional Conservative Judaism." Nevertheless, though passions ran high and there were threats of
wholesale defection, the parent organization remained intact. At the
same time, a series of polls disclosed that there was an unmistakable
growth of sentiment in the Rabbinical Assembly for the admission of
women. Perhaps some part in the change of attitude may be attributed
to the appearance of serious and urbane treatments of the subject, pro
and con.[12]

In 1981, Rabbi Beverly Magidson, who had been ordained by Hebrew Union College—Jewish Institute of Religion, applied for membership in the Rabbinical Assembly. Unanimously, the Membership Committee found her eminently qualified on all counts of character, learning, and commitment to Conservative Judaism, both in theory and in practice. The question of gender was excepted, since a minority of the Membership Committee were opposed to the ordination of women. In accordance with the constitution, the Executive Council voted on this report, and it endorsed her application 18–7. According to the constitution of the Rabbinical Assembly, her application now required an affirmative vote by three-quarters of the membership at the annual convention.

A vigorous campaign for and against Magidson's admission was waged in the months before the convention in Dallas in April 1983. On April 12, a full-fledged debate on the issue was held, with some thirty rabbis participating. The entire proceeding was conducted on a high level, with few lapses, though feelings were strong. The final roll call showed 206 members in favor, 72 against—three votes short of the three-quarters needed. When a second ballot was called for, the tally was 210 ayes and 75 nays, Rabbi Magidson's admission being rejected by four votes.

Prophecies of a split in the Assembly were not fulfilled. Both the right-wing "traditionalists," who had won, and the "center" majority, who had lost, remained within the movement. But those who opposed the admission of a woman rabbi to the Assembly had won only a pyrrhic victory, for the trend was unmistakeable. A survey taken in November 1979 showed that 47 percent of the Conservative rabbinate favored women rabbis and 45 percent were opposed. In April 1983, 74 percent of the members present at the convention voted for the admission of women to the Conservative rabbinate. The signal sent by the Rabbinical Assembly to the Seminary faculty was clear. In the spring of 1983, Chancellor Cohen announced that he would present the issue at a faculty meeting on October 24, 1983.

With the advent of the Jewish year 5744, in the fall of 1983, the issue of the ordination of women gathered momentum. A group of rabbis and laymen opposed to the idea organized a Union for Traditional Conservative Judaism. In large advertisements appearing in the Anglo-Jewish press in the United States and in Israel, they invited all who agreed with them on such issues as the authority of the Halakhah, the centrality of the family, and the importance of *kashrut* and the sabbath in Conservative Judaism to join their ranks.

Generally, their advertisement was flanked by another carrying the names of five members of the Talmud Department of the Seminary faculty. The latter called for a rejection of women's ordination in the name of obedience to a decision (*psak*) rendered by Saul Lieberman.

(Lieberman, one of the giant Talmudists of the age, was professor of Talmud at the Seminary until his death in April 1984.) According to some reports, the decision was embodied in a letter simply setting forth his opposition to the idea. According to others, his *psak* contained citations from Halakhic sources, from which he deduced that women's ordination was forbidden. It was also rumored that Lieberman had explicitly forbidden the publication of his statement. At this writing, this *psak* has not been published, and so it has not been subjected to the normal study, analysis, and criticism that is the lifeblood of the Halakhic process.

Finally, at the faculty meeting on October 24, 1983, after extensive discussion, the admission of women to the rabbinical program at the Seminary was adopted, 34–8, with one abstention. Chancellor Cohen then proceeded to implement the decision. Several women who had been taking courses in the rabbinical curriculum were given credit for them, thus shortening the period required for their ordination.

At the convention in the spring of 1985, Rabbi Magidson, whose gentle persistence was widely admired, was elected to the Rabbinical Assembly with the proviso that her membership begin after the Seminary commencement on May 12, 1985, so that the honor of being the first woman to be admitted to the Assembly would be accorded to a Seminary graduate, Amy Eilsberg-Schwartz.

There is obviously strong opposition, among both rabbis and laity, to the ordination of women, but all signs point to this being a minority and receding position. The women entering the Conservative rabbinate will undoubtedly find, as did their sisters in Reform and Reconstructionism, that they must surmount many obstacles in congregational life before their position as rabbis is taken for granted. But no congregation will be compelled to accept a woman rabbi against its will.

If history is any guide, it is clear that this move, important as it is, will prove neither as world-shaking as its proponents believe nor as catastrophic as its opponents maintain. The introduction of woman suffrage and the increasing election of women to political office in the United States did not transform the character of politics in America. However, the ordination of more women may modify the character and function of the rabbinate by bringing a new dimension of personal concern and sympathetic understanding to the relationship of rabbi and lay person.

The New Doctrine of Rabbinic Infallibility

Some opponents of women's ordination have continued to proclaim that "the Halakhah is opposed to the ordination of women," but they have rarely offered to present the evidence. Instead, they have nurtured the implication that the material is too recondite and complicated for examination by generally intelligent lay people. They have insisted that it can be fathomed only by a handful of Halakhic experts. Whoever disagrees with their conclusions is, by definition, not a Halakhic expert!

This tactic is one more illustration of a characteristic of contemporary Jewish life—a twenty- or thirty-year cultural, social, and ethical lag behind society at large. Thus, precisely at a time when the doctrine of papal infallibility has encountered growing opposition in Roman Catholic circles, the idea of rabbinic infallibility has become increasingly popular in the Jewish religious community: "The law is thus and so because we say so." The old Talmudic principle *neitei sepher veneheze*, "Let us take the book and see,"[13] is largely ignored. Instead, pronouncements are handed down in the name of a supreme authority who rarely deigns to disclose the basis for his decision. In the past, the Talmud encouraged students and colleagues to disagree with their masters so that the truth might emerge. Today, those who have had the temerity to question these august judgments are not refuted but are attacked as lacking in respect for the Torah and in deference for its only true expositors.

The sincerity of those opposed to rabbinic ordination for women is not being questioned—only their right to arrogate to themselves the sole authority to decide the issue by fiat. When the contention "the ordination of women is forbidden by the Halakhah" is examined in the light of the evidence, the absolute judgments pronounced on the subject bear an uncanny resemblance to the emperor's "new clothes."

Rabbis bear the oldest honorific in continuous use in human history. The title "rabbi" is far older than any honorary degree or academic distinction recognized today. At the same time, the rabbinate represents virtually a new calling, since the functions designated by this ancient title have undergone a great transformation. The term "rabbi" is an old label on a bottle of new wine. Elsewhere I have attempted to trace the five principal stages in the rabbinate from Talmudic times to the present; the end of the development of the office is not yet in sight.[14] The modern rabbi, for good or for ill, and perhaps for good *and* for ill, is a *novum* in Jewish experience. The subject of the ordination of women is not discussed in traditional sources because past generations never contemplated the possiblity. To offer an extreme analogy, nowhere do we encounter a discussion of whether Martians are obligated to put on *tefillin*, "phylacteries," or are required to observe the Noahide laws.

In the absence of any direct testimony on the subject, opponents of the ordination of women have drawn inferences of their own from various rabbinic passages, a procedure that is entirely legitimate. But do these passages really have any bearing on the issue? During the relatively brief time that the question of women's ordination has been actively discussed, many of the passages that were originally advanced with great assurance have been tacitly abandoned, and new texts have been offered in their place.

Some arguments against ordination are homiletic rather than Halakhic in character. Thus one rabbinic scholar cited the Mishnah, *Hakol shoḥatin usheḥitatan kesherah huz meḥeresh shoteh veqatan*, "Everyone is eligible to slaughter an animal, except a deaf-mute,[15] an insane person, or a minor,"[16] as proof that the Rabbis permitted a woman to be a *shoḥet*, "slaughterer," but not a rabbi.

One congregational rabbi published a letter in which he categorically declared, "The Halakhah is opposed to women's ordination," citing the Talmudic reference B. *Sotah* 20a. But this text deals with the biblical law regarding the ordeal of a woman accused by her husband of adultery (Num. 5). In this connection, the Talmud quotes two diametrically opposed opinions by Mishnaic teachers:

> Ben Azzai says, "A man is required to teach Torah to his daughter (so that if she should ever have occasion to undergo the ordeal of the accused wife, she would know that any merit she possesses would create a suspension of punishment for her)." Rabbi Eliezer says, "Whoever teaches his daughter the Torah is teaching her obscenity (because from the Torah she would learn how to circumvent the law and hide her immorality)" [M. *Sotah* 3:4].

The writer of the letter evidently wished to infer from Rabbi Eliezer's statement that since it is forbidden to teach the Torah to a girl, she obviously cannot be ordained as a rabbi. This view, however, is the opinion of only one Sage and is contradicted in the very same passage by that of another. Rabbi Eliezer, one of the most conservative and strong-willed of the scholars, held highly individual views. Time and again, the vast majority of his colleagues did not hesitate to overrule his judgment.

Undoubtedly the restrictive opinion of Rabbi Eliezer regarding the education of women was adopted in the Middle Ages, but would the author of the letter forbid the teaching of Torah to his own daughters or the enrollment of girls in his school? In general, few modern Orthodox Jews favor denying girls a meaningful Jewish education.

Maimonides, in his *Mishneh Torah*, repeats the substance of a Tannaitic midrash. The biblical laws regarding the qualifications of a king include the provision "You may indeed set as king over you him whom the Lord your God will choose. One from among your brethren you shall set as king over you, you may not put a foreigner over you who is not your brother."[17] The *Sifre* comments: "A king, not a queen."[18]

Maimonides broadens this statement to mean "every position of author-ity [*mesimut*] shall be limited to 'one of your brothers,' and therefore not a woman."[19] Adhering to this decision would effectively rule out the appointment or election of a woman to any government position or to any supervisory job.

In view of an Aggadic statement comparing rabbis to kings, Maimoni-des' judgment that women cannot be kings has been used to declare them ineligible to serve as rabbis.[20] It is difficult to believe that this homiletic passage is being seriously offered for deciding the Halakhah. It may be pointed out that the Pharisees, who were the predecessors of the Tannaim in the fashioning of traditional Judaism, had no difficulty in accepting Shelom-Zion (Salome Alexandra), the widow of King Alex-ander Janaeus, as the legitimate queen during the Second Temple (76–67 B.C.E.). Indeed, they praised her friendly relations with Simeon ben Shetah and her adherence to Pharisaic norms.[21] Similarly, in the first century of the Common Era, when the royal house of Adiabene adopted Judaism, Queen Helene was praised for her piety and philan-thropy; and no word of censure is raised against her rule, though, to be sure, she may have sat on the throne with her husband, King Monobaz.[22]

The argument is also raised that the laws of *niddah* (the separation the Halakhah enjoins for the period before, during, and after menstrua-tion), would effectively preclude a woman's officiating as a rabbi. This consideration might be appropriate in a right-wing community of Ha-sidim, where all the regulations of *niddah* are punctiliously observed and where women have no social contact at any time with men outside their immediate families. Exclusive of these enclaves, there is scant evi-dence that the total social segregation of women during their menstrual periods is observed today, even in Orthodox circles.

I worship in an Orthodox synagogue that is militant in its adherence to the Orthodox interpretation of the Halakhah and is attended by many women. After nearly two decades, I have yet to see a woman, be-cause of her menstrual period, refrain from shaking hands with a man who extended his hand in greeting. Moreover, most of these women, young and old, are gainfully employed or attend college or are active in the public sector. I doubt whether even those who observe the regula-tions regarding the *mikveh*, "ritual bath," adhere to the other traditional prohibitions in their daily lives. However persuasive the rationales that have been proposed for the laws of *niddah*,[23] the fact is that in Conserva-tive (and most Orthodox) circles, these bans on social contacts during the menstrual period are disregarded. On the other hand, if a woman wished to observe these prohibitions, she would be as free to do so in the rabbinate as in any other calling.

Women's Exemption from the *Mitzvot*

The strongest Halakhic argument against the ordination of women is the contention that the traditional Halakhah exempts women from the obligation (*ḥiyyubh*) of prayer. This exemption in turn is buttressed by the Talmudic principle that "women are free from commandments that must traditionally be performed at specific times" (*mitzvat ʿaseh shehazman gerama*).

Before we examine the implications that have been drawn from this rule, it should be noted that the principle itself was far from universally applied. Rituals to be performed at particular times, such as the kindling of sabbath and festival lights, were ruled obligatory for women. So, too, rabbinic law commanded women as well as men to hear the reading of the *Megillah* on Purim, "since they, too, were involved in that miracle of salvation."[24] Thus a generalization was made that women were excused from observing *mitzvot* having a specific time frame. But the principle represents only a few specific instances and is not universally binding. As often occurred, the Gemara, observing a series of concrete statements of the Mishnah on different subjects, sought to develop an underlying principle to cover them all.[25] The generalization may or may not have been in the minds of the authors of the various relevant rabbinic passages. In our case, the rule is clearly descriptive and not prescriptive, as the many exceptions make clear.[26]

With regard to prayer, the Mishnah (M. *Berakhot* 3:3) exempts women from reciting the *shema* and putting on *tefillin*, "phylacteries," but makes the recitation of the *tefillah* (i.e., the *amidah*, or silent prayer) obligatory for them. The Talmud (B. *Berakhot* 20b) explains the exemption here by the fact that women are free from *mitzvot* that must be performed at particular times, but it has trouble explaining the distinction. Since women were not expected to engage in statutory prayer services or to attend the synagogue, the rule exempting them from prayer, in whole or in part, is a rationalization after the fact. Apologetics aside, the retention of this rule is an expression of the inferior status of women and of their segregation from public life.[27] The justification offered by the fourteenth-century scholar David Abudraham for exempting women from the positive commandments tied to a specific time was that a husband has a prior claim on his wife's services at any time. This hardly comports with the realities of present-day life.

It has also been explained that the manifold tasks devolving upon women as homemakers made it impossible for them to observe prayer and other obligations at specific hours. This contention may been valid in the past, when a woman's household duties were onerous and unlimited, but it has little justification today. In this age of labor-saving devices, a woman who is a homemaker has as much free time as a man engaged all day in his occupation; and a woman who is gainfully employed outside the home is in exactly the same position as her male counterpart.

The American historian James Harvey Robinson once said that every event in history has a good reason and a real reason. In the case of the *mitzvah* of prayer and women's exclusion from the *minyan*, the real reason is no longer good and the good reason is not real.

Let us grant that the Talmudic principle was originally established by the Sages out of a sense of genuine compassion for women, whose working day coincided with their waking hours, with virtually no leisure. It would be ironic to invoke this principle as a basis for discriminating against them today. However, even if all these considerations are brushed aside and the principle is maintained that women are exempt from the obligation of prayer, its bearing on the ordination of women is tenuous in the extreme. None of the major functions of the modern rabbi—preaching, teaching, conducting funeral services, serving as *mesadder kiddushin* ("officiant" at marriage ceremonies), personal counseling, and adult education—are prohibited by extant rabbinic sources.

The speciousness of the argument becomes clear when it is recalled that it is the cantor not the rabbi who is the *sheliah zibbur*, "the messenger of the congregation." The rabbi may read some prayers in English or supplement the service, but the function of leading the congregation in prayer is essentially that of the cantor or other laity. One may also question the logic of the contention that one who is not *obligated* to pray cannot fulfil the function for one who is. Obviously, a woman is not *forbidden* to pray.

If we were to accept the principle that one who prays can exempt one who does not, there would be no logical ground for denying this role to women. When a fire breaks out, a fireman is obligated by his occupation to rush in and save the life of a child. The general citizen has no such obligation but is not *prohibited* from leaping into the building and saving the child. *Me ʿikkara dedina pirkhah*, "the original assumption is dubious."

The doctrine that the *sheliah zibbur* must be a person obligated to pray is subject to challenge from yet another direction. According to the Halakhah, the *sheliah zibbur* conducting a service is fulfilling the obligations for worshippers who cannot pray for themselves. The provision stems from a time, before the invention of printing, when prayer books were scarce and many Jews could not pray on their own. So, too, the law had in mind pious and observant Jews who, because of the pressures of their work, were unable to read their prayers at the proper time. Today prayer books are available everywhere, and the majority of Jews who do not engage in prayer are not prevented by preoccupation but by indifference. To deprive a community of the service of a woman rabbi for these anachronistic reasons certainly argues a strange scale of values.

The Ineligibility of Women as Witnesses

According to rabbinic law, women are ineligible to serve as witnesses; therefore, it is argued, a woman rabbi would be incapable of signing as an *edh* on a *ketubbah*, "witness to a wedding." The Halakhah still excludes women as witnesses and places them on a par with minors and deaf-mutes with regard to testifying before a religious court.

The ineligibility of women as witnesses derives from two passages in Deuteronomy: 19:15, which deals with witnesses but does not specify the male gender; and 19:17, which indicates the male gender but is concerned with litigants not witnesses. The Talmud bases its exclusion of women as witnesses on the latter; Maimonides on the former, which uses the masculine noun *edhim*, "witnesses," in the context. [28]

The exclusion of women as witnesses (and therefore as judges) was part of the established order in ancient and medieval society, for which the Talmud and the Codes sought a warrant in the text of the Torah, with less than total success. On this issue, the received Halakhah can therefore not be the sole determinant of our practice today. In a society where women were sheltered and had little experience or contact with the world at large, there might have been some basis for regarding their testimony as inexpert and therefore inadmissible. But for the modern Halakhah to perpetuate this status in a society where women participate in all areas of life is unconscionable. Even in Israel, where right-wing religious authorities dictate conduct in many areas of life, the exclusion of women as witnesses in the secular courts has not been proposed.

Strictly speaking, the issue of the ineligibility of women as witnesses is irrelevant to their ordination as rabbis. There is no necessity for the rabbi, male or female, to serve as a witness at a wedding. The rabbi's role is that of a *mesadder kiddushin*, "the arranger of the marriage ceremony." Two other witnesses can, and often do, sign the *ketubbah*.

At this point, the Halakhists who oppose the ordination of women invoke a "sociological" argument and ask us to consider the position of a small community in which the rabbi is the only religious functionary. If the rabbi were a woman, she might be called upon to act as the *ḥazzan*, "cantor." In the case of a marriage ceremony, she might need to serve as a witness for the *ketubbah*, especially because of the paucity of religiously observant witnesses. The response might be put as follows: The Rabbis of the Talmud, *shaqedu ʿal taqqanat benot yisraʾel*, "were diligent for the welfare of the daughters of Israel."[29] In such a special case, where the happiness and welfare of a bride and groom are involved and they wish to be married "according to the Law of Moses and Israel," the entire thrust of the Halakhah and its underlying spirit suggest the approach to be adopted. Where no other witness is available, it is entirely appropriate that a woman who is both religiously knowledgeable and observant be recognized as a legitimate witness. That is precisely what happened with the Mishnaic ruling accepting the testimony of an ʿagunah.

The Halakhah Is Silent

In conclusion, it is clear that these objections, ostensibly based on the Halakhah, are indirect at best and far-fetched at worst. In the face of major problems confronting the survival of Judaism, the role of women in contemporary society and the ethical issues involved, no Halakhic objections of substance have been adduced. The truth is that the Halakhah neither sanctions nor forbids the ordination of women—it never contemplated the possibility.

In the absence of Halakhic sources against the ordination of women, opponents of the idea have advanced another argument—it is a matter of *minhag*, "custom," and, as the popular saying has it, "custom supersedes a law."[30] Many customs are highly appealing because of the piety and ethical sensitivity they express or because of their colorful folk character. It is a far cry from this observation to the conclusion that *minhag qua minhag* is sacrosanct and not subject to analysis and critique. The customs, local and general, to be found in Jewish communities have different points of origin, serve diverse functions, and vary widely in their significance. In the history of Judaism, countless customs have arisen, flourished, and disappeared. To set up the *minhag* as the final arbiter is to violate the inner spirit of a religion that has produced the Talmud, which is dedicated to rational discussion, the establishment of consensus, and the practice of justice and equality.

The present work offers ample proof that throughout its history the Halakhah has always been responsive to emerging religious and ethical insights and aware of new social, economic, political, and cultural conditions. These considerations, far from being extra-Halakhic or anti-Halakhic, constitute an integral element in the Halakhic process. Our examination of the passages in traditional Halakhic sources, cited as allegedly opposing the ordination of women, demonstrates that they neither favor nor oppose the idea. The admission of women to the rabbinate is not a breach of the Halakhah.

Since the law virtually always codifies the positions attained by society in an earlier period, it is no wonder that the process of conferring full equality upon women has not been completed, either in secular law or in the Halakhah. Nevertheless, women have achieved positions far more advanced than contemporary law codes would indicate. To have ordained women as rabbis in an earlier age would have been counterproductive, since women had only a private role in society (though there have been women preachers and other charismatic women in Christianity). The appearance of a woman on a pulpit would have caused a sensation that would have disrupted the traditional values of communal prayer and the study of the Torah.

Today the situation is radically different. The issue is not that women must be ordained and that congregations must accept women rabbis, but that women should be free to be accepted or rejected as rabbis.

The Growing Need for Rabbis

Thirty to forty percent of the students enrolled in non-Orthodox seminaries are women, about the same percentage as in other professions in the United States today. The accession of women to the rabbinate will be particularly valuable in view of the shortage of dedicated and knowledgeable personnel in Jewish life. The rapid geographical and occupational mobility among American Jews has led to the decentralization of Jewish communities and the breakup of the large concentration of Jewish population into hundreds of smaller cities and towns. Many of them are bereft of competent Jewish leadership, and their survival is gravely imperiled.

In addition, there is an unmistakable movement in American Judaism to overcome the impersonalization and mass character of large congregations. In institutions whose memberships run into many hundreds, individuals, already stripped of much of their sense of personal worth in contemporary society, seek in vain to recover their sense of identity. Differing widely in orientation, background, and interests, *minyanim*, *shtiblach* (prayer huts), and *havurot* (fellowships) have proliferated. They are united by a quest for a "do-it-yourself" Judaism, with a large measure of personal participation and a warm feeling of community.

This renewed interest in Judaism deserves the enthusiasm with which it has been greeted. But the creation of small, independent groups completely unrelated to existing synagogues and therefore in competition with them is not the solution to the problem of the survival of Judaism. The abandoning of large synagogues and synagogue centers wastes many years of work by the dedicated men and women who founded and nurtured them.

The creation and maintenance of well-staffed, properly graded, adequately housed Jewish schools, on both the elementary and the high school level, requires substantial financial resources beyond the power of a *minyan*. Adequate adolescent and adult education programs also need substantial memberships and considerable funding. Attractive social and cultural programs for singles are a crying necessity today. Badly needed centers for personal counseling, geriatric services, and day care under religious auspices would also be virtually impossible if, for example, a congregation of a thousand families were to be dissolved and in its stead twenty independent groups of fifty families apiece were to emerge.

The solution, I believe, is the retention and restructuring of the synagogue so that it can serve as the base for all these activities and as the source and center for smaller "special interest" groups, such as *havurot*. All too often, the high hopes of these fellowships are not realized because of the lack of properly trained personnel to work with them. Women rabbis can help fill that need. If the recent experience, admittedly brief, of some Christian churches is any indication, many ordained women will gravitate to the fields of childhood, youth, and adult education and to personal counseling.

The needs of the Jewish community constitute only one element in the picture. The other includes the broad ethical dimension. To continue to exclude women from this area of service when they are admitted in virtually all others will surely alienate many ethically sensitive men and women, particularly among our youth, and drive potentially creative members of the community out of Jewish life. Judaism has always prided itself on being in the vanguard of ethical progress, whether it be in the areas of personal rights, universal education, political freedom, social justice, or international peace. On ethical and as well as pragmatic grounds—and the Halakhah is properly concerned with both—the ordination of women today is indispensable for the vitality of Judaism and the meaningful survival of the Jewish people.

XII

"BE FRUITFUL AND MULTIPLY"
BIOGRAPHY OF A *MITZVAH*

During its long career, as the Jewish community faced constant perils from without and within, it stressed the obligation to procreate in order to survive. If self-preservation is the first law of nature, the injunction "Be fruitful and multiply" is properly the first Commandment, not merely because it occurs in the opening chapter of Genesis but because it is the cornerstone of Jewish life, upon which all else depends.

It is therefore no wonder that both scholars and lay persons believe that throughout the centuries Judaism has demanded large families of its adherents, and that high fertility has always been a characteristic of traditional Jewish life. Actually the truth is more complicated than the truism. The *mitzvah* of procreation has undergone many vicissitudes, paralleling the shifting tides of Jewish history. There have been four principal stages in the history of the *mitzvah*.

The Biblical Blessing

In the biblical narrative of creation we read: "God blessed them, and God said to them, 'Be fruitful and multiply, and fill the earth and subdue it; and have dominion over the fish of the sea and over the birds of the air and over every living thing that moves upon the earth.'"[1] The same formula is addressed to the sons of Noah after the Flood. God blessed Noah and his sons, and said to them, "Be fruitful and multiply, and fill the earth."[2] The same blessing is also extended to Jacob and his descendants: "God said to him, 'I am God Almighty: be fruitful and multiply: a nation and a company of nations shall come from you, and kings shall spring from you'"[3]

The context makes it obvious that all three passages are blessings, not commandments.[4] Throughout the biblical period, when Jewish life was normal, exposed only to the usual hazards that are part of the human condition, the attitude toward procreation was relaxed; children were regarded as blessings. Thus the Psalmist declares: "Lo, sons are a heritage from the Lord; the fruit of the womb, God's reward."[5] The next Psalm offers a moving picture of the patriarchal family in biblical times: "Your wife is like a fruitful vine within the corners of your house; your children are like olive shoots around your table."[6]

Many factors converged to create the attitude toward children as a blessing. Economically, children assisted in running the household, tending the fields, and guarding the flocks. When parents reached old age, children were expected to maintain them.[7] Sons could be called upon to protect the head of the family in case of a quarrel or a lawsuit within the city gates.[8] Psychologically, children offered a support for parents in their old age. The Prophet described Mother Zion in exile as being drunk with the poison of God's anger:

> You have drunk from the Lord's hand, the cup of his wrath, drained to its dregs the bowl of drunkenness. Of all the sons you have borne, there is not one to guide you. Of all you have reared, not one to take you by the hand (Isa. 51:17–18].

The full force of the tragedy emerges from its Near Eastern background. In ancient Canaan and Egypt children were supposed to support a drunken father and lead him home after a feast.[9]

Finally, children were regarded as a blessing on religious grounds. A child surviving his parents conferred immortality upon them by "setting the name of the dead man over his inheritance" and thus keeping him alive. This theme may be implied in Rachel's anguished call to her husband, "Give me children, for otherwise I die."[10] This last factor should be stressed, because the drive to avoid oblivion answers deep human instincts that transitory fashion and fleeting life styles may obscure and even suppress, but not permanently destroy.

In the biblical period, polygamy was practiced, but for economic as well as biological reasons, it was restricted to heroes like Gideon, who had 70 sons, or affluent men like Elkanah, who had two wives. Above all, polygamy was a prerogative of the royal household, for whom political and dynastic considerations played a major role, as in the case of David and Solomon. The typical Jewish family was monogamous and not very large. Moderate-sized families were favored, and there was no pressure for unlimited procreation. Adam and Eve, the prototype of the human family, have two sons, with Seth being born after the tragic clash of Cain and Abel. Sarah and Abraham have only one son; Isaac and Rebecca have two. Amram and Jochebed beget two sons and a daughter; Aaron has four sons; Moses, two. In the desert period too, Zelophehad has five feminist daughters, but no sons.

After the settlement in the land, the priest Eli has two sons. Hannah bears three sons and two daughters to Elkanah following Samuel's birth. The Prophet Samuel himself is credited—if that is the word—with two sons. Zeruiah has three sons—Abishai, Joab, and Asahel. That there were daughters in all these families as well goes without saying, so that the number of offspring was somewhat larger than these figures would indicate.

The life story of the patriarch Jacob in Genesis must be read on two levels: first, that of a sharply delineated human individual who has two wives and two concubines and is the father of twelve sons and at least one daughter. On another level Jacob-Israel is an eponym, symbolizing the common ancestor for the twelve tribes of Israel. The same structure undoubtedly reflects tribal relationships in the twelve sons of Abraham's kinsman Nahor, the six sons of Abraham borne to him by Keturah, and the twelve sons of Ishmael.

Of course, larger families are also found. Jesse has seven sons and two daughters. Job, a patrician, is pictured as having seven sons and three daughters. After his restoration, all his possessions—his cattle, sheep, camels, and goats—are doubled in accordance with the law that establishes double restitution for one who has been robbed. Job fathers fourteen sons, twice the original number.[11] As for his three daughters, the author follows the philosophic principle that enough is sufficient. Their number is not increased, but they are beautiful—no civilization has ever been indifferent to beautiful women.

The reference to seven sons, in the case of Jesse and of Job, may have a folkloristic significance. Thus in a hymn praising God's power, the poet hyperbolically declares, "the barren woman has borne seven, but she that has many children, languishes."[12]

The Rabbinic Era

Between the Return after the Babylonian Exile until the end of the Tannaitic period, the third century c.e., the center of Jewish life was in Palestine. Politically Jews were either independent or autonomous. They faced the normal problems of poverty and disease, but there were no major threats to Jewish survival.

Spiritually, this period was marked by the institutionalization of Jewish belief and practice in the Halakhah. With the emergence of the Halakhah as the basic structure of Jewish life, the blessing of procreation was transformed into a *mitzvah*, an obligation incumbent upon the Jew. Yet even in this second stage there was no pressure for very large families, in view of the basic normality of Jewish life. The Halakhic evidence pointing to this conclusion is both extensive and impressive.

Shammai and Hillel, who flourished during the first century c.e., in the decades before the destruction of the Second Temple, were in agreement that the commandment was fulfilled by the birth of two children, Shammai requiring two sons, and Hillel a son and a daughter.[13] This ruling surely does not advocate a "population explosion." At least equally remarkable is the position adopted in the Mishnah that the man is commanded to engage in procreation but not the woman:

> Rabbi Johanan ben Beroka says: "The commandment applies to both, as the biblical text clearly indicates: 'And God blessed *them*, and said to *them* "be fruitful and multiply." ' "[14]

Nevertheless, the majority of the Sages (and hence the law) did not accept Rabbi Johanan's thoroughly justifiable deduction from the text and limits the obligation to the man.[15]

The exemption of women from the obligation to bear children is all the more striking since Judaism, from the biblical period onward, has always been free of the cant that has prevailed in the Western world to our own day, according to which respectable women have no sexual desires, and "nice girls don't need sex." Eve is told, "You will have an urge for your husband," and the same noun, *teshuqah*, "desire, urge," occurs in the Song of Songs, "I am my beloved's and his desire is for me." Indeed, the celebration of love between the sexes constitutes the theme of the entire Song of Songs, which Rabbi Akiba describes as the "Holy of Holies" in the Scriptures.[16]

The sexual desires and needs of the woman are recognized as a legal right in the Holiness Codes, the oldest biblical law code: "He [the husband] shall not deprive the first [his wife] of food, clothes and conjugal rights."[17] Nevertheless, while fully aware of the role of sex in a woman's life, rabbinic law exempts her from the obligation to bear children.

No reason is assigned in the Mishnah for the exemption. Various explanations have been proposed by modern scholars, but they seem unconvincing and far-fetched. J. Preuss declares that if such an obligation existed, women might be encouraged to practice prostitution.[18] Another scholar maintains that women have an "instinct" for childbearing, so that they require no specific commandment to that end.[19]

A much more reasonable explanation is that the Rabbis were well aware that the burden, the pain, and the peril involved in the *mitzvah* of procreation, both in child-bearing and child-rearing, fall primarily on the woman. They wished to minimize, or at least not increase, her problems in this area by not making procreation obligatory upon her.

The Rabbis of the Talmud voiced strong objections to the marriage of minors, possibly out of a concern for the health and well-being of the child that might be threatened by pregnancy, and a recognition of the existence of preferences and antipathies intrinsic to human nature. Thus Rab, the architect of the Babylonian Talmud, at the end of the Tannaitic period, declared: "A man is forbidden to marry off his daugh-

ter while she is a minor, until she is grown and says 'this man I want.' "[20]
Whatever motives entered into the negative judgment on child marriages, it is evident that forbidding them would limit the number of
child-bearing years for the mother and thus tend to reduce the size of
families.

The practice of birth control is discussed in the Talmud because of
the Rabbis' deep concern for the life and health of the woman and that
of her unborn child. The classic Tannaitic passage is quoted in the Talmud no fewer than seven times, once in the *Tosefta*, and six times in the
Gemara,[21] so that it is not an obscure or isolated utterance, but is clearly
in the mainstream of the tradition. The passage reads as follows:

> Rabbi Bebai recited a Tannaitic passage in the presence of Rabbi
> Nahman: Three types of women use an absorbent [to prevent concep-
> tion], a minor, a pregnant woman and a nursing mother: a minor, lest
> she become pregnant and die; a pregnant woman, lest her embryo be in-
> jured and become a [fish-shaped, flat] abortion; and a nursing mother,
> lest she wean her child too soon and it die.
> Who is meant by a "minor" [*ketannah*]? From the age of eleven years
> and a day to twelve and a day. Below this limit and above it, she cohabits
> in the normal manner, so says Rabbi Meir. The Sages say that [*ɔaḥat zo
> veɔaḥat zo*] if she is both within the limit [i.e., eleven to twelve years]
> and outside of it [below or above], she cohabits in the normal manner,
> and Heaven will have pity and protect her, as it is said, "The Lord guards
> the simple" [Psalms 116:6].[22]

There is no disagreement between Rabbi Meir and Sages with regard
to two of the three categories, the pregnant woman and the nursing
mother. They differ only on the first category, the minor, from the age
of eleven to twelve. Rabbi Meir permits a minor to use a contraceptive,
but rules that those outside this age bracket carry on sexual relations
in the normal manner, since they are not in danger, because the one
younger than eleven is not likely to conceive, while the one older than
twelve will not jeopardize her health if she becomes pregnant. But
Rabbi Meir's colleagues maintain that both those within the eleven-to-
twelve-year bracket and those outside it should carry on normal intercourse and trust to Heaven to protect them.

Medieval and modern authorities in many *Responsa* discuss whether
these three categories of women *may* use a *mokh* (and other women *may
not*), or whether these three *must* and others *may* employ the absorbent.
There are respected authorities on both sides of the issue. Later views
also differ as to whether the device may be used before, during, or after
coitus.[23] But it is obvious that there is a basically permissive attitude
in Tannaitic literature toward the practice of birth control by the

woman. This is entirely in harmony with the rabbinic view that she is exempt from the obligation to procreate.[24]

The Middle Ages—And the Need for Children

During the long period of the Galut, when Palestine was no longer the center of Jewish life and Jews were dispersed throughout Europe, North Africa, and western Asia, they were regarded as aliens, living at the pleasure of their hosts. Jews were perpetually victims of persecution, expropriation, expulsion, and massacre at the hands of their neighbors. While there were some peaceful interludes, Jewish survival was always precarious. Both natural and manmade factors brought about high levels of infant and child mortality among Jews during the Middle Ages. "There was no house without its dead" (Exod. 12:30). It should also be remembered that for the bulk of east European Jewry, the medieval era continued into the twentieth century.

The extent of this perpetual danger to the biological survival of the Jewish people may be gauged through some, admittedly rough, statistics. According to the famous New Testament scholar Adolf Harnack, there were four million Jews in the Roman Empire at the beginning of the Christian Era, approximately ten percent of the population. Salo W. Baron and other scholars give a considerably higher figure, up to eight million. It is estimated that in 1070, when Benjamin of Tudela set out on his travels, the world Jewish population had been reduced to one million. Not until the eighteenth century did it again reach four million.

Medieval Jewish leaders decided that the desperate situation required Draconian measures, that the procreation of more and more children was the only means for safeguarding the Jewish future. Hence the commandment "Be fruitful and multiply" had to take precedence over other considerations of health, convenience, or personal desire. Accordingly, the Rabbis concluded that the decisions of the earlier period could no longer be normative under the new and more perilous conditions of medieval life. With extraordinary courage, the post-Mishnaic authorities proceeded to review, modify, or completely set aside the four principal limiting provisions of the law that we have cited, in order to meet this overriding international need.

The view of Bet Hillel and Bet Shammai that two children suffice to fulfil the injunction "Be fruitful and multiply" was nullified by the introduction of two principles derived from biblical verses cited in the Talmud: "He created the earth not for chaos, but for habitation [*lashevet*]" (Isa. 45:18); and "In the morning sow your seed, and in the evening [la‹erev] do not be idle, for you cannot tell which will prosper, or whether both shall have equal success" (Eccles. 11:6). The first passage yielded the principle of *lashevet*, the obligation to have as many children as possible. The second provided the doctrine of *la‹erev*, that procreation is an activity that must be pursued throughout one's entire lifetime. Both became normative in traditional Jewry, and women continued to bear children as long as they were able.[25]

The urgency of this step is all the more apparent when we note that it sets aside the decision of the schools of both Hillel and Shammai. Moreover, the later authorities disregarded the generally accepted Talmudic principle, which, to be sure, is not without exception, that "Torahitic rules are not to be derived from the words of the Prophets or the Sacred Writings."[26] In this instance, the instructions from Isaiah and Ecclesiastes are not literal derivations from the text but Midrashic homiletics.[27]

The rabbinic attitude toward procreation, which became normative in traditional Judaism, was set forth by Maimonides with characteristic clarity and vigor:

> Even though a man has fulfilled the *mitzvah* of procreation, he is commanded by the Sages not to desist from procreating so long as he has the strength, for whoever adds a single soul in Israel it is as though he had built a world [*Mishneh Torah*, Hilkhot 'Ishut, 15,4].

That the obligation to procreate did not fall upon the woman was not denied. But it was argued that, as a good wife, she had an obligation to assist her husband in fulfilling the *mitzvah*.[28] In view of the subordinate position women occupied in the medieval world, no protest was forthcoming, at least in our extant sources.

As regards child marriage, the medieval authorities consciously set aside the Talmudic objections to the practice. They called attention to the rigors of the Exile and the uncertainties, economic and personal, that hovered over every potential match. In the words of the sixteenth-century Polish codifier, Rabbi Mordecai Jaffe:

> Some say that our present custom of betrothing minor daughters despite the Talmudic disapproval is due to the fact that we are in Exile, and do not always have enough for a dowry; therefore, we marry them while we are still able. Also we are few in number, and do not always find the proper match; our practice is to marry them early, when a proper match presents itself.[29]

Early marriages continued to be a feature of Jewish life in eastern Europe, until at least the beginning of the twentieth century. Boys showing high promise in their rabbinic studies were regarded as desirable matches for the daughters of affluent merchants. This practice was vigorously opposed by both the modernist *maskilim*, "enlightened," and government authorities. Nevertheless, traditionalist Jews continued to arrange *tenaim*, "engagements," for their children in their early teens, and the marriages were consummated a few years thereafter.[30]

The most radical procedures of all were adopted by the medieval authorities in dealing with the Tannaitic provisions regarding birth control. Medieval authorities disregarded the clear meaning of the common phrase, *ʾahat zo ve ʾahat zo*, "both the one and the other," which invariably refers to two categories and no more. Instead they applied the phrase to all three classes of women, the child-wife, the pregnant woman, and the nursing mother. They insisted that all three categories are forbidden to use an absorbent but must practice normal intercourse, trusting to Heaven to protect them.[31] Since Rabbi Meir gives his individual opinion and the Sages are the majority, the law would therefore effectively forbid the use of an absorbent for all women.

The Rabbis' knowledge of the Hebrew language and all its nuances was second to none. Had it been the intention of the *Baraita* to say that all three categories cohabit in the normal way, it would have said *kullan meshammeshot kedarkan*, "all of them practice intercourse in the normal manner [i.e., without the interposition of a *mokh*]." The idiom *ʾehad ʾehad* with its feminine counterpart, *ʾahat ʾahat*, occurs scores of times in the Mishnah and the Talmud and invariably refers to two categories and no more.[32]

What led the medieval commentators and the decisors to depart from the obvious meaning of the text? I submit that they were intent on preventing any procedure that would reduce the number of children in Jewish families. This surmise is supported not only by the abrogation of the Shammaite and the Hillelite limited interpretation of the commandment "Be fruitful and multiply" and of the clear-cut Talmudic opposition to child marriages, but by another remarkable fact. Though this *Baraita* on the three categories of women is quoted seven times in the Talmud, it is totally ignored in all the medieval law codes.

It is not referred to in the *Mishneh Torah* of Maimonides or in the *Shulhan Arukh* of Rabbi Joseph Karo. It is lacking in the *Sefer Mitzvot Gadol*, the *Tur*, the *Beth Joseph*, and several lesser codes. The suggestion has been offered that "it is possible that Maimonides saw no practical ruling at all emerging from the *Baraita*," but this is hardly convincing. The practical implications of the *Baraita* are obvious for every family.[33] Besides, Maimonides' Code contains many laws no longer operative in his time or in ours. A distinguished modern Orthodox scholar frankly writes, "The Codes *rather surprisingly* omit any direct reference to contraception altogether."[34]

Actually the omission is entirely congruent with the other aspects of family law already cited. The rabbinic leadership in the Middle Ages was convinced that Jewish group survival took precedence over individual health and personal desires and needs. In a sense, their reaction was similar to that of Ezra and Nehemiah, who, centuries earlier, forced the dissolution of mixed marriages in the Jewish community.

Far from deprecating the measures adopted by the Rabbis of the Middle Ages, I believe that they are to be honored—or at least respected—for recognizing the desperate need of the hour—an hour that lasted nearly two millennia—and for taking steps to meet the danger. To cite the rabbinic interpretation of the verse in Psalms 119:126: "It was time to act for the Lord—so they set aside 'Thy Law.'" Today we are in a position of comparable gravity, confronted by desperate dangers to which we dare not shut our eyes.

The Modern Era and the Vanishing Family

The fourth historical stage, the modern era of the Emancipation lasted only 150 years, from the French Revolution to the eruption of Nazism, from 1789 until 1939, and was basically limited to Western Jewry, the communities of central and western Europe and North America. In this period, the *mitzvah* of procreation suffered the same fate that overtook many other basic *mitzvot* in Judaism—it went into total eclipse. Modern Jews, highly urbanized, with an overpowering drive for upward mobility, reduced their birthrate far more than did the rest of the population. According to the most optimistic figures, American Jewish couples have an average of 1.7 children, not even enough to replace themselves let alone exhibit a pattern of growth.

Demographic studies have revealed the catastrophic decline of the Jewish population of the West during the Emancipation era. It was partly masked by the fact that the bulk of world Jewry, residing in Eastern Europe, had by and large not yet been exposed to the blessings and the temptations of the modern era and were still living within the framework of the medieval Jewish lifestyle. Hence East European Jewry was constantly engaged in replacing the diminishing ranks of Jews in Germany, Austria, Holland, Belgium, France, Great Britain, and Italy, as well as the United States. The Holocaust not only wiped out this source of replenishment but also reduced the world Jewish population from sixteen million to eleven million, the latter figure including the doomed Jewry of Soviet Russia, numbering two million or more.

At the height of the festivities celebrating the Bicentennial of the United States, two social scientists from the Harvard Center for Population Studies gave American Jewry a rude jolt. They projected that in the year 2076, if intermarriage were to remain constant at 15 percent, the U.S. Jewish population would be 944,000; if it rose to 50 percent, the Jewish population would be 420,000; and if it rose above 50 percent, the Jewish population would be only 10,240.[35]

These figures were vigorously disputed both in the community at large and by sociologists and demographers. The statistics may be unduly pessimistic, but the precise figures are not the issue—it is the trend that is indisputable and disturbing. The authors indicated that their projection was based on the assumption that no new factors would enter the picture—and new elements are always a possibility. But there is good authority in the tradition for the principle *ʾEin somekhin ʿal hanes*, "We do not depend upon miracles."[36] So far the trends toward intermarriage and small families seem to be continuing and indeed intensifying.

Much can and should be done to win over non-Jewish partners to Judaism. One direct consequence would be that the children of mixed marriages would be saved for Judaism and the Jewish people. Obviously a person who enters Jewish life as an adult will lack the childhood memories of a born Jew, even as a naturalized American citizen will not have the same background or experience as the native-born. But millions of naturalized Americans have demonstrated the depth of their attachment to their new country by their contributions to America in war and peace. Similarly, converts to Judaism often bring a new enthusiasm to Jewish commitment, especially when they receive from the community the warm welcome they deserve.

Every step taken toward enhancing the quality of Jewish life and making it attractive, to those both within and outside the Jewish community, helps to safeguard the Jewish future. Achieving this requires a broad program.

To be sure, hard statistical facts about American Jews are rare, but the U.S. Census figures for the general population between 1970 and 1980 are illuminating—and disquieting—for the future of the American family: Twenty-three percent of American households consist of one person; one child out of every five lives with only one parent; and the age at which people marry is rising steadily, thus reducing the number of childbearing years for American marriages. In addition, the incidence of premarital and extramarital sex militates against procreation; and homosexuals, estimated to constitute ten percent of the general population, are openly withdrawing from the procreative process.[37] Indeed, all the phenomena we associate with the "sexual revolution" have the effect of reducing the birthrate among Jews, as part of the general population.

Strategies for a Higher Jewish Birthrate

The traditional pattern of a large number of children is being maintained today almost entirely by Hasidic and other right-wing Orthodox families. "Modern Orthodox" families tend to be somewhat larger than those that are Conservative or Reform. Although this observation suggests that the power of tradition is not completely spent, its impact is limited. Nor will pious exhortations from the pulpit urging an increase in the number of children per family affect many members of the present generation. Today's complex socioeconomic and cultural factors are far more powerful than religious motivations. As we have seen, earlier great masters of Jewish law were highly sensitive to social, economic, and cultural conditions of their times in seeking to raise the Jewish birthrate. Through means appropriate to our day, I believe that modern Jewry must walk in their footsteps. There are three agencies that can be effective in this regard: individual Jewish communities, the rabbinate, and American Jewry on the national level.

Individual Jewish communities, through their synagogues and centers, are at long last beginning to make provisions for "singles." Efforts are being made to draw them into Jewish religious life and cultural activity. Basic to singles programs is the creation of facilities for social intercourse for its own sake, as well as for the purpose of stimulating marriages within the Jewish community. The synagogue could make itself a modern instrumentality for *shadhanut*, "matchmaking," which is an honorable, and today, an indispensable calling. The synagogue offers an excellent setting for these activities, which could go beyond the individual synagogue. For instance, some years ago the United Synagogue of America established a computer service especially useful in smaller Jewish communities. This program might be evaluated and extended.

The pulpit and the lecture platform, the study course and the discussion group, are invaluable instruments for dealing with the issue of the birthrate. The subject of increased family size could be an integral element in all educational projects dealing with personal problems and sexual issues. The rabbinate is uniquely equipped to perform a major service in this area. Rabbis from all sectors of American Jewry could launch a broad-based, ongoing campaign to change contemporary mores on family size, especially the current fashion of the two-child family. A not unimportant by-product of such an effort would be an instance of meaningful and cooperative activity by Orthodox, Conservative, and Reform Judaism on behalf of Jewish survival.

The premarital conference between the rabbi and the nuptial couple is an invaluable resource. Most rabbis have established a practice of meeting with the bride and groom to discuss various aspects of the ceremony and of the marriage to follow. This meeting, coming at a sensitive and significant hour in the life of the couple, offers an excellent opportunity to discuss the obligation and the privilege of becoming parents and bringing Jewish children into the world. This has rarely been done in the past.

Rather unexpectedly the "advanced" sex mores of the day offer another opening for broaching this basic issue. Very often, couples who come to the rabbi to be married have already been living together. The rabbi is now in a position to bring home to the couple that their new married status will give them the opportunity, the duty, and the joy of having children.

In my opinion zero population growth is not a universal ideal. I agree that family limitation is desirable in underdeveloped countries, where poor living conditions prevail and the basic necessities of life may be lacking. But this is not the case for the upper- and middle-class societies in industrialized nations like the United States. Since the Holocaust has reduced the number of Jews in the world by more than a third, zero population growth, to my mind, is hardly an appropriate goal for American Jews. Milton Himmelfarb has projected that if the average Jewish family were to have three children, the American Jewish population would rise to seven and a half million and the world Jewish population to twenty-two million.[38]

The Rebirth of the Family

In 1983 I persuaded the leadership of the American Jewish Committee to take the initiative in setting up and funding a National Conference on Jewish Population Growth. It was sponsored by twenty-four national organizations, representing the widest possible spectrum. The three-day conference attracted a large attendance of scientific experts, community leaders, and interested laity. It dealt with all aspects of Jewish survival and gave consideration to the biological, social, economic, cultural, and religious aspects of procreation and the building of larger Jewish families. Many excellent papers were presented with constructive suggestions for dealing with the issue.

To urge a campaign for larger families today may seem quixotic in the extreme. I do not think so. I believe that there are important and unsuspected resources available for such an effort. One is broadly human, the other specifically Jewish; the first is rooted in human nature, the second, in Jewish loyalties.

Some of these universal human factors are only now beginning to surface. There is growing evidence that the profound human instinct for children, which has been out of fashion during the recent past, has not been destroyed. Rachel's pathetic cry to Jacob, "Give me children or I perish," resonates in the hearts of many men and women today, as evidenced by normal and abnormal behavior patterns reported daily in the press.

Recent statistical evidence, including some phenomena that we may personally find distasteful, indicate the strength of this natural love for children. According to the U.S. Bureau of the Census, seventeen percent of all children born out of wedlock are kept and raised by their mothers. Undoubtedly, the change of attitude toward marriage is a significant factor.

More and more single people uninterested in marriage are eager to have children of their own. The number of applications to the courts by single people who want to adopt children is rising constantly. This trend offers an oblique testimony to the strength of the desire for a child as a passport to immortality.

In a recent article, an English journalist describes her experiences. For twenty years she was afraid of becoming pregnant. Now she urges women, including those past their twenties, to experience the joys of fertility. With undisguised joy she writes:

> For a woman a child late in life—odd phrase when by most averages a 40 year old woman is only halfway to the grave—is a triumph of the will, not of ovarian longevity. How to explain to a friend who exclaims at the news—"Well, there goes another twenty years of your life!"—that fertility at this time of life restores all the traditional associations of abundance, power, productivity and strength. Must women's struggle for self-determination of their sexuality end not with a bang but a whimper . . . ? Human reproduction, with all its passions, is more rewarding than many of us, trained to sublimate desire for achievement and independence will concede.[39]

Betty Friedan, perhaps the most-influential voice in American feminism, has modified her earlier emphasis upon careers and independence for women outside the home in a book significantly called *The Second Stage*.[40] She argues that in "the first stage" many women fought to escape from the conventional image of a woman as "completely fulfilled in her role as husband's wife, children's mother, server of physical needs of husband, children, and home." As a result, Friedan now recognizes, many women suppressed or denied the human longing for home, mate, and family, and she calls upon her comrades-in-arms to recognize this indestructible need.

Obviously women will not—and in view of economic realities cannot—surrender their careers outside the home; it will not be a case of career versus family, but career and family for the overwhelming majority of women. Ways and means must be found for accommodating both goals. Friedan is not alone in suggesting that husband and wife will need to share the responsibilities of home-building and child-rearing. They may well discover a new, more equitable and rewarding life style. Social programs such as government subsidies for children and child-care facilities by employers are common in many countries, and flexible work schedules for women with families have been instituted.

Synagogues and Jewish centers can also play a role. They ought to be more active in providing child-care centers, which could be staffed by volunteers as well as by professionals. Older citizens in the community can perform a major service as "voluntary grandparents" and in the process bring healing to themselves through a unique form of occupational therapy. The astronomical costs of education are undoubtedly a major deterrent to larger families. Provisions should be made to assist large families with regard to both Jewish religious education and general schooling.

The synagogue could take the lead in honoring larger Jewish families by some form of public recognition. The *shabbat* of *Parshat Shemot*, when the account of Pharaoh's attempt to decimate the Jewish population at birth is part of the Torah reading, might become a universally observed "Jewish Family Sabbath."

There is also a special Jewish dimension that enters the picture. The past few decades have seen the intensification of Jewish loyalty among Jewish youth. At every hand, there is evidence of the influence the Holocaust has had in strengthening Jewish consciousness for hundreds of thousands of Jews, though to be sure it has encouraged a small minority to desert Judaism altogether. Even more powerful has been the positive impact of the state of Israel both directly on those who live or have lived in the land, and indirectly on Jewish youth and adults in the Diaspora who take pride in the achievements of Israel and feel concerned and involved in its problems.

It is increasingly evident that the revulsion against anti-Semitism that developed in the Western world in the wake of Hitler has largely evaporated; hatred of the Jews is becoming respectable again. The mounting terrorism against Jews in the democratic West—Italy, France, Belgium, the Netherlands, and Scandinavia—has its parallel in the growth of anti-Semitic propaganda in the United States. Both manifestations are linked in diverse ways to the rise of terrorist acts against the state of Israel. It may well be that the worldwide growth of anti-Jewish prejudice is the harbinger of a new era of hostility to the Jewish people. Even this black cloud, however, may have a silver lining. The Talmud quotes Rabbi Abba bar Kahana as observing,

> The ring of King Ahashuerus given by him to Haman [with the authority to destroy the Jews] was more effective than the forty-eight prophets and seven prophetesses who prophesied to Israel, because they all were unable to bring the people back to the right road, while that ring succeeded in doing so.[41]

Experience teaches that the efforts to combat these ugly manifestations of man's brutality to man can stimulate and deepen Jewish loyalty among alienated or indifferent Jews. Their new activism and loyalty emphasize again that it is not enough to protest the oppression and murder of Jewish men, women, and children. Each Jewish couple must see in larger families a personal commandment.

The Rabbis of the medieval period, with their boundless reverence for the tradition they had inherited, did not hesitate to set aside basic elements of earlier Jewish teaching that, under new conditions, were not conducive to the survival of their people. Modern Jews may hope to be spared the massacre, spoliation, and expulsion that was the lot of earlier generations, but the dangers that confront them are no less real and their situation is no less desperate. Our generation requires some of their courage, insight, and dedication so that we may not fail in our historic duty to safeguard the life of an eternal people.

During the past two millennia, our ancestors were taught that the blessing of procreation is a *mitzvah*. Their descendants need to learn anew that the *mitzvah* of procreation is a blessing.

XIII

SAFEGUARDING JEWISH SURVIVAL

The Eternal Covenant

One of the hallmarks of modern Jews is their preoccupation—or obsession—with Jewish survival and the preservation of Jewish identity. Their ancestors faced countless perils through the centuries—discrimination, persecution, and massacre—but the possibility of the extinction of the Jewish presence in the world played little or no part in their thinking, particularly in earlier periods.

For the Jewish tradition, the relationship between God and Israel was subsumed under the concept of *brit*, "the covenant," a reciprocal compact entered into by two parties, setting forth their obligations to each other. Preeminently the *brit* was the covenant between God and Israel. Its essence is embodied in the succinct formula frequently set forth in the Bible, "You shall be My people, and I will be your God."[1] Under the terms of the covenant, Israel undertook to obey the will of God as embodied in His law, while He would protect Israel against human enemies and natural disasters, thus safeguarding it against annihilation.

The term *brit* was not applied to the conditions governing Adam's sojourn in the Garden of Eden,[2] perhaps because the compact was of short duration and was soon abrogated by Adam. The term *brit* is first applied to God's promise to Noah and his descendants after the Flood not to destroy the world. In return mankind is forbidden to eat the blood of animals or to commit murder.[3] This rudimentary covenant with Noah, as well as the earlier commandment to Adam (Gen. 2:15), served in the Book of Jubilees and in the Talmud as the basis for the important concept of the Noahide laws, the basic moral principles binding upon all people, by virtue of their human character.[4]

The *brit* became central to the patriarchs Abraham, Isaac, and Jacob, who were promised that their seed would multiply and that they would inherit the land of Canaan and be a blessing to the nations.[5] The covenant *par excellence* took place at Sinai[6] and was confirmed by a sacrifice (Exod. 19:5). It is embodied primarily in the Decalogue, the Ten Words of the covenant.[7]

Israel's subsequent history was a record of violations of the covenant with condign punishment coming upon it. In an angry moment, Hosea might declare, in the name of his God, "You are not My people, and I am not your God" (Hos. 1:9),[8] but this was exceptional. The covenant was irrevocable. This is the theme of Moses' "Farewell Song" to his people in Deuteronomy[9] and the burden of the denunciations of Israel's offenses by the later Prophets. The nation's sins would bring war, famine, disease, and exile, but not its total destruction.

A subsequent covenant was entered into with David,[10] who was promised that his seed would enjoy an everlasting kingdom if it remained faithful to God. After the end of the Davidic kingdom, hope refused to die, largely under the inspiration of Prophets like Jeremiah (chap. 31) and Ezekiel (chap. 37). As a result, a faith in a supernatural Messiah ben David arose among the people and became a fundamental article of belief.[11] However, the exact time of the arrival of the redeemer was unknown and in large degree was dependent on the character of the people.[12]

The same term, *brit*, was applied to the two great movements of religious reformation in pre-exilic Judaism, in the reigns of Hezekiah (II Chron. 29:10) and Josiah (II Kings 23:3). After the Return from the Babylonian Exile, Ezra entered into a covenant with the people, the central feature of which was the agreement to put away foreign wives and the undertaking to observe various ritual ordinances in the Torah (Ezra 10:3).

For the Prophets, the essence of the covenant was obedience to the moral law (Jer. 31:30–33), the high standards of which would require "a new heart and a new spirit" (Ezek. 11:19; 18:31; 36:26). No matter how the covenant was conceived of, whether in ritual or ethical terms or both, its basic character endured—it was unbreakable, and Israel was, therefore, indestructible. Malachi, the last of the biblical Prophets, declares, "For I the Lord have not changed, and you, children of Jacob have not ceased to be" (3:6).

Even the destruction of the Northern Kingdom in 722 B.C.E. and the disappearance of the Ten Tribes, leaving only Judah and Benjamin, did not destroy this faith. It required a massive deterioration in the status of the Jewish people and an active campaign by its enemies for its extermination to suggest that total Jewish annihilation was a real possibility.

O God, do not keep silence; Do not hold Your peace or be still, O God, For lo, our enemies are in tumult; those who hate You have raised their heads. They lay crafty plans against Your people; They consult together against your protected ones. They say, "Come let us wipe them out as a nation; Let the name of Israel be remembered no more" [Psalm 83:1–4].

Such descriptions of attempts to obliterate the Jewish people are rare; since the enemies of Israel, as this passage indicates, are the foes of God, they are doomed to failure. During the Babylonian Exile it was those of little faith who declared, "Our bones are dried up, our hope is lost, we are utterly cut off" (Ezek. 37:11), a lament that proved, for them alone, to be a self-fulfilling prophecy.

The Role of the Halakhah

The vast majority of the people in every generation never doubted the eternity of Israel; individual Jews might perish—and thousands of them did—but the people of Israel was safeguarded by its covenant sealed by the Torah. In the Daily Service and the blessings recited at the reading of the Torah, God was praised because "He planted in us everlasting life." Nonetheless, this faith led to no quietism on the part of Jewish leadership, which was actively concerned with preserving the life and welfare of every individual. The Book of Esther is paradigmatic for the zeal and energy that communal leaders displayed through millennia of exile in order to protect their people against spoliation and destruction.

The Rabbis of the Mishnah were fundamentally concerned with the observance of the Torah by the people. Nevertheless, when a Jew was confronted by the choice of transgressing the commandments or losing his life, the Halakhah declared that he was to violate the law and save his life. Only when one of the three major sins—murder, sexual immorality, or idolatry—was involved was he to accept martyrdom rather than transgress. Rabbi Ishmael went further and ruled that only if the idolatry would take place in public and thus serve to encourage others to transgress, must he undergo martyrdom; if the act is private, he may violate the law rather than die.[13] To be sure, many "disobeyed" the injunction of the Sages rather than commit even lesser offenses; they died as martyrs ʿal kiddush Hashem, "for the sanctification of the divine name."

What emerges clearly is the profound concern of the Halakhah and its spokesmen to defend the lives of the people, in both its spiritual integrity and its material interests. The guiding principle was set down in the Bible and the Talmud. The Psalmist proclaimed, "Grievous in the eyes of the Lord is the death of His faithful ones" (Psalm 116:15). The Talmud declares, "The Torah seeks to spare (and safeguard) the money of Jews" (B. *Yoma* 39a). More than once these objectives required change, sometimes even a major modification in accepted theory and practice.

The Threat of the Twentieth Century

The long centuries of Jewish exile were frequently punctuated by persecution and massacre. But these episodes of murder, even mass murder—like the slaughter of the Rhineland communities during the First Crusade in 1096, the Chmelnicki massacres in 1648–49, or the pogroms in eastern Europe—affected individuals but did not threaten the survival of the Jewish people as an entity. That sorry mark of distinction was reserved for the twentieth century. Hitler's "final solution" nearly achieved its objective—six of the seven million Jews alive in Europe in 1933 were cruelly done to death by 1945, the end of the Second World War.

Nor was this all. The bloody tactics employed in the Nazi work camps, the crematoria, and the gas chambers came to an end, but new and equally insidious dangers appeared. In the Soviet Union the campaign of spiritual genocide against Jewish survival, taking the form of the persecution of the Jewish religion and culture has been going on almost from the inception of the Bolshevik Revolution in 1917. Signs of *glasnost* in this area of Soviet policy are only now beginning to appear.

In the democratic West, the threat to survival takes on impersonal, automatic, and even attractive forms. The protean shapes of assimilation, particularly the increase in intermarriage and the low birthrate in the Jewish community, have deeply shaken the previously all-but-universal confidence in the eternity of Israel.

Patrilineal and Matrilineal Descent: History of the Question

The problem of intermarriage, which has grown so acute in the modern world, is as old as the Jewish people itself, since, as the Book of Deuteronomy reminds us, "Not because you are the most numerous of people has the Lord set His heart on you and chosen you, indeed you are the smallest of peoples" (7:7).

Perhaps the greatest threat to Jewish survival posed by intermarriage, which led to the most radical innovation ever adopted to deal with it, took place in the fifth century B.C.E. That ancient event has come to general notice in our time because of the current controversy in the American Jewish community engendered by the adoption in Reform Judaism and Reconstructionism of the patrilineal principle: the descent of a child of a mixed marriage is determined by that of the father.[14]

The Bible offers abundant evidence that in the pre-Exilic period patrilineal descent was followed, the child inheriting the lineage of the father. For the Second Temple era, the picture is less clear. It would seem that some sects, such as the Qumranites and a few outlying communities, continued to maintain the earlier biblical practice of patrilineality. What is certain is that by the third century c.e., when the Mishnah was compiled, the matrilineal principle was fully operative in rabbinic Judaism: the child born of a Jewish mother and a gentile father was regarded as fully Jewish, while a child born of a Jewish father and a gentile mother was regarded as gentile. Nor was there any sense of an innovation in the practice.

When did this drastic about-face in so fundamental a law take place?[15] There is no explicit reference in our sources to the change. It is clear that the answer must satisfy several criteria: It must have originated in a crisis situation requiring radical measures in the existing law; the period must have possessed a leader of sufficient prestige and force to carry the change through successfully; and there must be a reasonable explanation for the total silence in our sources on an issue of such magnitude.

The one period that satisfies all these conditions is the time of Ezra and Nehemiah (fifth century b.c.e.), which offers an ideal *Sitz im Leben* for the introduction of the matrilineal principle. The books of Ezra and Nehemiah make it clear that in the period of the Return, after the Babylonian Exile, intermarriage with gentile women by Jewish men, including members of the priesthood, was widespread.[16] Ezra, his colleagues, and the governor (Nehemiah) felt that drastic action was called for. They proceeded to force all Jewish men married to gentile women to divorce them or to leave the community.

However, we find no reference to Ezra's expelling Jewish women married to gentile husbands. It has been suggested that the reason lies in the fact that the patrilineal principle was operating, so that children born of a Jewish father and a gentile mother were regarded as authentically Jewish. But this can hardly be the reason, since Deuteronomy, which was clearly the biblical source of Ezra's drastic action (23:4–9), forbids with equal force the marriage of both males and females with outsiders: "You shall not enter into marriage with them [i.e., the seven nations in the Promised Land]; you shall not give your daughter to his son, nor take his daughter for your son" (7:3).

How can we explain Ezra's apparently ignoring the marriage of Jewish women to gentile men? In a patriarchal society the woman would leave her own community and join that of her husband, thus exogamous marriages of this kind, however painful for the family, did not pose a threat to the religious integrity and cultural homogeneity of the community. The opposite, foreign women married to Jewish men and living in the Jewish community, did pose a challenge to the small, struggling Jewish settlement seeking to preserve its own ethnic character. As Nehemiah 13:23–24 explicity indicates:

> In those days also I saw the Jews that had married women of Ashdod,
> of Ammon, and of Moab; and their children spoke half in the speech of
> Ashdod, and could not speak in the Jews' language, but according to the
> language of each people.

It was a critical hour for the preservation of Jewish identity, since the
Jewish people was a tiny island in a vast pagan sea, and intermarriages
that involved important members of the community would undermine
its homogeneity and survival. It is plausible that, to meet this challenge,
Ezra and Nehemiah modified the older patrilineal principle, which operated in the First Temple period, and imposed the ruling that the offspring of a gentile woman would not be Jewish. On that basis, they proceeded to expel all families that insisted upon retaining gentile wives
in their midst.[17] The objections to intermarriage during this period were
basically national-cultural rather than religious.[18] The women were
blamed for teaching their children alien languages, but at no point were
they charged with idolatrous beliefs or practices.

The prestige of Ezra as "a scribe skilled in the law of Moses" (Ezra
7:6) was paralleled by the secular authority of Nehemiah, the governor
appointed by the Persian authority. The two biblical books bearing
their names testify to the extent of their power in reviving practices and
creating new ones for the fledgling Jewish community. Rabbinic tradition pronounces the supreme encomium upon Ezra, whom it regarded
as the fountainhead of the Pharisaic-rabbinic tradition, by declaring,
"Ezra was worthy of having the Torah given through him, had not Moses
preceded him" (B. *Sanhedrin* 21b). He is credited with changing the old
Hebrew script to the Aramaic square letters universally used in his
time; and many other provisions and enactments of rabbinic Judaism
have been attributed to him.

The ban on gentile wives encountered considerable opposition from
people of influence. There would, therefore, be every inducement for
Ezra and Nehemiah not to call attention to the innovative character of
the ruling but to relate it to the Torah's total prohibition of marriages
with the Canaanites and the somewhat less stringent interdict on the
Moabites and the Ammonites.[19]

It is reasonable to believe that later dissident sects opposed to the
Pharisees did not share this enthusiasm for Ezra; they might well reject
his radical change from the patrilineal descent established in scripture
to the new matrilineal principle. Thus the Book of Jubilees categorically
forbids both types of out-marriage, as does Philo. The marriage of
Simon and Judah to Canaanite women (Jubilees 34:20) and Joseph's
marriage to the daughter of an Egyptian priest (Testament of Joseph
18:3) are not commented on adversely, nor is Moses' Ethiopian wife;

the children of all these unions are regarded as Jews. These writers of the Second Commonwealth period apparently retain the patrilineal principle of the biblical era, long after Ezra's time.

Second Temple Judaism was far from being monolithic; on the contrary, it was characterized by a multiplicity of sects. Communities that were either geographically or ideologically distant from Pharisaic-rabbinic Judaism in Palestine preserved their own traditions and practices. As these groups ultimately disappeared, especially after the destruction of the Temple, and rabbinic Judaism became normative, the innovative character of Ezra's rule was forgotten and the matrilineal principle became universal.

While there have been some dissenting voices, the consensus through the centuries has been that the peril of total assimilation and disappearance that threatened the tiny Jewish community in the days of Ezra and Nehemiah justified the severe measures they adopted. As the Jewish community gained in numbers and strength, the threat of wholesale intermarriage abated, but the change introduced to combat it remained normative. By the time of the Mishnah, 600 years later, the matrilineal principle had acquired the force of tradition, which it retains to the present day, while the historical origin of the change was forgotten.

In later periods decisions regarding authenticity of lineage and Halakhic legitimacy arose with regard to several communities. Rabbinic opinions have been divided since the Middle Ages on the status of such sects as the Karaites and of exotic branches of the Jewish people, such as the Beni-Israel of India and the Falashas of Ethiopia.

The current decision of the Reform (and the Reconstructionist) leadership to adopt the patrilineal principle has precipitated passionate controversy and a major division in the Jewish community. Considerations rooted in ethics, demography, and law have been advanced on both sides of the question. The opposition of Orthodox and Conservative groups to this innovation poses a major obstacle to its implementation.

The matrilineal principle has prevailed from the fifth century B.C.E. to the present. Even on the basis of a later date of adoption proposed by some scholars, it would be at least 1,600 years old. No faction in the Jewish people has ever violated the rule. When Reform Judaism arose in the middle of the nineteenth century, it surrendered many practices, including such fundamentals as observance of the sabbath and of the dietary laws—but not until today has it challenged the matrilineal principle. So radical a step should not be undertaken except under dire necessity, and that is precisely the contention of the Reform rabbinate, who view the change as an appropriate and necessary response to intermarriage. However, I see the adoption of the patrilineal principle as having grave drawbacks from the standpoint of the mother, the child, and the Jewish community.

First, it is not a function of Judaism to break down the unity and stability of the family, which is already under siege. Let us assume that the mother has agreed to have "the child raised Jewishly," or, in the language of the Reform rabbinic statement, that the parents express a wish to have the child regarded as Jewish "by appropriate and timely public and formal acts of identification with the Jewish faith and people." In that event, either the phrase is a hollow formula, or the mother is being asked to submerge part of her background and personality and surrender her child to a tradition not her own.

Second, the patrilineal descent principle would introduce a multiplicity of religious and cultural backgrounds into the family and prevent the child from achieving the sense of rootedness and belonging that the home is designed to foster.

Third, when a non-Jewish woman marries a Jewish man, her act reflects a desire or willingness to share to some degree his Jewish destiny. It presupposes a friendly attitude toward his Jewish background; anti-Semites do not usually practice intermarriage. In such instances, an outreach program is eminently in order. Building upon these foundations, the rabbi might try to persuade the mother to undertake the study of Judaism with a view to her conversion, thus laying the foundation for a harmonious atmosphere in the home. If she cannot bring herself to convert, her decision should certainly be respected, but clearly "raising the child as a Jew" is virtually meaningless, and counting the child as a Jew is little more than a form of self-deception.

Finally, the advocates of patrilineal descent do not argue in favor of having the children of a mixed marriage considered Jews if the non-Jewish mother is opposed to the idea. They seek to invoke the patrilineal principle in the case of a Jewish husband and a non-Jewish wife who is willing to have her children "raised Jewishly" but is unwilling to be converted herself. Under these circumstances it should be pointed out that the process of integrating the children of such a union into the Jewish community could be completed by having them formally converted to Judaism. Thus, they would be spared any future questions regarding their Jewish status and possible anguish if they seek marriage with Jewish partners.

Children who know that their mother is not Jewish and that they are being raised as Jews will have no difficulty understanding why they need to undergo a special ceremony in order to make them completely Jewish. Upon attaining majority they will, in accordance with Jewish law, have the option of deciding their religious affiliation. In other words, the optimum procedure would be the conversion of both the mother and the children; the minimum would be the conversion of the children alone.[20]

At the present writing the issue has not been resolved and passions run high. It is clear, however, that in spite of their radical divergences, the protagonists on both sides have a deep desire to preserve the Jewish identity and safeguard the survival of the Jewish people. Indeed, this has been the motive behind the centuries of Jewish suffering and striving underlying the law and the lore, the ritual and the ethics of Judaism—that the Jewish people may not only be blessed with the gift of eternal life, but that it may be worthy of the blessing.

AFTERWORD

This book has reached its end, but the process it has sought to delineate and analyze has not. The Jewish tradition, which has been contemporaneous with virtually the entire significant history of the human race, proved adequate to serve the needs of the Jewish people through all the vicissitudes of its history. Jewish law will survive into the future on precisely the same terms—and the task has become incomparably more challenging today because of the vastly enlarged possibilities and the massive problems of the nuclear age.

From the biblical era to the present, the process of growth and development in Jewish tradition and law, though varying in extent and creativity in differing epochs, remains clear. The prophetic insistence that righteousness, individual and collective, is the categorical imperative for humankind dominated all succeeding stages in the history of Judaism and imbued the Jewish people with a strong ethical consciousness, which played a decisive role in the later formulations of Jewish law. Succeeding generations, inheriting an extensive body of Jewish lore and law, found that the blend of idealistic aspiration and realistic understanding made the tradition effective and relevant, so that most of it could be maintained virtually intact from generation to generation.

Stability was one of the pillars on which Judaism rested; the other was its dynamism, its capacity to grow and develop with time. When confronted by changed social, economic, and political conditions, on the one hand, and by new ethical attitudes and insights on the other, its leaders reacted with insight and resilience to undertake the necessary accommodations between past and future to ensure a viable future.

Particularly during the earlier period, that of the Mishnah and the Talmud, when the Halakhah was actively in the making, the task of adjustment was undertaken by the recognized rabbinic authorities of the age. When the survival of their people was threatened, the Jewish leaders took steps to counter the danger, even if they called for a radical break with earlier, accepted attitudes. In later periods, particularly in the Middle Ages, the new patterns were sometimes felt more keenly by the masses of the people. While the Sages and scholars might not subscribe to the formula *Vox populi vox Dei*, they were astute enough to reckon with the popular will and adjust the law to conform with the people's *minhag* when the custom served to strengthen loyalty to Judaism. All these factors will continue to operate in the future with even greater strength than in the past, since the tempo of change is far greater in our century than in the preceding 2,000 years.

I have refrained from discussing problems created by the scientific and technological revolution of the twentieth century. New questions of great complexity for both the individual and society have emerged in many fields, from the exploration of outer space to research in subatomic physics, from bio-genetics to electronics. The definitions of life and death have become increasingly complicated and controversial, challenging the traditional concepts of the past. The ethical issues cannot be logically addressed since there is no unanimity, often not even consensus, on many scientific questions resulting from new discoveries. The widely differing responses of ethicists and theologians bear witness to the tentative and inconclusive nature of current thinking.

What is more, the traditional sources contemporary thinkers cite are all too often interpreted in a literalistic and uncritical spirit, with no recognition of the role that new insights and unprecedented conditions must play in finding proper solutions to our problems. It is no wonder, therefore, that religious tradition is frequently invoked to hamper progress rather than to advance it, thus bringing the wisdom of the past into disrepute among intelligent and sensitive people.

If the Halakhah is to remain alive and meaningful, and the Jewish people is not to become what Toynbee called it, "a fossilized relic of Syriac society," its scholars, thinkers, and leaders must demonstrate the three attributes of loyalty to traditional standards, moral sensitivity, and common sense.

The intellectual and spiritual enterprise of restoring a creative and relevant Halakhah is only the first element in building the Jewish future. A people needs a law, but the law need a people. All the resources of education and persuasion must be used to attract modern Jews to a deeper personal attachment to the pattern of Jewish living in accordance with the tradition. Many other elements, such as literature, scholarship, folkways, music, and art, all contribute to the richness of the Jewish experience and need to be cultivated with energy and zest. But the Jewish people cannot survive for long without religion at its center. A vital Judaism requires a living Halakhah. Growth is the law of life, and the Law is the life of Judaism.

NOTES

1. The Basic Traits of the Jewish Tradition

1. Medieval Jewish philosophy, from Saadia to Crescas, represents a major synthesis, varying in pattern between biblical-rabbinic thought and Greek philosophy, that of Plato and preeminently that of Aristotle. Both were refracted through the great Muslim thinkers ibn Sina, ibn Roshd, and their colleagues. The subject is surveyed in I. Husik, *Medieval Jewish Philosophy* (New York, 1930); and J. Gutmann, *The Philosophies of Judaism*, translated by David W. Silverman (New York, 1964). It has been suggested that Maimonides, the greatest figure in medieval Jewish philosophy, aspired to achieve the status of the prophet. See A. J. Heschel, "Did Maimonides Believe That He Had Attained to Prophecy?" (Hebrew) in *Louis Ginzberg Jubilee Volume: On the Occasion of His Seventieth Brithday*, 2 vols. (New York: American Academy for Jewish Research, 1945), pp. 159–89.

2. Though Abraham Geiger's pioneering study, "Was hat Mohammed aus dem Judentum aufgenommen?" was published in 1834, and much significant research has been done since, the definitive study of the impact of Jews and Judaism on Islam remains to be written. On this subject, see A. Guillaume, "Judaism and Islam," in I. Abrahams, C. Singer, and A. R. Bevan, eds., *The Legacy of Israel* (Oxford, 1927); A. I. Katsh, *Judaism in Islam* (New York, 1954); Joel Carmichael, *The Shaping of the Arabs* (New York, 1967), pp. 3–60; Bernard Lewis, *Islam in History* (London, 1973), pp. 123–76.

3. For an exposition of Koheleth's authentic world view, long obscured by theological misreading, see R. Gordis, *Koheleth—The Man and His World* (New York, 1951, 1955, 1968).

4. On the entire subject, see George Foot Moore, *Judaism in the First Centuries of the Christian Era* (New York, 1971), vol. I, pp. 474–80; and the comprehensive study by Samuel S. Cohon, "Original Sin," *Hebrew Union College Annual* 21 (1948): 275–330. A brief account may be found in R. Gordis, "The Nature of Man," in *Judaism for the Modern Age* (New York, 1955), pp. 229–76.

5. In the Apocrypha, in I Enoch, some passages attribute man's propensity for sin to the machinations of Satan (54:6; 69:5; 8:1ff.; 9:8), while others deny that sin is man's inheritance from Adam and therefore unavoidable (9:14; 98:4).

6. See Apocrypha, IV Ezra 7:116–131; 9:32–37.

7. Cf. Apocrypha, II Baruch 54:15, 19; 56:6.

8. Cf. Rom. 5:12ff.; 7:17; I Cor. 15; also II Cor. 11:3.

9. For a detailed treatment of this subject, see R. Gordis: *Love and Sex: A Modern Jewish Perspective* (New York, 1978).

10. See Ch. B. Chavel, ed., *Kitbei Haramban*, 2 vols. (Jerusalem, 1959, 1960), for the text of the *Iggeret*, the authorship of which is in doubt. For an English translation, see Seymour Cohen, *The Holy Letter* (New York, 1976).

11. Rashi, on B. *Ketubbot* 62b.

12. Nahmanides, on *Iggeret Hakodesh* sec. 3.

13. For a presentation of the principal elements of the ethics of self-abnegation in the New Testament as opposed to the ethics of self-fulfilment in normative Judaism, with particular reference to its impact on the perennial is-

sues of politics and ethics, see R. Gordis: *The Root and the Branch: Judaism and the Free Society* (Chicago, 1962), chap. 10.

14. For the various stages in the biblical doctrine of reward and punishment, moving from collective solidarity to individual responsibility and, consequently, to the acute problem of suffering for biblical religion, see R. Gordis, *The Book of God and Man: A Study of Job* (Chicago, 1965), chap. 20, "Job and the Mystery of Suffering."

15. For the traditional doctrine of retribution interpreted as "the law of consequence," the concept of "moral inpenetrability," and my own approach to the problem of evil, see R. Gordis, *A Faith for Moderns* (New York, 1960, 1971), particularly chap. 10, "Evil in God's World, " reprinted in *God in Conservative Jewish Thought*, edited by S. Siegel and E. Gertel (New York, 1986).

16. See Reinhold Niebuhr, *Moral Man and Immoral Society*, (New York, 1932).

17. There was a brief efflorescence of Jewish studies, naturally along Marxist lines, in White Russia soon after the Bolshevik Revolution in 1917. Two instances of Communist-Jewish scholarship may be cited: The Communist biblical scholar Luria explained that forbidding the lender to enter the poor man's hovel was a way of protecting the rich man from being beaten or killed by the indignant borrower.

In modern Jewish history, the Soviet Jewish historian Uditsky explained that the nineteenth-century East European Maskilim, the advocates of modernization, were spokesmen for bourgeois economic interests. The Maskilim urged Jews to enter Czarist military service because the bourgeosie were engaged in the manufacture of textiles and a larger army would mean more substantial contracts for uniforms! See Steve J. Zipperstein, "Haskalah, Cultural Change and Nineteenth Century Russian Jewry: A Reassessment," *Journal of Jewish Studies* 35 (1983): 194–95.

18. Gedalya Alon, *The Jews in Their Land in the Talmudic Age* (Jerusalem, 1980), vol. I, pp. 174–75.

19. See George Bernard Shaw, Preface to *Mrs. Warren's Profession*, in *Complete Plays* (New York, 1963), vol. 3, pp. 15ff.

20. See James A. Montgomery, "Ascetic Strains in Ancient Judaism," *Journal of Biblical Literature* 61 (1932): 183–213. Steven D. Fraade, "Ascetical Aspects of Ancient Judaism," in *Jewish Spirituality From the Bible Through to the Middle Ages*, edited by Arthur Green (New York, 1986), pp. 253–82, deals primarily with the medieval period. The asceticism characteristic of medieval German-Jewish pietism is treated in Ivan G. Marcus, *Piety and Society* (Leiden, 1980); and Joseph Dan, *Jewish Mysticism and Jewish Ethics* (Philadelphia, 1980), chap. 3.

21. Scholem's individual articles in the *Encyclopedia Judaica* on various aspects of Jewish mysticism have been collected in a 495-page volume simply entitled *Kabbalah* (New York, 1974). His classic work, *Major Trends in Jewish Mysticism* (New York, 1954), was preceded and followed by a dozen important books and scores of scholarly papers.

22. This section, which acknowledges the seminal contribution of Gershom Scholem as well as a critical attitude toward his fundamental views on the centrality of mysticism in Judaism, was written in 1984. A full-length treatment of Scholem's philosophy of Judaism and a trenchant critique of his approach is now available in Eliezer Schweid, *Judaism and Mysticism According to Gershom Scholem: A Critical Aanlysis and Programmatic Discussion*, translated by David A. Weiner (Atlanta, 1985). This detailed and meticulous analysis of

Scholem's standpoint brings Schweid to conclusions largely identical with mine.

23. The principal works of Max Kadushin are *The Theology of Seder Eliyahu: A Study in Organic Thinking* (New York, 1932); *Organic Thinking: A Study in Rabbinic Thought* (New York, 1938); *The Rabbinic Mind* (New York, 1952, 1965); *Worship and Ethics: A Study in Rabbinic Judaism* (New York, 1964); and *Conceptual Approach to the Mekilta* (New York, 1969).

2. Bondage and Liberation

1. For a spirited account of the Exodus, enriched by the fuller perspective of rabbinic Midrash and the exegesis of medieval and modern preachers, see Michael Walzer, *Exodus and Revolution* (New York, 1984), which interprets the Exodus as a guide to the general pattern of political and social revolution.

2. See, for example, Lincoln Steffens, *Moses in Red, the Revolt of Israel as a Typical Revolution* (Philadelphia, 1926); Ernst Bloch, *Atheism in Christianity: The Religion of the Exodus and the Kingdom*, translated by J. T. Swann (New York, 1972); J. Severino Croatto, *Exodus: A Hermeneutics of Freedom*, translated by S. Attanasio (New York, 1981). See also Lewis Feuer's negative assessment of the "Mosaic Revolutionary Myth," in *Ideology and the Ideologists* (New York, 1975).

3. B. *Kiddushin* 20a and elsewhere.

4. For the biblical philosophy of history, its later transformation, and its significance for our day, see R. Gordis, *A Faith For Moderns*, 2d Augumented Edition (New York, 1971), chaps. 7 and 10; and Gordis, *The Book of God and Man* (Chicago, 1965; 5th ed., 1978), chaps. 2 and 11.

5. For the people's continual complaints about the rigors of desert life and the wish to return to Egypt, see Exod. 5:21; 14:12; 15:24; 16:3; 17:1–3; Deut. 1:25–28; and especially the Book of Numbers, which might well be called *The Trials of Moses* or *the Chronicle of Rebellion*, chaps. 11; 12; 13; 16; 17; 20:1–13; 21:4–10. All this aside from the Rebellion of the Golden Calf (Exod. 34) and the Hebrews' general recalcitrance decried by Moses before his death (Deut. 31:14–30; 32:15–31).

3. The Primacy of Ethics

1. See K. Budde, "Das nomadische Ideal im A.T.," *Preussische Jahrbucher*, 1896; published earlier in English in *New World* 4 (1895):726–45. The concept was expanded by J. W. Flight, "The Nomadic Idea and Ideal," *Journal of Biblical Literature* 42 (1923):158–226.

2. The concept of a nomadic stage for ancient Middle Eastern society in general was maintained by A. Alt, M. Noth, M. Weippert, and others. It has been questioned more recently by J. R. Kupper, J. T. Luke, and M. B. Rowton.

Its validity for the history of the Hebrews has been vigorously denied by S. Talmon in "The Desert Motif and Qumran Literature," in *Biblical Motifs*, edited by A. Altman (Cambridge, Mass., 1966). This paper offers a valuable analysis of the "desert motif" in the Bible as a whole. Talmon is undoubtedly right in rebutting the extreme form that the "nomadic theory" received at the hands of Flight and other scholars. He has also called attention to the common error, to which Budde also fell victim, of exaggerating the importance of the Rechabites.

However, several major considerations that have not been given their due by either the proponents or the opponents of the "nomadic" theory need to be taken into account:

A. While Budde recognized that the Rechabites and the Prophets were dissimilar, the full extent of the differences needs to be reckoned with. As has already been noted, what the two groups shared in common was a protest against contemporary conditions in the rural-urban stage of Israelite society. However, the Rechabites were essentially a reactionary movement, expressing themselves by a mechanical retroversion to the externals of the past; the Prophets sought to preserve, reinterpret and extend the ideals that they saw in the earlier period and to apply them to their own age. See chap. 1 above. I had pointed out this fundamental distinction between them in "The Bible as a Cultural Monument," in *The Jews*, edited by Louis Finkelstein (New York, 1949), pp. 783–822, reprinted in R. Gordis, *Poets, Prophets and Sages: Essays in Biblical Interpretation* (Bloomington: Indiana University Press, 1971), esp. pp. 24–30.

B. It is important to recognize that the perception of the past and its idealization by later generations, particularly the concept of a simpler and more ideal period, is no novelty in the history of culture. Thus the *Idylls* of Theocritus and the *Eclogues* of Virgil, in the ancient world, and the glorification of "rustic simplicity" and "the happy peasant" in Rousseau and in the Romantic movement, during the eighteenth and nineteenth centuries, bore scant resemblance to the hard facts of agricultural life in western Europe.

C. If all the biblical sources are taken into account, it is clear that there are two concepts of the "desert generation," not one. In much of Exodus (5:21; 14:11ff.; 16; 17; 32; 33), the first part of Numbers, and Deuteronomy (*passim*), the picture is generally negative, that of a rebellious, cowardly, and ungrateful generation. This is thoroughly at variance with the view of Hosea and Jeremiah, who see the desert period as the Golden Age in the relationship of God and Israel, and with the implications of Elijah's flight to Horeb (I Kings 19). Talmon argues that the passages in Hosea 2:17 and Jeremiah 2:2 are quantitatively insignificant as against Exodus-Deuteronomy and that Elijah fled to Horeb out of fear and not in search of inspiration.

However, two observations are in order: Had there been no "favorable" tradition of the desert era familiar to the people, the Prophets' glowing references to it would have been meaningless or, worse, self-defeating. If Elijah were simply in search of a refuge, as Talmon has suggested, he could have sought it much nearer to home, by traveling across the northern or eastern border of Israel instead of traversing all of Judah into the Sinai Desert.

D. Moreover, the positive assessment of the wilderness generation is actually much greater then Talmon alleges. The Sinai pericope and the Decalogue, so influential ever after, cannot be dismissed in evaluating the later conception of the desert period. They certainly reflect a favorable view of the sojourn in the wilderness.

E. In another favorable reading of the wilderness era, a dissertation by Benjamin E. Scolnic suggests very plausibly that the latter section of the Book of Numbers is primarily concerned with the second, desert-born generation, which was free from the sins of rebelliousness and cowardice that marked their parents. The second census (chap. 26), the assertiveness of the daughters of Zelophehad (chaps. 27 and 36), the prescriptions for a permanent sacrificial system (chaps. 28–29), and the ordinances regarding vows (chap. 30) all presuppose an obedient people. More explicitly, the victories over Midian (chap. 31) the sense of mutual responsibility displayed by the tribes of Reuben, Gad, and half of Manasseh (chap. 32), and the demarcation of the boundaries of the Promised Land, including the cities of refuge (chaps. 34–35), presuppose a self-reliant and courageous generation prepared for the responsibilites of freedom. In particular, Scolnic sees in the "stations of wandering" (chap. 33) the record of a triumphal march of the children of Israel toward their destined home.

Modern research has demonstrated that a rough egalitarianism, at least, was a historical reality in primitive nomadism among the Semites and the Indo-Europeans and therefore was not a mere product of nostalgia or the imagination. Cf. Th. Jacobsen, "Primitive Democracy in Ancient Mesopotamia," *Journal of Near Eastern Studies* II (1943):159–72; R. Gordis, "Primitive Democracy in Ancient Israel," in *Poets, Prophets and Sages*, pp. 45–60 and the sources cited there.

F. The two divergent traditions regarding the desert period have been studied most recently by R. Adamiak, *Justice and Mercy in the Old Testament: The Evolution of Divine Retribution in the Historiographies of the Wilderness Generation* (Cleveland, 1982).

3. The theory of a socioeconomic revolt was proposed by G. E. Mendenhall in "The Hebrew Conquest of Palestine," *Biblical Archaeologist* 25, no. 1 (Feb. 1962):66–87, reprinted in *The Biblical Archaeologist Reader*, vol. 3, edited by David Freedman and Edward Campbell (New York, 1970), pp. 100–20, and elaborated in Mendenhall, *The Tenth Generation* (Baltimore, 1973). It has served as the point of departure for a massive reinterpretation of biblical history by Norman K. Gottwald, *The Tribes of Yahweh—A Sociology of the Religion of Liberated Israel* (New York, 1979). The validity of a socioeconomic approach as an important but not an exclusive resource for understanding biblical history is undeniable, even if one is not persuaded by the details of the reconstruction of biblical history proposed by Mendenhall or Gottwald. An earlier scholar whose work in this area has been undeservedly forgotten is Louis Wallis, author of *The Bible is Human* (Chicago, 1925) and *The Sociological Study of the Bible* (New York, 1940).

4. See R. Gordis, "Primitive Democracy in Ancient Israel," in *Poets, Prophets, and Sages*, pp. 45–61.

5. I hope to be able to return to a detailed investigation of the important stage in the history of Judaism represented by the Second Commandment. It does not deny—nor does it concede—the reality of other gods; it merely forbids Israelites to worship them. (The categorical denial of the reality of other deities is to be found in Deut. 4:39 and I Kings 18:24; note the use there of the definite article.) Other nations are expressly permitted to worship the heavenly bodies (Deut. 4:19; 29:2).

So, too, the Second Commandment does not deny any physical form to the deity; it merely prohibits the Hebrews from fashioning any physical likeness of their God. Thus the Second Commandment exhibits "pragmatic monotheism" and "pragmatic aniconism," which served as the point of departure for a process of religious thought that culminated in the later recognition of one universal God, spiritual in essence. It also was the starting point for the idea that God has no physical shape or attributes, a principle that did not emerge fully until the Middle Ages and was not universally accepted even then, as Rabbi Abraham ben David of Posquières makes abundantly clear in his strictures on Maimonides (*Mishneh Torah, Hilkhot Teshuvah* 3:7).

At no time do all the communicants of a given religion stand on the same level of insight. There is every reason to believe that Moses' conception of God was higher than that of the masses, who were ready to see their God in the

Golden Calf. Nevertheless the Second Commandment represented a significant step forward in the history of biblical religion.

6. Midrash, Genesis Rabbah 44.

7. The incident is reported in both the Palestinian and the Babylonian Talmuds with some variations (P. *Baba Mezia* 6:8, B. *Baba Mezia* 83a). They have been given a "close reading" and the significance of the divergences has been acutely pointed out in Daniel H. Gordis, "Scripture and Halakhah in Parallel Aggadot," *Prooftexts* 5 (1985):183–90.

8. *The Encyclopedia of Philosophy* (New York and London, 1967), vol. 3, p. 73.

9. A noteworthy exception to the harmony between the Halakhah and ethics that the Rabbis found particularly difficult to contemplate was the permanent exclusion of a *mamzer* (illegitimate child) from the community, derived from Deut. 23:2. "No bastard shall enter the assembly of the Lord; even to the tenth generation, none of his descendants shall enter the assembly of the Lord." See chap. 7 below.

This subject is by no means of purely scholastic interest today. Aside from clear instances of adultery in our society, the horrors of the Holocaust have produced heartrending instances of women, informed that their husbands were dead, who in all innocence remarried and bore children who are technically illegitimate. In the state of Israel, where the religious Establishment is the ultimate authority in the area of personal status, the reactions have run the gamut from total indifference toward the plight of the principals to the use of various legal technicalities to resolve the situation.

It should be added that some Halakhic scholars, sensitive to the ethical issues and the human suffering involved, believe that resources may be found within the traditional Halakhah for solving or at least alleviating the problem. The question deserves a fresh scholarly and legal investigation in our time.

4. Revelation and Authority

1. In the Passover Haggadah, the term is used to describe the redemptive power of God in freeing Israel from Egyptian bondage.

2. For an analysis of fundamentalism see R. Gordis, "The Revival of Religion and the Decay of Ethics," originally published in *Christian Century*, Nov. 28, 1984, and incorporated in Gordis, *Judaic Ethics for a Lawless World* (New York, 1986), pp. 85–94.

3. Maimonides, *Introduction to Mishneh Torah* (New York, 1947), p. 4.

4. J. David Bleich, "Halakhah as an Absolute," *Judaism* 29 (1980): 31. My observations occur on p. 93. Bleich's paper is part of an extensive symposium, "Halakhah, Authority and the Future of Judaism," pp. 4–109, in which eighteen scholars react to my paper "A Dynamic Halakhah," *Judaism* 28 (1979): 263–82.

5. The literal view of revelation, with which, as has been noted, Bleich has difficulty, is rarely expressed today without paraphrases and circumlocutions. The rare exception is this statement by Rabbi Bernard Weinberger:

> Reform and Conservative Judaism, simply stated, do not accept the fundamental principle that the Torah is the literal work of God revealed to Moses and transmitted from generation to generation. That Torah is eternal and immutable and applicable to all societies, cultures, and epochs. That is the heart of the matter, all the rest is commentary. Our tradition struggles to explain how Moses wrote the last eight sentences of the Bible

which deal with the death of Moses, but, nonetheless it indicates that the totality of the Pentateuch was dictated by God and transcribed by Moses. Anything less than that is, in the eyes of Rabbinic-Orthodox Judaism, heresy [*Sh'ma*, Dec. 25, 1987].

6. S. Behrmann in his Hebrew commentary on Isaiah, *Or Bahir* (Warsaw, 1924).

5. The Halakhic Process: The Scholars' Role

1. Comprehensive treatments of the history of Jewish law are presented in I. H. Weiss, *Dor Dor Vedorshav*, 5 vols. (Vienna, 1871–91); Ch. Tchernowitz, *Toledot Ha Halakhah*, 4 vols. (New York, 1935–50); and Tchernowitz, *Toledot Haposkim*, 3 vols. (New York, 1946–47). Weiss's work was subjected to detailed criticism by I. Halevy, *Dorot Rishonim*, 6 vols. (1897–1939), but Weiss's basic positions remain essentially valid.

Important later studies are L. Finkelstein, *The Pharisees*, 2 vols. (Philadelphia, 1st ed., 1938; 2d ed., with significant changes in emphasis, 1966); Finkelstein, *Akiba* (Philadelphia, 1936); J. Z. Lauterbach, *Rabbinic Essays* (Cincinnati, 1951); A. Guttmann, *Rabbinic Judaism in the Making* (Detroit, 1974); S. Zeitlin, *The Rise and Fall of the Judean State* (New York, 1968); and many papers in *Jewish Quarterly Review*.

The significance of economic and political factors in the development of rabbinic law is underscored in L. Ginzberg, *Of Jewish Law and Lore* (Philadelphia, 1955), which includes his epoch-making essay, "The Role of Halakhah in Jewish Scholarship." A work intended for the general reader and undeservedly forgotten is S. Zucrow, *The Adjustment of Law to Life in Rabbinic Literature* (Boston, 1928). Several works in this area have recently appeared. Joel Roth, *The Halakhic Process: A Systemic Analysis* (New York, 1986), discusses legal principles adopted by the Halakhah itself for arriving at decisions in view of the multiplicity of views expressed in the literature. Elliot Dorff and Arthur Rosett, *A Living Tree: The Roots and Growth of Jewish Law* (New York, 1988) traces the stages in the history of Jewish law and compares it with current American jurisprudence.

2. The passages are B. *Yebamot* 12b, 100b; B. *Ketubbot* 39a; B. *Nedarim* 35a, 45b; B. *Niddah* 45a; T. *Nedarim* 2:6. The Hebrew participle *meshammeshot* simply means "practice," "use." It is given permissive force, "may use," by Rashi (on B. *Yebamot* 100b) and compulsive force, "must use," by Rabbenu Jacob Tam (*Tosafot* on B. *Ketubbot* 39a), Asheri, and Rabbenu Nissim (on *Nedarim* 35b). Both interpretations are grammatically sound.

3. For a discussion of the obviously strained meaning assigned to the passage in the desire to limit its application, see R. Gordis, *Love and Sex: A Modern Jewish Perspective* (New York, 1978), chap. 8, esp. Note 12. See also chap. 12 below.

4. It is also omitted in the *Sefer Mitzvot Gadol, Tur, Beth Josef,* and several lesser codes.

5. See *Shulḥan Arukh, Oraḥ Ḥayyim* 282, 3.

6. He bases his comment on earlier authorities, Rabbi Isaac ben Sheshet and Rabenu Nissim.

7. See I. H. Weiss, *Dor Dor Vedorshav*, vol. 2, pp. 49–65.

8. This view of the career and activity of Rabban Johanan follows W. Bacher, *Die Haggadah der Tannaiten* I (Berlin, 1884–90), p. 74; and J. Dérenbourg, *Essai sur l'histoire et la géographie de la Palestine* (Paris, 1867), pp.

306ff. The mass of traditions recorded about Rabban Johanan ben Zakkai have been subjected to a radical critique by J. Neusner, *Development of a Legend: Studies in the Traditions Concerning Johanan ben Zakkai* (Leiden, 1970). The Israeli historian G. Alon has offered a revisionist interpretation of Rabban Johanan's ideas and activities in *The Jews and Their Land in the Talmudic Age*, edited and translated by Gershon Levi (Jerusalem, 1984), vol. 1, pp. 86–118. His view was criticized by E. Urbach, "Class Status and Leadership in the World of Palestinian Sages," *Proceedings of the Israel Academy of Sciences and Humanities*, 1966.

I find both the revisionist views and those opposed to them not much removed from those of Bacher and Dérenbourg. Alon points out that Rabban Johanan was not a member of the extreme anti-Roman party during the rebellion against Rome and was thus *persona grata* to the Romans. He believes that Rabban Johanan "did not ask for Jabneh and its sages" but was sent by the Romans to this half-gentile village during the hostilities. Alon makes the reasonable suggestion that Johanan's act was disapproved of by some members of the Jewish community, especially by the priests and the scholars, who saw his departure from Jerusalem as a desertion of the Holy City during its final agonies.

Alon suggests further that the priests' hostility to Johanan evoked a negative attitude on his part toward their desire for authority; and that there were scholars who regarded his attempts to give Jabneh a central position an unwarranted assertion of authority. These views seem very plausible.

6. The Halakhic Process: Responsiveness to the Popular Will

1. The literature on the origin and history of the synagogue is enormous. See W. Bacher, "Synagogue," *Jewish Encyclopedia*, vol. XI, pp. 619–28; *Encyclopedia Judaica*, vol. XV, pp. 579–620; I. Levy, *The Synagogue, Its History and Functions* (London, 1963); J. Weingren, *The Origin of the Synagogue* (London, 1964); J. Gutmann, "The Origin of the Synagogue," *Archäologisher Anzeiger*, 1972, pp. 36–40. For the later architectural history of the synagogue see R. Krautheimer, *Mittelalterliche Synagogen* (Berlin, 1927); Lee I. Levine, ed., *Ancient Synagogues Revealed* (Detroit, 1982); Carol Herselle Krinsky, *Synagogues of Europe: Architecture, History, Meaning* (Cambridge, Mass., 1985).

2. For a brief and brilliant exposition of the social and economic background of rabbinic legislation, see Louis Ginzberg, "The Place of the Halakhah in Jewish Research," in *On Jewish Law and Lore* (Philadelphia, 1970); and Louis Finkelstein, *The Pharisees* (Philadelphia, 1938, 1966), who consistently relates the Pharisaic teaching to social and economic norms. See also S. Zeitlin, "The Origin of the Synagogue," *Proceedings of the American Academy for Jewish Research* 2 (1930–31):72ff; and Alexander Guttmann, *Rabbinic Judaism in the Making* (Detroit, 1970).

3. For a balanced description of Jewish sects in the Second Commonwealth period, see the standard work by Emil Schürer, *The History of the Jewish People in the Age of Jesus Christ* (Edinburgh, 1976–86), now completely revised and updated by Geza Vermes, Fergus Miller, Matthew Black, and Martin Goodman.

4. See Alexander Guttmann, "Participation of the Common People in Pharisaic and Rabbinic Legislative Processes," in *Jewish Law Association Studies* I (Touro Conference Volume), edited by B. S. Jackson (Chico, CA, 1985), pp. 41–52.

5. Ibid., pp. 42–43.

6. As, e.g., B. *Baba Kamma* 79b; B. *Baba Batra* 60b; P. *Shebiʿit* 4:2 (35b).

7. A comprehensive survey of the Karaites is presented by the leading con-

temporary authority on the subject, Leon Nemoy, in *Encyclopedia Judaica*, vol. 10, col. 761–85. It registers the progress in research on Karaism in this century since Abraham Harkavy's classic article in *Jewish Encyclopedia*, vol. VII, pp. 438a–446b (with an addendum by K. Kohler). See Leon Nemoy, *Karaite Anthology* (New Haven, 1952), for a selection of Karaite literature. A socioeconomic interpretation of the sect is given by R. Mahler, *Haqara>im* (Jerusalem, 1949).

8. The saying is quoted by Rabbi Ben-Zion Uziel, a former Sephardic Chief Rabbi of Israel, in *Mishpetei Uziel, Even Ha< ezer* (Jerusalem, 1964), pp. 431–32. He declares, "Whenever the original form and intent of a *minhag* is changed, it changes into the gates of Gehinnom."

9. Adret opposed it because of its similarity to the *Azazel* rite on *Yom Kippur* (Lev. 16:5–22). He called it a "heathen superstition" (*darkhei ha> emori, Responsa*, Part I, no. 395).

10. *Shulḥan Arukh, Oraḥ Ḥayyim* sec. 605. Karo's language was later toned down to read, "It is best to avoid the custom." Rabbi Moses Isserles, however, declares that it has been practiced "in these lands" (i.e., the Polish-German communities) and therefore defends its retention. See Jacob Z. Lauterbach's comprehensive study of the rite in his *Rabbinic Essays* (Cincinnati, 1951), pp. 354–76.

11. On the primitive origins of many aspects of the rite, see Lauterbach's exhaustive study, "Tashlik," ibid., pp. 299–433.

12. Abudraham, *Hamanhig, Tefillot Sukkot*, sec. 55, cited in S. J. Zevin, *Hamo<adim Bahalkhah* (Jerusalem, 1944), p. 32; and Jacob ben Asher, *Tur, Oraḥ Hayyim*, sec. 669.

13. *Or Zaru>a*, part 2, no. 398; *Tosafot, Megillah* 31a, s. v. *lemaḥar*.

14. *Oraḥ Hayyim*, sec. 669.

15. Cited by Zevin, p. 128.

16. Ibid., pp. 129–30.

17. Ibid., p. 129

18. For the references, see ibid., p. 131.

19. *Minhagim* of Meir of Rothenberg; *Maharil*; Isserles, gloss on the *Shulḥan Arukh*.

20. See *Noda> Biyehudah Tinyana* (Prague, 1776); *Yoreh De>ah, Responsum* 54.

21. Cited in Hatam Sofer, *Even Ha<ezer, Responsum* 78 (reprint, Jerusalem, 1969–70).

22. *Alphei Menashe* 186, p. 75b, cited by I. Barzilay, *Proceedings of the American Academy for Jewish Research* 50 (1983):12.

23. The basis for the prohibition is the statement by the Talmudic sage Rab Sheshet, *se<ar be>ishah <erwah*, "a woman's hair is sexually suggestive" (B. *Berakhot* 24a). It was originally held to apply only to the time that the *Shema* was being recited (Maimonides, *Mishneh Torah, Issurei Bi>ah* 21, 2; *Shulḥan Arukh, Oraḥ Hayyim* 75, 2; and the gloss of Moses Isserles). As was frequently the case in the history of Judaism, religious practices were "democratized" by being extended in scope.

Rabbi Jacob Emden strongly condemned the wearing of wigs (*Responsum* 69). See S. Carlebach, "References to the Prohibition of Women's Uncovering Their Own Hair or Wearing a Wig" (Hebrew), in *Festschrift zum 70ten Geburtstage D. Hoffmann*, edited by Louis Lamm (Berlin, 1914), pp. 242, 248. He cites Isaac Lampronti, *Paḥad Yizhak*, s. v. *pe>ah nokhrit*, who quotes Rabbi Isaac Katzenellenbogen, who opposes the practice and "proves with clear evidence that is impermissible."

The Hatam Sofer, in his ethical will to his family, published in his book *Torat*

Moshe (3¢ ed.), asks of his daughters and daughters-in-law "to observe these prohibitions which are totally forbidden."

On the other hand, Rabbi Aaron Halevi of Barcelona, in his *Sepher Hahinukh*, does not list this prohibition among the negative precepts. Conceivably the Sephardic tradition was less strict in this regard, as in many others.

The *Encyclopedia Judaica*, vol. 6, p. 222, states: "The wig or sheitel (made of natural hair) was *never* considered proper wear for the very Orthodox women in Poland." This is in contrast to the undeniable fact that in central and western Europe (and now in America) many Orthodox women regard the wig as a mark of great piety.

(I owe some of these references to my colleagues Professor David Weiss Halivni and Rabbi Theodore Friedman.)

24. See M. *Sukkah* 5:1–4. The festival ritual refers explicitly to the earlier worship of the sun, see 5:4. Both its name and the rites associated with it demonstrate that it was part of a rain ritual, an aspect still reflected in the early medieval piyyut *Geshem*, "the Prayer for Rain," recited on the closing days of the *Succot* holiday.

The Mishnah declares, "He who did not behold the joy of the Festival of the Drawing of the Water never saw true joy in his life" (M. *Sukkah* 5:1). After allowance is made for hyperbole, it is clear that it bore a carnival-like folk character. Thus the priests and the Levites "came down" from the "Court of the Israelites" to "the women's court" for the celebration. There was elaborate illumination by torches and candelabra. Men distinguished for piety danced, throwing torches into the air and catching them. Rabbi Simeon ben Gamaliel is reported to have tossed eight torches upward and to have retrieved them. Rabbi Joshua ben Hananiah declares that "during the festival we never saw sleep in our eyes."

25. Philo, *The Contemplative Life*, translated by F. H. Colson, Loeb Classics, vol. IX (Harvard, 1941).

26. M. Baillet, *Qumran Grotte IV, Documents of the Judean Desert* VII (Oxford, 1982), text 502, pp. 81–105.

27. The editor, M. Baillet, suggests that the text is a marriage ritual. J. M. Baumgarten, "4 Q 502: Marriage or Golden Age Ritual?" *Journal of Jewish Studies* 35 (1983):125–35, argues convincingly against this interpretation but does not clearly present an alternative.

28. On the excavated synagogue at Rehov, see F. Vitto, in *Ancient Synagogues Revealed*, edited by Israel Exploration Society and Lee I. Levine (Detroit, 1982), pp. 90–94; J. Sussman, "Inscription in the Synagogue at Rehov," ibid., pp. 146–50; and Sussman, *Tarbiz* 43 (1974):88–158; 45 (1976): 213–57.

29. On the history of synagogue architecture in Europe, see Krautheimer, pp. 132–35. See Krinsky, pp. 28–30, for a survey of the known history of the women's area in the synagogue.

30. See David Philipson, *The Reform Movement in Judaism* (New York, 1931): "In the Berlin congregation men and women were not seated together, simply because this is not the Continental custom. Family pews were introduced by a congregation on the other side of the Atlantic" (p. 250). "Later a Berlin Reform Congregation, the liberal synagogue in Frankfort and the liberal synagogue in Paris dispensed with the women's gallery" (p. 250).

31. Rabbi W. Gunther Plaut, in a private communication dated January 28, 1985: "I did not do any research into that area when I prepared my two volumes, and I do not remember why. I probably didn't think about it."

Rabbi Walter Jacob, in a letter dated January 11, 1985: "To the best of my knowledge, the separation of the sexes was practiced in German liberal synagogues. I do not know about this matter in the single ultra-Reform congregation of Berlin. In contemporary Great Britain, some congregations permit mixed seating and others do not. Let me add on the other side, that I was quite surprised as a military Chaplain some thirty years ago, to note that mixed seating was permitted by some Orthodox congregations in the Western part of the United States. I remember vividly that one congregation in San Antonio, Texas, prohibited women from sitting in the first five rows, but further back, mixed seating was allowed."

32. The material on the Mount Clemens case is conveniently assembled in Baruch Litvin, *The Sanctity of the Synagogue* (New York, 1959), p. 83. The depositions and other statements in the Cincinnati case are collected in *Conservative Judaism* 11 (1956–57):Fall, pp. 1–73; Spring, pp. 33–37.

There had been a controversy concerning mixed seating in the 1870s in Congregation B'nai Jeshurun in New York. The case was decided in the courts by the canons of American law rather than in terms of the Halakhah.

My earlier treatment of the subject is incorporated in this chapter. See now Jonathan D. Sarna, "The Debate over Mixed Seating in the American Synagogue," in *The American Synagogue: A Sanctuary Transformed*, edited by Jack Wertheimer (New York, 1987), pp. 364–94, especially pp. 365ff.

33. See the comprehensive *Responsum* of R. Aaron Kotler, in Litvin, pp. 125–38, which assembles a large variety of sources. The *Responsa* of Maharam Schick (*Oraḥ Ḥayyim* 77), and of Hatam Sofer (*Responsum Hoshen Mishpat* 190 and *Oraḥ Ḥayyim* 28) are reprinted in Litvin, pp. 193–96.

34. The only biblical source adduced to support the practice of segregated seating is the enigmatic prophecy of a mass ritual of mourning at "the end of days" (Zech. 12:9–14). It speaks of all the families of David, Nathan, Levi, the Shimᶜei, and all "the remaining families" being separated from one another and their women being set apart from them during this mourning rite.

35. This basic quotation is cited in Litvin, p. 194; see also R. Hillel Lichtenstein, in Litvin, pp. 196–98.

36. Rabbi Moshe Feinstein's letter (Litvin, pp. 118–25) also discusses the height of the *meḥizah*, which he declares must be at least three ᵓammot, or eighteen handbreadths, "although the heads are visible in such a case, when people stand. For it is highly unlikely that such circumstances can lead to frivolity" (pp. 123–24).

37. See Ira Robinson, "Because of Our Many Sins: The Contemporary Jewish World as Reflected in the Responsa of Moses Feinstein," *Judaism* 35 (1986):35–46, esp. p. 44.

38. See David Regensburg in Litvin, pp. 207–208; R. Ezekiel Grobnei, pp. 208–20.

7. Abiding Principles and Changing Conditions

1. For a brief compartive study of fundamentalism in both communities, see "The Revival of Religion and the Decay of Ethics," in R. Gordis, *Judaic Ethics for a Lawless World* (New York, 1986), pp. 85–94.

2. See David Weiss Halivni, "Can Religious Law be Immoral?" in *Perspectives on Jews and Judaism: Essays in Honor of Wolfe Kelman*, edited by Arthur A. Chiel (New York, 1978), pp. 165–70. The author answers his question in the affirmative, thus offering a kind of Jewish version of Kierkegaard's doctrine of

the teleological suspension of the ethical. Nevertheless he is constrained to admit that "the conflict with morality subconsciously played a major if not a decisive role in [the rabbinic] interpretation" (pp. 165, 168).

For a critique from a biblical perspective of this popular Kierkegaardian concept, see R. Gordis, "The Faith of Abraham—A Case Study," in *Judaic Ethics for a Lawless World*, pp. 103–10.

3. Sifra, *Kedoshim* 19:1.

4. The significance of new concepts and the terms used to express them in rabbinic theology and ethics is stressed in five books by Max Kadushin: *The Theology of Seder Eliahu: A Study in Organic Thinking* (New York, 1932); *Organic Thinking, A Study of Rabbinic Thought* (New York, 1938); *The Rabbinic Mind* (New York, 1952, 1965); *Worship and Ethics: A Study in Rabbinic Judaism* (New York, 1964); and *A Conceptual Approach to the Mekilta* (New York, 1969).

5. The sources for the theological and ethical conceptual terms in rabbinic literature are assembled in M. D. Gross, *Otzar Ha>aggadah*, 3 vols. (Jerusalem, 5714–1954). They are discussed in G. F. Moore, *Judaism in the First Centuries of the Christian Era*, vol. I (New York, 1971); C. G. Montefiore and H. Loewe, *A Rabbinic Anthology* (Philadelphia, 1960); and Ephraim E. Urbach, *Hazal— Pirge Emunot Vede-ot* (Jerusalem, 1971).

6. For the extraordinary development of philanthropy in the Middle Ages see Israel Abrahams, *Jewish Life in the Middle Ages*, 2d ed., edited by Cecil Roth (Philadelphia, 1932); S. W. Baron, *The Jewish Community*, 3 vol. (Philadelphia, 1942).

7. This principle is frequently invoked in the Talmud, e.g., in B. *Baba Kamma* 79b; B. *Baba Batra* 60b; and B. *Horayot* 3b.

8. The Impact of New Economic and Social Factors

1. Bul occurs in I Kings 6:39. Ethanim in I Kings 8:2, and Ziv in I Kings 6:1, 37. Whether Abib is the earlier name of the month of Nisan is in doubt, since it occurs as a common noun, meaning "fresh ear of corn" in Exod. 9:31 and Lev. 2:14. Moreover, unlike the others, it is joined not to *yerah*, "moon-period," but to *hodesh*, "new time."

2. See W. F. Albright, in J. B. Pritchard, *Ancient Near Eastern Texts Relating to the Old Testament* (Princeton, 1950), p. 320. Albright believes that the Gezer calendar was a mnemonic, written in verse for the teaching of children. He dates it at the beginning of the ninth century B.C.E.

3. B. *Sanhedrin* 21b.

4. M. *Sheviit* 10:3: "This is the text of the Prosbul, 'I declare [*mosrani*] to you, judges in this place, that any debt owing to me, I may collect whenever I choose.' The judges or the witnesses sign below." See also B. *Sanhedrin* 32a, b; *Arakhin* 28b.

5. Cf. Deut. 23:20–21.

6. For a conspectus of the history of interest ("usury" in its older meaning), see *Jewish Encyclopedia*, vol. X, pp. 388–92; and *Encyclopedia Judaica*, s. v. "Usury," vol. 16, pp. 27–32.

7. On "The Eighteen Decrees" designed to restrict intercourse between Jews and pagans, see P. *Shabbat* 1, 7, 3c; B. *Shabbat* 13b, 17b; and Solomon Zeitlin, "Les dix-huit mésures," *Revue des Etudes Juives* 68 (1914): 22–36. See also Zeitlin's other detailed studies, especially *The Rise and Fall of the Judean State*, 2 vols. (Philadelphia, 1968).

8. B. *Shabbat* 15a. Glass, as a foreign importation, was also declared unclean.

9. Num. 18:18–32.

10. Lev. 25:1–7.

11. B. *Hagigah* 3b; B. *Megillah* 10b; B. *Zebahim* 60d. See also B. *Yebamot* 92b on "three inheritances" and Rashi ad loc.

12. See chap. 6, note 28. For a less-technical presentation, see Sussman, "The Inscription in the Synagogue of Rehov," in Levine, pp. 146–50.

13. P. *Demai* II, 22c; B. *Hullin* 6b.

14. B. *Gittin* 36a; P. *Shevi‹it* X, 39c.

15. Gedalya Alon, *The Jews in Their Land in the Talmudic Age* (Jerusalem, 1980), vol. II, p. 73.

16. Lev. 12:1–8.

17. P. *Demai* II, 22c.

18. B. *Pesahim*, 10a.

19. Amos 2:6–8; Isa. 3:13; and Mic. 3:1–4 may be cited among many.

20. To be sure, the doctrine *divrei Torah midivrei quabbalah lo yalphinan*, "We do not derive laws from sections of the Bible outside the Pentateuch" (B. *Hagigah* 10b and elsewhere), though often invoked, was also frequently set aside.

21. The relevance of this subject to contemporary sexual mores is discussed in R. Gordis, *Love and Sex: A Modern Jewish Perspective* (New York, 1978), pp. 167–68.

22. Raphael Patai and Jennifer P. Wing, *The Myth of the Jewish Race* (New York, 1976), p. 131.

23. Rabbi Abraham cites Nahmanides' view in his *Responsa*, no. 6, 398. Nahmanides, in his correspondence with Rabbi Jonah Gerondi (cited in *Zedah Laderekh*, III 1, 2, 122b), permits concubinage "because there are many in this country who take concubines."

See Rabbi Abraham's comment on Maimonides, *Mishneh Torah, Nashim, Hilkot Ishut* 1:4: "In the case of the woman who dedicates herself exclusively to one man, there is neither flagellation [*malqot*] nor a negative prohibition [*issur lav*]. This is the *pilegesh* referred to in the [biblical] text." Maimonides, on the contrary, equates these extramarital unions with prostitution (ibid.).

Cf. also S. Halberstam, *Kevuzat miktavim be-inyanei hamahloket al dvar Sepher Hamoreh Vehamada* (Bamberg, 1875; Haifa, 1969). See I. M. Epstein, *The Jewish Marriage Contact* (New York, 1927). On the etymology of *pilegesh* and the categories of concubinage in ancient times, see E. Neufeld, *Ancient Hebrew Marriage Laws* (London, 1944), pp. 123ff.

24. The Hebrew phrase is *pelonit penuyah muteret*.

25. *Responsum* 425; see also No. 6 and No. 398, on concubinage. Cf. A. M. Hershman, *Rabbi Isaac bar Sheshet Perfet and His Times* (New York, 1942), esp. pp. 143–45; and Yitzhak Baer, *A History of the Jews in Christian Spain* (Philadelphia, 1966), vol. II, pp. 465–66; I. M. Epstein, "The Institution of Concubinage Among the Jews," *Proceedings of the American Academy for Jewish Research* 6 (1934–35):153–88.

26. Cf. *She›elot Yavez*, Part II, *Responsum* 15. Emden declares that it is his own view that "it is a *mitzvah* to proclaim publicly the permissibility of concubinage." But he "does not wish to have anyone rely on his own individual opinion." The motive he gives for his eccentric opinion is the desire to increase the population of God's holy people. On this objective in the Halakhah generally, see chap. 12 below.

9. New Ethical Attitudes and Insights

1. The Seven Rules of Hillel were expanded into the Thirteen Rules of Rabbi Ishmael and the Thirty-two Rules of Rabbi Eliezer ben Jose, the Galilean.

2. For the two major modes in the formulation of biblical law, casuistic and apodictic, see A. Alt, *Der Ursprung des Israelitesches Rechts*, appearing in English as "The Origins of Israelite Law," in A. Alt, *Essays on Old Testament History and Religion*, translated by R. A. Wilson (New York, 1967), pp. 161–71.

3. *Sifrei, Devarim*, edited by L. Finkelstein (Jerusalem, 1969), sec. 117, p. 250. In B. *Baba Batra* 122b, 123a, the same reasoning is presented in slightly different form.

4. Gen. 49:22 and I Chron. 5:1–2.

5. For the plethora of limitations introduced by the Rabbis, see M. *Sanhedrin* 8:1–4 and the Gemara, B. *Sanhedrin* 71a.

6. B. *Sanhedrin* 71a. A parallel statement was made regarding the biblical law commanding the destruction of an idolatrous city (Deut. 13:12ff.).

7. Hos. 2:21.

8. *Sifre, Shofetim*, sec. 173, B. *Sanhedrin* 8b. "Warning was established to distinguish between wilful and accidental murder."

9. M. *Makkot* 1:10—on *huvlanit*, "a murderous (court)."

10. Gen. 9:17, esp. vv. 4–6.

11. B. *Sotah* 8b; B. *Sanhedrin* 90a; Midrash Bereshit Rabbah 9:11. See also M. *Abot* 2:6.

12. Exod. 21:23; Lev. 24:20. See also Deut. 19:21.

13. B. *Ketubbot* 38a.

14. B. *Baba Kamma* 84a.

15. *Atem heyitem ʿimmanu ʾotto hayom bimekom peloni* (M. *Makkot* 1:4).

16. B. *Hullin* 11b; Rashi ad loc. The reasons advanced for this limitation are discussed by Barukh Halevi Epstein, *Torah Temimah* (New York, 1928), on Deut. 19:19, note 73. He concludes, "The greatest of the Sages tried greatly to reduce the number of people executed by the court."

17. It has been argued that no moral considerations entered into the modifications of biblical law introduced by the Rabbis, because religious law, *ipso facto*, can never be immoral, since it is the will of God. See, e.g., David Weiss Halivni, "Can Religious Law Be Immoral?" in *Perspectives on Jews and Judaism: Essays in Honor of Wolfe Kelman*, edited by Arthur A. Chiel (New York, 1978), pp. 165–71; see also chap. 7, note 2, above.

In view of the relationship between rabbinic reinterpretation of biblical law and undeniable ethical norms, Halivni assumes that moral motives did operate with the Rabbis, "subconsciously." Hence, he argues, they kept the letter of the law, but interpreted it out of existence. Aside from the impossibility of penetrating the subconscious of other human beings, one would have to assume a high degree of naiveté on the part of the Sages, which is belied by many of the sources in the present text. See the discussion in chap. 3, note 9, above; and the fuller treatment in R. Gordis, "The Faith of Abraham: A Case Study," in *Judaic Ethics for a Lawless World* (New York, 1986).

18. See L. Finkelstein, *Jewish Self-Government in the Middle Ages* (New York, 1924); S. W. Baron, *The Jewish Community: Its History and Structure*, 3 vols. (Philadelphia, 1942). The standard work on the *taqqanot* in Jewish law is M. Bloch, *Sefer Shaʿarei Torat Hataqqanot* (Vienna and Cracow, 1879–1902). See also two articles by M. Elon and I. Levitats in *Encyclopedia Judaica*, vol. 15, col. 712–37.

19. The recently published *Temple Scroll* from the Qumranite sectaries for-

bids polygamy even to kings. The Scroll is dated at the beginning of the Christian era.

20. See *Shulḥan Arukh, Even Ha‹ezer* 1:10; Asheri, *Responsum* 42:1, *Tashbetz, Responsum* 94.

21. In 1951 the Israeli Knesset formally banned new polygamous marriages with its Law on Equal Rights for Women.

22. As David Aronson has acutely noted, this ruling is a clear application to contemporary conditions of the Talmudic dictum enunciated (B. *Sanhedrin* 58b) by Raba: *Mi ›ikka› middei veyisra›el lo› meḥuyyab venokhri meḥuyyab,* "Is there any act for which a Jew is free from guilt and a non-Jew is guilty?" See David Aronson, "The Authority of the Halakhah and the Halakhah of Our Authority," *Proceedings of the Rabbinical Assembly* XL (1979): 42–56 (the quotation on p. 51 is not cited exactly).

10. Women's Status in Marriage and Divorce

1. The status of women in Judaism is treated, from various perspectives, in Elizabeth Koltun, ed., *The Jewish Woman* (New York, 1976); R. Gordis, *Love and Sex: A Modern Jewish Perspective* (New York, 1978); esp. pp. 191–208; Blu Greenberg, *On Woman and Judaism: A View from Tradition* (Philadelphia, 1983); and Susannah Heschel, *On Being a Jewish Feminist* (New York, 1983). M. Meiselman, *Jewish Women in Jewish Law* (New York, 1983), sets forth the provisions of the traditional Halakhah, ignoring the results of historical-critical scholarship; the impact of social, economic, political, and cultural factors; and the existence of major problems in this area. A similar approach, though with a measure of ambivalence, is to be found in R. Biale, *Women and Jewish Law* (New York, 1984), which presents a selection of biblical, Talmudic, medieval, and modern sources. A still useful survey is Moses Mielziner, *The Jewish Law of Marriage and Divorce*, 2d ed. (New York, 1901).

2. See Susan Brownmiller, *Against Our Will* (New York, 1975).

3. Cf. B. *Kiddushin* 31a; B. *Keritot* 28a; and Rashi on Lev. 19:3.

4. The first is the translation of the Revised Standard Version; the second, of the New English Bible and the New Jewish Publication Society Version; the third, of the New American Bible.

5. The rendering is that of the New Jewish Version.

6. B. *Baba Batra* 115a; *Abodah Zarah* 25b.

7. B. *Kiddushin* 70a.

8. See below, p. 182.

9. Most modern interpretations and translators treat all the clauses in vv. 1–3 as the *protasis* ("*if* he takes . . . and writes . . . and she goes to another man . . . and he dislikes her . . . and he writes a bill of divorce") and only v. 4 as the apodosis ("then he shall not be able to take her back"); see the Revised Standard Version, the New English Bible, the New American Bible, and the New Jewish Publication Society Version. Thus the verb *vekhatabh* in v. 3 means "if he writes or wrote," not "he shall write." This reading of the text would suggest that a written bill of divorce was one of several recognized methods for dissolving a marriage, perhaps the most authoritative and legally acceptable. From the standpoint of the woman's rights, however, this variant in the interpretation of the verse is unimportant, since the passage takes as self-evident that a bill of divorce is written by the husband. The biblical passage seems concerned not with the bill of divorce, which is taken for granted, but with prohibiting the woman's remarriage to her first husband after

her marriage to another, an act that would appear to be bordering on promiscuity.

10. See E. Westermarck, *The History of Human Marriage*, 5th ed. (New York, 1922), vol. 3, pp. 216–20, 261–66, for a survey of the practice throughout the world.

11. The various stages of the levirate in Jewish law and their bearing on the Book of Ruth are traced in detail in R. Gordis, "Love, Marriage and Business in the Book of Ruth," in *A Light unto My Path: Old Testament Studies in Honor of Jacob M. Myers*, edited by Elizabeth Achtemeier, H. N. Bream, R. D. Heim, and C. A. Moore (Philadelphia, 1974). This chapter is reprinted in R. Gordis, *The Word and the Book: Essays in Jewish Biblical Language and Literature* (New York, 1976), pp. 84–107; the history of the levirate is surveyed on pp. 246–52.

12. A superstitious dread of the widow may have played a part in the brother's refusal to marry her. See Mordechai A. Friedman, "The Killer-Wife Motif in Biblical and Post Biblical Literature" (in press), for a comprehensive survey of the folkloristic background of the belief.

13. P. *Nedarim* 3, 5.

14. Other sectarian groups like the Samaritans and the Karaites resolved the contradiction in other ways. See Gordis, *The Word and the Book*, pp. 89–93 and notes.

15. B. *Yebamot* 39b, 109a; B. *Yebamot* 3a, a citation from *Tosefta* 6.

16. B. *Yebamot*, 39b; 109a.

17. See Barukh Halevi Epstein, *Torah Temimah* (New York, 1928), vol. 5, p. 386, no. 52, which calls attention to this unusually broad interpretation of *ben*. The rabbinic exegesis of the biblical pericope on the levirate is systematically presented in the same work, pp. 384–404.

18. There are, however, sporadic references to the performance of the levirate rite in the *Responsa* literature in Christian Europe after the period of Rabbi Gershom.

19. The literature on the *Ketubbah* is enormous, cf. L. M. Epstein, *The Jewish Marriage Contract* (New York, 1927) and articles in *Jewish Encyclopedia* and *Encyclopedia Judaica*, s. v. "Ketubbah."

20. See J. B. Pritchard, *Ancient Near Eastern Texts* (Princeton, 1956), p. 171. For the differing explanations of this divergence, the "leniency" in Babylonian law as against the severity of Hebrew law, see R. Sonsino and R. Gordis, "A Note on Adultery," *Judaism* 33 (1984): 202–11.

21. From the vast literature on the subject, see, e.g., the commentaries of W. R. Harper, *Amos and Hosea*, International Critical Commentary series (New York, 1905); F. I. Andersen and D. N. Freedman, *Hosea* (New York, 1980), for critical treatments; and Yehuda Kol, *Sepher Hosea* (Daʾat Miqra) (Jerusalem, 1973), for a traditional approach to the problems involved.

22. For an analysis of the principal views and my approach, see R. Gordis, "Hosea's Marriage and Message," *Hebrew Union College Annual* 27 (1954): 9–35; reprinted in *Poets, Prophets and Sages*, (Bloomington, 1971), pp. 230–54.

23. The basic problem with the alleged "sale" is the impression made by the book that Naomi and Ruth are destitute and that the younger woman, therefore, goes to glean in the fields of strangers, a customary practice of the poor in the biblical era. Moreover, Elimelech would surely have disposed of any property he owned before leaving Bethlehem, and so there would be no land now available for Naomi to sell.

For these reasons and other considerations, I believe that Naomi is not selling land but the "obligation right" to redeem the land that Elimelech had sold to strangers outside the clan, and which relatives were duty bound to redeem. On this transaction, and the various modes of land redemption, see R. Gordis, "Love, Marriage and Business in the Book of Ruth—A Chapter in Hebrew Customary Law," in *The Word and the Book*, pp. 84–107.

24. Cf. B. Porten, *Archives From Elephantine* (Berkeley, 1968) pp. 209–10, 261–62, for the divorce formula in Elephantine and its relationship to other evidence for this practice.

25. Chaim Grade, *The Agunah*, translated from the Yiddish by Curt Leviant (New York, 1978). See also Louis M. Epstein, *The Jewish Marriage Contract* (New York, 1925); *Marriage Laws in the Bible and the Talmud* (New York, 1942); *Sex Laws and Customs in Judaism* (New York, 1948); and *Lishe ᵓelat Haᶜagunah* (New York, 1940) as well as various papers in *Proceedings of the Committee on Jewish Law and Standards*, edited by Nina Cardin (New York, 1984).

26. For the earlier history of the efforts to deal with the ᶜagunah problem, see A. H. Freiman, *Seder Kiddushin uNesuin* (Jerusalem, 1945). Different perspectives and more-recent efforts to deal with the problem are to be found in various volumes of the *Proceedings of the Rabbinical Assembly*, 1936–1976; in J. David Bleich, *Contemporary Halakhic Problems*, 2 vols. (New York, 1977, 1983); and in Irwin H. Haut, *Divorce in Jewish Law and Life* (New York, 1984).

27. See M. *Yebamot* 16:7. Here the stricter opinions of Rabbi Eliezer and Rabbi Joshua, who insist on two witnesses to a man's death in order to free a woman to remarry, and of Rabbi Akiba, who does not wish to accept the woman's testimony in such a case, are overridden by the majority of the Sages. Cf. M. *Yebamot* 15:8, B. *Yebamot* 13b, 114b.

28. *Sanhedrin* 9b and elsewhere.

29. The literature on the difficulties confronting Jewish women in the rabbinical courts in the state of Israel is enormous. See, for example, R. Gordis, "Jewish Womanhood," *The Jerusalem Post*, Sept. 18, 1986.

30. On the Lieberman clause, see *Proceedings of the Committee on Jewish Law and Standards* (New York, 1984).

31. The doctrine is referred to in the Talmud frequently: B. *Yebamot* 19a, 110a; B. *Ketubbot* 3a; B. *Gittin* 33a, 73a; B. *Baba Batra* 48b.

32. See Michael Corinaldi, "The Problem of Divorce by Judicial Decree in Karaite Halakhah," in *Dine Israel—An Annual of Jewish Law: Past and Present*, vol. IX, edited by A. Kirschenbaum (Tel Aviv, 1980).

33. According to Rabbi Edward Gershfield, the Beth Din of New York has used the provision only 50–75 times over the course of a decade.

11. Women's Role in Religious Life

1. *Tos. Kelim, Baba Mezia* 1:6.

2. See chap. 6, note 29.

3. The passion engendered by this ban on women's *minyanim* is reflected in the various articles defending the practice by Michael Chernick, David Singer, and Rivkah Haut in *Sh'ma*, May 17, 1985.

4. Louis Ginzberg has called attention to a liturgical fragment found in the Cairo Genizah: "Blessed are You, O Lord our God, King of the universe, who created me human, and not an animal, a man and not a woman, an Israelite and not a Gentile, circumcised and not uncircumcised, free and not a slave. Blessed are You, O Lord our God, King of the universe, who created Adam in Your likeness and image" (*Bidemuto uvezalmo*); it was published by Jacob Mann, *Hebrew Union College Annual* 2 (1925):269.

5. It has been adopted in the prayer book issued by the Reform rabbinate in Israel and in the Mahzor for *Rosh Hashanah* and *Yom Kippur*. It is the text in all subsequent liturgical publications of the Rabbinical Assembly and the United Synagogue. See *On the Wings of Awe*, edited and translated by Richard N. Levy (Washington, D.C., 1985), p. 85.

6. The concept is expressed in the Seven Blessings recited in the wedding ceremony.

7. On the important theological and ethical implications of the concept, see R. Gordis, *Judaic Ethics for a Lawless World* (New York, 1986), chap. 7, "The Truths of Genesis."

8. The Rabbis were conscious of the use of plural suffixes in these passages, which would imply the equality of the sexes. They therefore speculated that the first human being was either androgynous or a Siamese twin, later separated. See, for example, Midrash Leviticus Rabbah, sec. 14, *Tazria*, beginning.

9. Samuel Belkin, a modern Orthodox scholar and president of Yeshiva University, entitled his presentation of the philosophy of the Halakhah *In His Image* (New York, 1961).

10. These papers and others subsequently submitted by faculty members are collected in Simon Greenberg, ed., *On the Ordination of Women as Rabbis* (New York, 1987). A comprehensive discussion of the issue from varying points of view—Orthodox, Conservative, Reform, Reconstructionist, and secular—is to be found in the symposium "Women as Rabbis," *Judaism* 33 (1984): 6–90.

11. The struggles and frustrations of these women are movingly described by a member of the group, Debra Cantor, in "Get Ready, Set, . . . Wait," *Moment* VIII 9 (1983): 38–42.

12. See Note 10 Above.

13. B. *Sanhedrin* 6b.

14. Cf. R. Gordis, *Understanding Conservative Judaism* (New York, 1978), chap. 16, "The Rabbinate—Its History, Functions and Future."

15. This provision, like others in Talmudic law that treat deaf people as mentally deficient, reflects older attitudes that are still widely held but are now known to be mistaken. These legal disabilities were based on the inability of the deaf to speak, but modern education and technology have made it possible for the deaf to take an active role in contemporary life. Thus the Halakhah is in urgent need of revision. See Jerome Schein and Lester Waldman, eds., *The Deaf Jew in the Modern World* (New York, 1986); and Alan Henkin, "To Hear Deaf Jews," *Judaism* 36 (1987): 489–98.

16. B. *Hullin* 1:1.

17. Deut. 23:20–21.

18. *Sifre, Shofetim*, sec. 157. Cf. *inter alia* B. *Berakhot* 49a: "Rab said, 'The covenant, Torah, and royal rule—do not apply to women.'"

19. *Mishneh Torah, Hilkhot Melakhim*, 1, 4.

20. B. *Gittin* 62a.

21. B. *Bezah* 48a, Midrash Bereshit Rabbah 91:3.

22. See B. *Baba Batra* 11a; P. *Pe'ah* 1:1, 15b; *Tos Pe'ah* 4:18; and Josephus, *Antiquities* 21:17.

23. A sophisticated argument for the laws on *niddah* on mystical and philosophic grounds is offered by Rachel Adler, "Tumah and Taharah, End and Beginnings," with an appendix, comment, and response in *Jewish Women*, edited by Elizabeth Koltun (New York, 1976), pp. 63–71.

24. B. *Megillah* 4a.

25. That the generalization is not a hard-and-fast rule becomes even clearer

from a careful examination of the sources. Of eight *mitzvot* tied to specific times from which women are ultimately exempted, only three are based on incontrovertible Talmudic law—*sukkah, lulav,* and *shofar* (B. *Sukkah* 38a; B. *Kiddushin* 33b), and there is substantial debate on two others, *zizit* and *tefillin* (B. *Erubin* 96b; B. *Kiddushin* 35a; B. *Menahot* 43a). On the ʿomer there is no Talmudic exemption; on the *shema,* the Babylonian Talmud exempts women (B. *Berakhot* 20a, b) but the Palestinian Talmud implies the existence of dissenting opinions (P. *Berakhot* 25b). Nevertheless, Maimonides lists all of them among positive commandments to be performed at specific times from which women are exempt (*Sepher Hamitzvot,* end of "Affirmative Precepts"). Out of 60 positive commandments listed by him as incumbent on the individual, women are exempt from fourteen. Eight are affirmative precepts limited by time—*shema, tefillin* (head and arm), *zizit,* the counting of the ʿomer, living in a *sukkah,* taking the *lulav,* and hearing the *shofar.* The other six, which are not limited by time, include the study of Torah and the commandment to procreate.

On the other hand, the Talmud lists other affirmative precepts equally linked to time from which women are not exempt: *kiddush* (B. *Berakhot* 20a), fasting (M. *Sukkah* 29a), *mazah* (B. *Kiddushin* 34a); rejoicing on festivals (ibid.), *haqhel,* "assembling [once in seven years]" (see Deut. 31:12; B. *Kiddushin* 34a), and sacrificing and eating the Paschal lamb (B. *Pesahim* 91b).

Finally, there are four affirmative precepts of rabbinic origin limited in time that are obligatory for women: lighting Hanukkah lights (B. *Shabbat* 23a), reading *Megillat Esther* (B. *Megillah* 4a), drinking the four cups of wine (B. *Pesahim* 108a), and reciting *Hallel* on *Pesah* night (B. *Sukkah* 38a).

26. This judgment coincides with that of Rabbi Saul J. Berman in "The Status of Women in Halakhic Judaism," *Tradition* 26/Fall (1973). He writes, "So the Mishnah is descriptive of *some* of the laws regulating the status of women, but is inaccurate as a general description and is certainly not a useful prediction principle."

27. Berman (ibid.) argues that only the motive for keeping women out of the public sphere explains their ineligibility to serve as witnesses and their exclusion from many *mitzvot.* But this motive takes for granted a conception of the inferiority of women.

28. Maimonides, *Hilkhot ʿEdut* 9, 2. The *Keseph Mishneh* points out, however, the Maimonides' derivation is also unsatisfactory because although the noun ʿedhim is masculine in grammatical form, it includes women. The Palestinian Talmud solves the difficulty by identifying the two passages on the basis of the word *shnei,* "two," as a *gezerah shawah,* "a deduction based on the use of an identical term in both passages" (P. *Yoma* 6, 1). See Barukh Halevi Epstein, *Torah Temimah* (New York, 1928), for a clear analysis of the problem (pp. 126a, b) and some special instances in rabbinic law where a woman's testimony is valid (pp. 249–55).

29. B. *Ketubbot* 10a and parallels.

30. P. *Yebamot* 12:1; P. *Baba Mezia* 7:1; B. *Sopherim* 14. See also chap. 10 for a detailed discussion of *minhag.*

12. "Be Fruitful and Multiply"

1. Gen. 1:28.
2. Gen. 9:1.
3. Gen. 35:11.
4. It is so treated by R. Moses Hagiz in his *Minyan Hamitzvot* and by the

Sepher Hahinukh, but not by Maimonides, who cites Gen. 9:1 and Gen. 35:11 as the source of the commandment.

5. Psalms 127:3.

6. Psalms 128:3.

7. See Gen. 45:11 and 47:12 for Joseph and Jacob, and Ruth 4:15 for Boaz and Naomi.

8. Psalms 127:4–5.

9. This relationship between the biblical passage and the Near Eastern background was pointed out by my colleague H. L. Ginsberg.

10. Gen. 30:1.

11. See Job 42:13. On *shibh‹anah* as "double seven" and not as an error for *shib‹ah*, see R. Gordis, *The Book of Job: Commentary, New Translation and Special Notes* (New York, 1978), p. 498.

12. See I. Sam. 2:5.

13. M. *Yebamot* 6:6.

14. M. *Yebamot* 6:6, B. *Yebamot* 61b.

15. The Talmud (B. *Yebamot* 65b) and the post-Talmudic commentators have great difficulty in justifying this procedure. They fall back upon the defective spelling of the word *vekhibshuhah* (without a Vav), "and subdue her" (i.e., the earth), in Gen. 1:28, so that it could be read, for homiletic purposes, as a masculine singular (*vekhabeshah*) and is therefore addressed only to males. It is also claimed that the verb "subdue" applies to the male subduing the female Bertinoro, *Commentary on the Mishnah*). Barukh Halevi Epstein, *Torah Temimah* (New York, 1928), vol. 1, p. 38, note 65, finds this argument unsatisfactory and interprets the verb to refer to military conquest, which is a masculine activity.

16. Although Rabbi Akiba interpreted the book as an allegory depicting the love of God and Israel, he was well aware of the fact that the book was widely understood in a secular, erotic sense. See his strong statement in *Tosefta, Sanhedrin* 12:10; "He who trills his voice [*hamena‹ne‹a Kolo*] in 'The Song of Songs' in the drinking halls and makes it a secular song [*kemin zemer*] has no share in the world to come." On *zemer*, see R. Gordis, *The Song of Songs and Lamentations* (New York, 1974), p. 6.

17. Exod. 21:10.

18. See J. Preuss, *Biblisch-Talmudisches Medizin* (Berlin, 1911), p. 479.

19. D. M. Feldman, *Birth Control in Jewish Law* (New York, 1968), p. 54. Feldman's book is indispensable for every serious student of Jewish sexual mores and law from the beginning of the rabbinic period to modern times. His comprehensive collection of the sources and the systematic discussion of the various issues involved in each area are invaluable. I am greatly indebted to Feldman's work, even when there are divergences in our approach and conclusions.

20. B. *Kiddushin* 41a, see also 82b.

21. The passages are T. *Niddah* 2:6; B. *Yebamot* 12b, 100b; B. *Ketubbot* 39a; B. *Nedarim* 35a, 45b; *Niddah* 45a.

22. That the Sages differ with Rabbi Meir only on the child-wife is also supported by the biblical verse they cite. The noun *peta›im*, "fools, simple-minded," is appropriate for a minor but not for a pregnant woman or a nursing mother. The Arab cognate *fata* means "youth."

23. See Feldman, pp. 169–75, 227–34 for the divergent views of medieval and modern authorities.

24. The passage does not make a distinction, as do Catholic theologians and some Jewish decisors, between chemical means, which do not interfere with

"natural intercourse," and which, therefore, might *perhaps* be permitted, and "mechanical devices" such as the absorbent (*mokh*) mentioned in the *Baraita*.

25. B. *Yebamot* 62a, b; the citation in the text is from Maimonides, *Mishneh Torah, Hilkhot, Ishut* 15, 16. See the excellent discussion in Feldman, pp. 48–53. However, in accordance with his general preference for a formalistic-casuistic interpretation rather than a historical approach, Feldman describes the establishment of the two new principles as an instance of "rabbinic definition" rather than an example of historical change.

26. B. *Baba Kamma* 2b; B. *Hagigah* 10b; see also B. *Niddah* 53a.

27. Thus, while the passage in Ecclesiastes is interpreted by Rabbi Joshua as a call for begetting many children, Rabbi Akiba deduces from it the obligation to study the Torah in old age as well as in youth.

28. See Rabbi Nissim on B. *Kiddushin* 41a, cited by Feldman, p. 55.

29. See *Levush* 37, 8 in Feldman, pp. 178–79.

30. A list of some early marriages at the ages of eleven to fifteen is given by I. Barzilay, "The Life of Menashe of Ilya (1767–1831)," *Proceedings of the American Academy for Jewish Research* 50 (1983):8, note 26. He also offers a bibliography on the agitation pro and con aroused by the practice.

31. Feldman evidently overlooked the insuperable problems confronting the "traditional" interpretation of the phrase. Thus he writes, "R. Meir taught that *the three women* (must or may) use the *mokh* in their cohabitation, the other sages, that *these* carry out their marital intercourse in the usual manner," p. 134 (italics mine).

32. For example, M. *Temurah* 1:1 reads: *Hakkol memirin ꜣehad ꜣanashim veꜣehad nashim*, "all have the power to exchange a consecrated object, both men and women." All the Mishnaic examples of the use of the masculine *ꜣehad . . . ꜣehad* and the feminine *ꜣahat . . . ꜣahat*, meaning "both A and B; A and B alike" are listed in Ch. J. Kosovsky, *ꜣOtsar Leshon Hamishnah* (Concordance to the Mishnah) (Jerusalem, 1952), pp. 56–57, 83.

33. Many of the authorities who adopted the usual view of the text saw in it a warning of the hazards of childbirth. See Feldman, pp. 199ff.

34. See I. Jacobovits, *Jewish Medical Ethics* (New York, 1959), p. 169 (italics mine). Maimonides' omission of the *Baraita* had been noted earlier by the eighteenth-century scholar Rabbi Meir Posner, in *Bet Meir* on *ꜣEben Haꜥezer*, sec. 23. On the opposite conclusions that were derived from Maimonides' silence on the subject, see Feldman, pp. 203–208.

35. See Harvey Liebenstein and Samuel S. Lieberman, *Unpublished Data and Analysis* (Cambridge, Mass., 1975). The data are summarized and various conclusions, many of which are questionable, are discussed in Elihu Bergman, "The American Jewish Population Erosion," *Midstream*, October 1977, pp. 2–12.

36. See B. *Pesahim* 64b.

37. *New York Times*, October 10, 1981.

38. Milton Himmelfarb and Victor Baras, eds., *Zero Population Growth—For Whom?* (Westport, Conn., 1978), pp. 167–78.

39. Claudia Wright, *New York Times*, September 17, 1981.

40. Betty Friedan, *The Second Stage* (New York, 1981).

41. B. *Megillah* 14b.

13. Safeguarding Jewish Survival

1. The covenant formula occurs, at times with slight variations, in Exod. 6:7; Lev. 26:12; Deut. 29:12; I. Chron. 17:22. It is a basic concept in Hosea (2:25),

in his spiritual descendant Jeremiah (7:23; 11:4; 24:7; 30:22; 31:32; 32:38), and in Ezekiel (11:20; 14:11; 36:28; 37:23, 27).

2. A possible exception is an oblique reference in Hos. 6:7, which I believe should be rendered, "And they, like Adam, have transgressed the covenant."

3. Gen. 9:1–17.

4. The Noahide laws attracted considerable attention among Jewish and Christian scholars. Theologians and legalists saw them as adumbrating a doctrine of natural law to govern the actions of people and the relationships among nations. In addition, the Noahide laws offer a basis for a theory of religious tolerance in a pluralistic world. See R. Gordis, "Natural Law in the Modern World," in *The Root and the Branch: Judaism and the Free Society* (Chicago, 1962), pp. 204–35 and the more-extended analysis of natural law and its Hebraic component in R. Gordis, *Judaic Ethics for a Lawless World* (New York, 1986), pp. 47–76. For a recent study of the Noahide laws, see David Novak, *The Image of the Non-Jew in Judaism* (New York, 1983).

5. The covenant is made with Abraham, including the rite of circumcision (Gen. 15:18; 17:2–21) and with all the Patriarchs (Exod. 2:24; 6:4, 5; Lev. 26:42; II Kings 2:13; 23; I Chron. 16:15; Ps. 105:8–10; Neh. 9:8).

6. Exod. 19:5; 24:7, 8; 34:10, 27, 28; Lev. 26:9, 15, 25, 44, 45; Deut. 4:13. The covenant was renewed near the Plains of Moab (Deut. 29:1), accompanied with blessings and curses (29:20). It is frequently referred to in the Prophets and the Psalms, the sabbath being preeminently the sign of the covenant (Exod. 31:16; Lev. 24:8).

7. The "traditional" Ten Commandments in Exod. 20 and Deut. 5 are largely ethical. Since Goethe, many scholars have found other "ritual Decalogues," in Exod. 23 and especially in Exod. 34. (Note the proximity to the phrase "the ten words" in 34:28.) I regard these alleged Decalogues as less than convincing, since the proposed passages do not contain ten commandments but many more; and they are not couched in the expected apodictic form but in expanded hortatory style.

8. That this is the correct reading of the Masoretic text is demonstrated anew by Carl S. Ehrlich, "The Text of Hosea 1:9," *Journal of Biblical Literature* 104/March (1985):13–19.

9. Moses describes God's care and protection of Israel, who is blessed with prosperity and well-being (Deut. 32: 1–14) but the backsliding of the people (32:15–18) brings on the wrath of God and the decision to annihilate them (32:19–26). However, lest Israel's destruction reflect upon His power, God decides instead to bring calamity upon them (32:27–28). As the result of its suffering, Israel will recognize the boundless power of its God (32:29–38), who will bring punishment upon its enemies and restoration to Israel (32:39–43).

10. See II Sam. 7; I. Chron. 17; Jer. 33:21; Ps. 2, 89, 132. The dating of Psalm 2 is uncertain; it has been assigned to various periods from the time of Saul to the Maccabean age. I believe it belongs to the period of Solomon.

11. The Messianic doctrine is treated in many histories and studies of Judaism. See the full-length treatment in J. H. Greenstone, *The Messiah Idea in Jewish History* (Philadelphia, 1906); and J. Klausner, *The Messianic Idea in Israel* (New York, 1955). For another perspective see G. Scholem, *The Messiah Idea in Judaism* (New York, 1967).

12. While "calculating the time" (*kez̧*) was frowned upon by most responsible authorities in Talmudic and post-Talmudic eras, it exerted a powerful fascination on both the elite and the masses; see A. H. Silver, *A History of Messianic Speculations in Israel* (New York, 1927). For a collection of the rabbinic sources

depicting the varied hopes and fantasies anticipated in the Messianic future, see M. Higger, *The Jewish Utopia* (New York, 1932); and J. Even-Shmud, *Midreshei Geulah* (Tel-Aviv, 1954).

13. I. H. Weiss, ed., *Sifra* (Vienna, 1865), *Aḥarei* on Lev. 18:5, p. 86a; B. *Sanhedrin* 74a; Midrash Shir Hashirim Rabbah 15:8; B. *Sanhedrin* 74a.

14. The history of patrilineal and matrilineal descent is the subject of painstaking and exemplary research by Shaye J. D. Cohen. See his papers, "The Matrilineal Principle in Historical Perspective," *Judaism* 34 (1985):5–19; "The Origins of the Matrilineal Principle in Rabbinic Law," *Association for Jewish Studies Review* 10 (1985):19–53; "Was Timothy Jewish (Acts 16:1–3)?" *Journal of Biblical Literature* 105 (1986):251–68. The first of these papers served as the point of departure for a comprehensive symposium, "The Issue of Patrilineal Descent," *Judaism* 34 (1985):3–134. The symposium presents the attitudes of Orthodox, Conservative, Reform, Reconstructionist, and secular scholars and thinkers.

15. Shaye J. D. Cohen maintains that the matrilineal principle was introduced in the Tannaitic period (second–third century C.E.). He believes that it was caused by the impact of Roman law, which traces descent in mixed marriages after the mother. The Rabbis were also motivated, he suggests, by a desire to avoid "mixtures" in procreation, similar to the prohibitions against mixing flax and wool (Deut. 22:11) in clothes and crops (*Kilayim*, Lev. 19:19; Deut. 22:9) and the eating of meat and milk together (based on Exod. 23:19; 34:26; Deut. 14:21).

I find Cohen's theory as to the date of the adoption of the matrilineal principle unconvincing, on the following grounds: 1. It is difficult to believe that the Rabbis, who regarded Rome as "the evil empire," would have set aside the patrilineal principle operating in biblical law in favor of one emanating from their pagan conquerors. 2. It is, I believe, incredible that so radical a change could have been introduced without leaving a trace in the voluminous rabbinic literature of the period (Mishnah, Tosefta, Tannaitic Midrashim). 3. There is no evidence that the Rabbis regarded intermarriage as a form of hybridization, with Jews and gentiles representing different species. 4. But if they did, they should have ruled that the offspring of both types of intermarriage were outside the Jewish pale. This is precisely the position adopted by the *Book of Jubilees* and by Philo with regard to intermarriage of either category. 5. No historical circumstance or other factor has been adduced to explain so radical a change from accepted biblical practice.

To my knowledge, Cohen has not addressed these problems, which were originally set forth in R. Gordis, "Patrilineal Descent—The Problem or the Solution," *Judaism* 34 (1985):32–40. In my view only the period of Ezra and Nehemiah (fifth century B.C.E.) meets all the criteria for the change far more satisfactorily.

16. Ezra 9:1ff.; 10:1–4; Neh. 10:30–31; 13:23ff. See also Mal. 2:11–16; Deut. 7:3; 23:4–9.

17. Ezra 10; Neh. 13:23 in conjunction with 13:1–3.

18. See R. Gordis, *Love and Sex: A Modern Jewish Perspective* (New York, 1978), pp. 191–247.

19. Deut. 7:3 and 23:4–9.

20. The various aspects of this problem are discussed by the twenty-three contributors to the symposium "The Issue of Patrilineal Descent," *Judaism* 34 (1985):3–134.

SUBJECT INDEX

INDEX OF BIBLICAL PASSAGES

Old Testament

INDEX OF TALMUDIC
AND MIDRASHIC PASSAGES

Midrash Rabbah